The Path of the WAY

End Days Field Manual for the Ekklesia of N...

NAVIGATING LIFE IN B'ACHARIT HA-YAMIM

Salt & Lyte Gypsy Ministry
Awake Aware No Fear!

Amaliyah Siler

I dedicate this to Adonai Elohim, my ABBA Daddy who called me back into HIS loving arms! To Yahusha my Messiah who showed me with love and sacrifice to whom adore!! And to the Ruach HaKodesh who has been so very faithful to guide me in spirit and truth with wisdom. Whom so graciously and patiently peeled back the veil and on the Father's que revealed the ancient path. MY LOVE.

To my wonderful strong, handsome, loving and faithful husband. Who believes and supports me in all I do. I love you so very very much and I would not want to do heaven and life with anyone else! You are my covering and my shield!! I am so honored to be your wife. You are my blessing and my rock to be with in the last days!

To my amazing children who have gone through many tribulations and sufferings that they should not have had to endure at their ages!! I am so grateful to ABBA for giving me each of YOU! You are my heart and my song and I love each of you to the moon and back!!!

I prophesy this day that we are a KINGDOM FAMILY advancing to the tribulation with our ARMOR ON!! WE pray together, heal the sick; together, cast out demons together, prophesy together, evangelize together, and WORSHIP and PRAISE YAHUAH TOGETHER!

BARAK YAHUSHA! MARANATHA!!

Tudah ABBA YAHUAH!

Warrior's Rise!

YOU ARE A WARRIOR! YOU MUST ARMOR UP DAILY! BE READY FOR
WAR!
Son or Daughter of Zadok/Melchizedek
Temple of Righteousness/Set Apart
Worshipping/ Honoring Yahuah with our Body/Mind/Spirit
Love, Passion, Emunah, Wisdom, Self Control, Gratitude,
Servitude,Grace,Patience,
Honor of the Temple
Weaving in around and through the **WORD** to come full circle.
The representation of the Melchizedek Priesthood,
King Yahusha. King of Righteousness

The
Tent of
Meeting

We are empowered, consecrated, anointed, gifted, and obedient,Hebrews have always been the dew of Hermon and it rests on us like a mantle. We are the NATSARIM. **NATSARIM** as a whole will be the **ARMOR OF YAHUAH** .

Sons and Daughters of Zadok , Natsarim dominion starts first with yourself. It means mastery over oneself first. Overcoming SELF is the main mission given to each of us. We can because HE did. HIS example is our desire. Let us first inquire within ourselves the need for temperance, balance, and more self- discipline. We must set our own house in order first. Judgement comes to the HOUSE OF YAH first! Our bodies are that house HE comes to inspect with a white glove.

"And as he reasoned about righteousness, and self-control, and the judgment to come, Felix became frightened and said, "For the present, go. And when I find time I shall send for you. " Felix chose to wait." Acts 24:25

Felix's time never came because the enemy made sure of it. Natsarim, I speak to you and myself now when I say there is **NO MORE TIME!** We must examine ourselves first, and daily submit to Yahuah, repent, and practice self-control and discipline!

Dominion= Mastery over oneself.

Dominion is only established, strengthened and secured by the spirit. You do not do this under your own strength lest you get yourself into legalistic bondage – by trying to be good – the good is placed in your heart by the spirit as you yield the pollution to Yahuah. Most of us know the basics of discipleship. The sad truth is that the younger generations do not. Those that came through the modern church do not know the skills of survival for a Believer. They have not been taught how to be overcomers or their authority. Most do not even really know ABBA. This is just a fact. It is up to the mature to train and prepare them while there is still some time. I saw as the Ruach leads me that teaching Believers their authority is #1 above all for survival for the coming days! I pray you will use this manual as you need and share it with everyone! I pray you are blessed!! Natsarim are Watchmen also known as Branches (Acts 24:5, Jer. 31:6) and consider **all** believers to be on the path to redemption through repentance, immersion and obedience to the renewed **Covenant** through the **WORD** of **Rabbi/Teacher Yahusha** HaMashiach, the Maker of Heaven and Earth. We *do not* **judge** ,but steadfastly press on toward the perfecting of the saints.

A true Testimony of what has been, what is, and what will be. Record of the Earth that was as Yahuah said. You are **MY DISCIPLES,** saith Yahuah. You are the Remnant that has been brought back together in this place of supernatural protection to dwell in these last days. **STAY IN ME, LET ME LEAD, I WILL GUIDE YOU BY A PILLAR OF FIRE BY NIGHT AND CLOUD BY DAY!**

" A recorded account of HIS PLAN, HIS CREATION, of HIS FAITHFUL SERVANTS, HIS MIRACLES, SIGNS AND WONDERS, OF YAHUSHA, of the Beast (hasatan) who I WILL DESTROY! Of HIS redemptive plan, Exodus to New Jerusalem, and the coming AGE."

A Prayer of Ahavah-

Truly, truly, I say to you, I love you YAHUAH Truly, truly, I say to you, I love you YAHUSHA My EL, YAHUSHA, Son of Man YAHUAH TSEVA'OTH, our Eternal Father!

The Disciples Discipline

It is the reflection of Yahusha and the simplicity is an inward reality that results in an outward life joyful unconcern for possessions!

To be a true **DISCIPLE of YAHUSHA-** Self Discipline is Faith in Action. To truly **LOVE YAHUAH** means to exude discipline, to exude a spirit of joy, to worship in ruach/spirit and truth and to always be in a posture of surrender and submission, allowing Yahuah to sanctify us day after day after day.

Hebrew word for work or occupation — **melachah (מְלָאכָה),**

"… the Yahuah your Elohim will bless you in all the work [ma'aseh} of your hand that you will do [ta'aseh]." Deuteronomy 14:29

In Hebrew it is: **לְמַעַן יְבָרֶכְךָ֩ יְהוָ֨ה אֱלֹהֶ֜יךָ בְּכָל־מַעֲשֵׂה יָדְךָ אֲשֶׁר תַּעֲשֶׂה**

How are we to **PRAY?** Yahusha said to pray like this;

Our Father/ Abba who is in the shamayim;

Let YOUR NAME be set apart,

Let YOUR reign come,

Let YOUR desire be done on earth as it is in the shamayims.

Give us today our daily bread;

And forgive us our debts as we forgive our debtors.

DO NOT lead us into trial nor temptation;

But, **DELIVER** and save us from the wicked one.

YOURS is the **REIGN** , the **POWER** , and the **ESTEEM;**

NOW and **FOREVER!**

AMEIN

But know this, that **in the last days, hard times shall come.** For men shall be *lovers of self, lovers of money, boasters, proud, blasphemers, disobedient to parents, thankless, wrong-doers, unloving, unforgiving, slanderers, without self-control, fierce, haters of good, betrayers, reckless, puffed up, lovers of pleasure* rather than lovers of Elohim, having a form of reverence but denying its power. And turn away from these! For among them are those who creep into households and captivate silly women loaded down with sins, led away by various lusts, always learning and never able to come to the knowledge of the truth. And as Yoḥane and Mamrě opposed Mosheh, so do these also oppose the truth – men of corrupt minds, found worthless concerning the belief; but they shall not go on further, for their folly shall be obvious to all, as also that of those men became. But you did closely follow my teaching, the way of life, the purpose, the belief, the patience, the love, the endurance, the persecutions, the sufferings, which came to me at Antioch, at Ikonion, *and* at Lustra – what persecutions I bore. Yet out of them all the Master delivered me. And indeed, all those wishing to live reverently in Messiah יהושע, shall be persecuted. But evil men and impostors shall go on to the worse, leading astray and being led astray. But you, stay in what you have learned and trusted, having known from whom you have learned, and that from a babe you have known the Set-apart Scriptures, which are able to make you wise for deliverance through belief in Messiah יהושע. All Scripture is breathed by Elohim and profitable for teaching, for reproof, for setting straight, for instruction in righteousness, that the man of Elohim might be fitted, equipped for every good work.

2 Timothy 3

We are true and loyal **Servants of Adonai, lovers of Yahusha,** and adorners of the Ruach HaKodesh. We will serve to the end and beyond because of our great **LOVE** and

FEAR of Yahuah! I have been on a journey discovering these new titles and names describing just who we are in truth. But, the words mean nothing if there is no action behind them. You can call yourself a Son or Daughter of Zadok but, you had better be walking that out daily before the world so they may see your truth. You can call yourself a Natsarim but, you better be living and doing as the disciples did when they walked with Yahusha!! I began this book excited about telling you what I have discovered through the promptings of the Ruach, that I know I am **YaH's** Scribe, a Daughter of Zadok and part of the Ekklesia of Natsarim yet, I find myself now in a bit of a shock because I know that to whom much is given much is required. Excellence is required to walk this walk! I am more humble now after the scope of this realization and I am deeply honored that **ABBA** would even consider me for anything at all.

So, if you are reading this then you too have a similar call on your life.

Congratulations Brother or Sister! YOU HAVE JUST BEEN ACTIVATED!

It is important to understand that each person in the Kingdom YaH has a different position, calling, and assignment. Each has been created from the beginning and assigned his or her duties; as long as one comes to the saving knowledge of Yahusha HaMashiach and complete repentance of sins. What I mean is the 144,000 have been chosen since the very beginning just as you and I have been chosen for the time we are living in.If you do not know what you have been assigned; I encourage you to seek and ask. Press in. **YaH** will reveal it to you through the Ruach that lives in you!

Isaiah 32:17

"The work of righteousness will be peace; the service of righteousness will be quiet confidence forever."

Exodus 33:7-9

"And Mosheh took his tent and pitched it outside the camp, far from the camp, and called it the Tent of Meeting. And it came to be that everyone who sought יהוה went out to the Tent of Meeting which was outside the camp.

And it came to be, whenever Mosheh went out to the Tent, that all the people rose, and each man stood at his tent door and watched Mosheh until he entered the Tent.

And it came to be, when Mosheh entered the Tent, that the column of cloud descended and stood at the door of the Tent, and He spoke with Mosheh."

Exodus 33: 13-23

"And now, please, if I have found favour in Your eyes, please show me Your way, and let me know You, so that I find favour in Your eyes. And consider that this nation is Your people." And He said, "My Presence does go, and I shall give you rest."

And he said to Him, "If Your Presence is not going, do not lead us up from here.

"For how then shall it be known that I have found favour in Your eyes, I and Your people, except You go with us? Then we shall be distinguished, I and Your people, from all the people who are upon the face of the earth."

And יהוה said to Mosheh , "Even this word you have spoken I shall do, for you have found favour in My eyes, and I know you by name."

Then he said, "Please, show me Your esteem."

And He said, "I shall cause all My goodness to pass before you, and I shall proclaim the Name of יהוה before you. And I shall favour him whom I favour, and shall have compassion on him whom I have compassion."

But He said, "You are unable to see My face, for no man does see Me and live."

And יהוה said, "See, there is a place with Me! And you shall stand on the rock.

"And it shall be, while My esteem passes by, that I shall put you in the cleft of the rock and cover you with My hand while I pass by.

"Then I shall take away My hand and you shall see My back, but My face shall not be seen."

KEYS are powerful symbols in any story. They symbolize opening and closing powers—for instance, when a character might use a key to lock someone in, depriving that person of his freedom. Or the character might use a key to unlock the door and free whoever is inside. Key are frequently mentioned in Scripture. It is called in Hebrew " *maphteah*" , i.e., the opener (Judges 3:25); and in the Greek New Testament kleis , from its use in shutting (Matthew 16:19 ; Luke 11:52 ; Revelation 1:18 , etc.).The " *key of knowledge* " (Luke 11:52 ; Compare Matthew 23:13) is the means of attaining the knowledge regarding the **Kingdom of YAHUAH.** The *"power of the keys"* is a phrase in general use to denote the extent of ecclesiastical authority. This manual contains many **KEYS OF POWER** for these last days and tribulation given by the Ruach HaKodesh. We can access these **KEYS** to open the door to the deeper things of **YaH** and seek **WISDOM** for how to live in this hour and the end days.

We are **OVERCOMERS** just as Yahusha overcame.

OVERCOMER = **Yakol** = succeed, prevail, victory, be bold, declare, have an attitude of confidence, understand, to grasp, processing information about a subject.

Hebrews 12:1, Numbers 13:30, Matthew 24: 12, 13, Revelation 2:5, Revelation 2:26 (these are only a few verses of overcoming)

"He who has an ear, let him hear what the Spirit says to the assemblies. To him who overcomes I shall give some of the hidden manna to eat. And I shall give him a white stone, and on the stone a renewed Name written which no one knows except him who receives it." Revelation 2:17

Principles of the OVERCOMER

Romans 12:1 - overcome evil with good

1 John 4:4 - The one who is in us is greater than he who is in the world

1 John 5:4- our faith (emunah)

John 1:5- Light shines in the darkness

Zechariah 9:15 - sling stones/ physical weapons

Luke 10:19 - the authority Yahusha has given us

John 16:33- for HE has overcome the world

"Then a voice came from the throne, saying: "Praise **Yahuah** , all you who serve **HIM** , and those who fear **HIM** , small and great alike!"... Revelation 19:5

KING YAHUSHA OUR MaShiach--(below terms from Teshuvah Ministries)

Yahusha has a wild freedom born out of profound holiness.

Yahusha has a freedom based on a holiness much deeper than any religion ever concocted. Yahusha moves holiness from external to internal! Ruach HaKodesh pulls it in. Yahusha is unable to speak nonsense. He would lead others to talk about what was truly important. Yahusha always told people the truth in the best possible way to hear it. Yahusha is disruptive honesty. Yahusha has the courage to always say what others will not say. We are Image Bearers.

KEY OF SURRENDERING (this key must be opened daily to keep us yielded to the Ruach HaKodesh)

PRAYER OF SURRENDER

Abba, I surrender all of my opinions, perceptions, desires for outcomes that are not your will. I want only what you want for me. What your will is and your truth is. I pray for clarity and wisdom. Create in me a clean heart. Thank you for your gracious mercies. Forgive me. Guide me, lead me and teach me your truth. I love you. I trust you. I honor you. Thank you Abba Yahuah!

Sabbath is Yahuah's declaration of freedom from slavery. (Deut.5:12-15)

We are authentic servants of **Yahuah** by resolute perseverance in times of: hardships, difficulties, distress, mobbed, labored, sleepless, starving, in purity, in patience, in knowledge, in kindness, love free of affection, word of truth, power of **Yahuah** . We wash ourselves clean of everything that pollutes either body or spirit bringing our sanctification to completion in the fear of **Yahuah** . **Yahuah** is drawing us back to the Garden of Eden to become organic spiritual beings.

Sons and Daughters of Zadok the Ekklesia of Natsarim in these Last Days

To those in training:

Order of Yahuah's Priesthoods:

Melchizedek = Supernatural Order of Priesthood Heavenly

Zadok =Righteous on Earth

Levite = Law of Obedience

You shall love Yahuah Eloheinu, Yahuah is ONE and you shall LOVE, (AHAVAH) with all your heart, all your soul and all your strength and you shall love your neighbor as yourself.

You are standing today, **ALL OF YOU** , before **Yahuah, your Elohim** …to pass into a covenant with **Yahuah, your Elohim** and to establish you as His people, and He as your **Elohim** …Not with you alone do I seal this covenant and this obligation, but also with whoever are not [yet] here with us today" Devarim 29:9-14

The Mature Order Of Melchizedek-Zadok Priesthood

Time for the Warriors of Prayer to RISE!

Come Forth And Call For The Power Of Yahuah our Elohim

YaH spoke to me on my walk and said, "Gimel" And so I looked this up as to its true meaning. I felt HE spoke that WORD as and assignment and a calling to us who call ourselves *Natsarim under the Zadok Anointing.*

Gimel- *The 'Sent One'- carries a message, or burden – Goes 'back and forth'; to Deliver, and Retrieve back; navigation, Boomerang dispatched and expected to return, Emissary, Messenger, Camel, import / export*

1. Remove **all** names of other "gods" from this land and restore **My Name,** why
.
2. Keep **My Sabbaths** beginning with **Passover**

3. **understand My** fear and **seek Me** for **My** laws, **My** for **given** ess, **My fresh, teaching** and **My** "unleavened" bread.
4. **Set-apart** the ***seventh day*** Sabbath and rest in your homes. "Sunday" is not **My Sabbath** Learn about **Me** and from **Me.** *Do* no work. Give **Me** the **same** amount of time that you want from **Me.**
5. Remove **all** evidence of *idolatry* or **pagan** *traditions* and **customs** from your lips, bodies, homes, businesses and government buildings. **Flee** *idolatry* which is idiot-ry! "Do your best," Paul wrote,"to present yourself to **Yahuah** as one approved, a workman who does not need to be ashamed and who correctly handles the **WORD** of truth" 2 Tim.2:15.

Our focus is on the **WORD** of truth." Like Peter, we ought to say, "Yahuah Elohim, to whom shall we go? You have the WORDS of eternal life" (John 6:68). We ought to be driven by a hunger and thirst for righteousness (Matt. 5:6); we ought to be longing or the life-transforming, "living and active" **WORD** of the Most High (Heb. 4:12).
Those who want to master the handling of Yahuah's **WORD** must be like the apprentice of a master craftsperson. Overtime, and through practice, that apprentice will learn to skillfully use many tools. Likewise, the biblical interpreter must know what interpretive tools to use and how to use them. This is what it means to "correctly handle" the **WORD of TRUTH.**
PRIORITY- PURPOSE - PERCEPTION
It is only **Yahuah's** approval we seek, no other. This is the priority, purpose and perception we must maintain as we peel the layers of interpretation and move from the natural realm of understanding to the supernatural realm in befriending **WISDOM** for the

correct application of our understanding of the most precious **WORDS** of The **Most High** ---seeking at all times to maintain that all revelation comes from the **Shekinah of Yahuah** ---the Ruach HaKodesh.

The committed servant must always remain in a state of humility. We must come before the **WORD** ready and willing to obey all it says. We must remain subject to correction and instruction. As Paul instructs to Timothy, "all Scripture is **YaH** -breathed and is useful for teaching, rebuking, correcting and training in righteousness, so that the man of The **Most High** may be thoroughly equipped or every good work" (2 Tim. 3:16–17).

Another quality is that we must listen attentively to the **WORD** and study it perceptively. We are to be quick to listen and slow to speak. (Jas. 1:19)

Listening requires **DISCIPLINE, SELF RESTRAINT, WISDOM and LOVE for Yahuah.** We must be led by the **Set Apart Spirit, Ruach HaKodesh** in all study of Scripture.

It is the Spirit that searches all things, even the deep things of **The Most High** . For who among men knows the thoughts of a man except the man's spirit within him? In the same way no one knows the thoughts of **Yahuah** except the Spirit of **YaH** . . . The man without the Spirit does not accept the things that come from the Spirit of **Yahuah** for they are foolish to him, and he cannot understand them because they are spiritually discerned. The spiritual man makes judgments about all things, but he himself is not subject to any man's judgment.

Totally dependent on the **Spirit of Yahuah** to direct our every movement even to our mouths. That we must walk humbly before **Yahuah Elohim.** As a Son or Daughter of Zadok, we must respond to each Word from **Yahuah.** Our posture is to remain totally submitted and yielded to the Spirit without hesitation day after day, even to go beyond our own human abilities to enter the world of extraordinary possibilities. To live as a Son or Daughter of Zadok is to truly live the supernatural life!

The True Altar Call ---what has **HE** asked **YOU** to put on the altar??

Yahuah spoke and said, "Listen carefully, minister to me. Keep in my presence and seek my face. Our intimacy is key. ``what is most precious to me must be Yahuah, Yahusha and our vows to **HIM.** The Zadok/Melchizedek Priesthood is not by blood but by spiritual inheritance.

GATHERING OF NATSARIM:
RISE UP ACTIVATED ANOINTED SERVANTS OF YAHUAH! LEADERSHIP IS LIFE.
ACTS 2 & JOEL 3
MISSIONARY OF RIGHTEOUSNESS

Psalm 127

If יהוה does not build the house, Its builders have laboured in vain. If יהוה does not guard the city, The watchman has stayed awake in vain.

In vain do you rise up early, To sit up late, to eat the bread of toil; So He gives His beloved sleep.

Look, children are an inheritance from יהוה, The fruit of the womb is the reward.

As arrows in the hand of a mighty man, So are the children of one's youth.

Blessed is the man Who has filled his quiver with them. They are not ashamed, When they speak with their enemies in the gate.

Hard work and captivity have been a part of my own life as long as I have been alive and perhaps this has led me to a deep and passionate desire to go beyond all ideas, all traditions of man, all perceptions of "Christianity" that I had believed for so long to seek the truth and to search for the "deeper" things of **Yahuah** . I decided that I wanted more and just could not continue to live life as "business as usual". The day it all changed for me was the day I lay ill in bed and without warning, suddenly hit by the Spirit of **Yahuah** . I heard **WORDS** and saw visions that forever changed me. **The Fear of The Most High** YaH, overcame the fear of everything else. Just like that, I was for the first time seeing the truth of "real world".   **The Most High, Yahuah Elohim** is gathering many of us together--those who **HE** has given a deep passion for the truth of **HIS WORD** , who desire to return to the ancient paths, who aspire to live as the disciples once did, who do not want to chase after the things of this world any longer but, to chase after **Yahuah** , gleaning wisdom from the Ruach Hakodesh. We are a Gathering of the Natsarim in these last days! This is what **YaH** as clearly called the Salt & Lyte Gypsy Ministry too. To be teachers of righteousness as **Yahusha** exemplified to us while walking this earth.

To become Sons and Daughters of Zadok and lead by example, to teach the true scriptures as Bereans, for together we are branches from the vine of **Messiah Yahusha.** We love (ahavah) YHWH, and we love (ahavah) our neighbors. We walk the narrow path which is " **The WAY** " of   **Yahuah Elohim's WILL** . Ignited with the **FLAME & FIRE** of the Ruach HaKodesh, we heal the sick, cast out demons, pray and intercede, serve the poor, feed the hungry, share all we have with one another in brotherly **LOVE.** We hold Shabbat and keep it **HOLY** . We speak the **TRUTH** , live the **TRUTH** , and breathe the TRUTH to all. We operate in the Melchizedek/ Zadok Priesthood with **EXCELLENCE, INTEGRITY, and WISDOM.** We break bread together with our lamps full of oil. We truly walk out Acts (MA'ASIYM) 2 and hold to **ABBA's** rhythm for the year by celebrating **HIS APPOINTED TIMES/ FEAST DAYS** . We honor mitzvah and are continuously learning as Natsarim and Bereans.

We practice teshuvah daily to stay in the right alignment with **ABBA** . We offer Mikvah to those who are ready to cross over or need to be healed. We as the Bride are preparing ourselves for the **RETURN of our KING YAHUSHA** and look forward to the day we are seated at the banquet table feasting with our Beloved!

Acts 2 Ministry--Living the Natsarim Life obtaining the Zadok Anointing

We are to continuously pray for **YaH's SHALOM** . for others and ourselves. When there is **SHALOM** there is tranquility which is just as sufficient food, clothing, and housing. There is divine health, where there is no sickness. **SHALOM** means an absence of disorder, injustice, bribery, corruption, conflict, flat, hatred, abuse, violence, pain, suffering, immorality, and all the other negative forces. **SHALOM** comes from the root **SHALEM** which means complete. **SHALEM** means to restore. Let us go to the mistar (secret place) and abide there until the Return of **OUR KING YAHUSHA!**

Notes on John the Immerser= Yohanan ben Zekaryah

Fire and Brimstone message of repentance *(teshuvah).*

John the Baptist wrote some of the Dead Sea Scrolls---and Qumran was Bethabara (*hidden name not listed today*)

Immerser = Teacher of righteousness and purity.

Just as John who was a Zadok Priest, we are now in training and have been activated as **Yahuah's** Warriors.

Mark 1:3

"A voice calling in the wilderness; **PREPARE the WAY** for Yahusha ! Make straight the paths for HIM!"

Joel 3:9

"Proclaim this among the nations. **PREPARE FOR WAR!** Rouse the mighty men; let all the men of war advance!"

Jeremiah 51:11

"Sharpen the arrows! Take up the shields! The Most High has aroused the spirit of the kings of the Medes, because **HIS PLAN** is aimed at Babylon to destroy her, for it is the vengeance of Yahuah--vengeance for **HIS TEMPLE!** " (aka, temple can also mean our bodies!)

Order of Melchizedek

John 3:22-26 and they questioned John about purifying---John's father was a temple Priest of **ABBA** --and his mother a daughter of Aaron.

Practised purification rituals (mikvah)

He did not go to the temple because he said it was defiled.

Greatest of all Prophets----He was the voice crying out in the wilderness when the Dead Sea Scrolls were found. Yet, many have been led to believe he was only the cousin of **Yahusha** , who baptized **Yahusha** ---when the Dead Sea Scrolls were found they were not "good enough" or "true enough" for us to read. This was the great deception and hidden truth for so long. hasatan's wicked plan to bury the truth of precious John the Immerser!

The place of Aenon/Salim where John and **Yahusha** were immersing in the river. At one point, the two of them were very close to each other immersing at the same time, when some of John's followers came to him and said that **Yahusha** had a larger crowd and the people were more drawn to **HIM.** John said to them, HE is greater than I and remember, I came only to prepare the way for **HIM** . So, I must **DECREASE** so that HE may **INCREASE! Yahusha** and his disciples were not baptized in the Jordan River as some believe, they were baptized in freshwater. In my studies, I found that the Jordan is really muddy, and not likely the place where our **Messiah** was immersed.

My Continuous Prayer and it should be YOURS TOO;

"Continue to transform me and change every part of me to conform me into the image of Yahusha, and that I will/am a true Image Bearer.

Lead me, teach me to live only in a way that is pleasing to you, Yahuah.

Give me the mantle of the Overcoming Spirit!"

Psalm 29

Ascribe to יהוה, O you sons of the mighty, Ascribe to יהוה esteem and strength.

Ascribe to יהוה the esteem of **HIS NAME** ; Bow yourselves to יהוה in the splendour of set-apartness.

The voice of יהוה is over the waters; The Ěl of esteem thunders; יהוה is over many waters.

The voice of יהוה is with power, The voice of יהוה is with greatness.

The voice of יהוה is breaking the cedars, יהוה is breaking the cedars of Leḇanon in pieces.

And He makes them skip like a calf, Leḇanon and Siryon like a young wild ox.

The voice of יהוה cuts through the flames of fire.

The voice of יהוה shakes the wilderness; יהוה shakes the Wilderness of Qaḏěsh.

The voice of יהוה makes the deer give birth, And strips the forests bare; And in His Hěḵal everyone says, "Esteem!"

יהוה sat enthroned at the Flood, And יהוה sits as Sovereign forever.

יהוה gives strength to His people; יהוה blesses His people with peace.

WHY ZADOK?

"Zadok, you have the gift of discernment! You know what is evil and what is holy. You are strong enough, faithful and committed enough to Me to go into that realm of rebellion and idolatry and save the kingdom!" The king said, "Return to the city!" **Yahuah** now had a holy priest to guard the house of **Adonai** from ruin! Zadok stayed true, holy, committed, blameless, and faithful! He knew **Yahuah's WORD**; he trusted his life and future to it — **DAVID WAS THE ONLY KING**! The Zadok ministry is separated from the world and has but **ONE** mission in life:

TO BE AT THE YAHUAH'S TABLE TO MINISTER TO HIM!

"You also, as living *stones*, are being built up as a spiritual house for a holy priesthood, to offer up spiritual sacrifices acceptable to YaH through Messiah Yahusha. But you are a **CHOSEN RACE, a royal PRIESTHOOD, A HOLY NATION, A PEOPLE FOR YAHUAH'S OWN POSSESSION,** that you may proclaim the excellencies of Him who has called you out of darkness into His marvelous light" (1 Peter 2:5,9).

We are called to a ministry **TO YAHUAH!**

"But you will be called the priests of the **MOST HIGH**; you will be spoken of as ministers of our **YAHUAH**" (Isaiah 61:6).

Zadok remnant is coming forth — visible and anointed. Those of the Zadok remnant all speak the same language: faithfulness to King Yahusha, repentance/teshuvah as a way of life, separation from all that is touched or represented by the world, an intense hunger and thirst for righteousness, purging, and refining, and a pure heart wholly given to Him.

As A Son or Daughter of Zadok and a Natsarim we are:

Pioneering the Frontier of Yahuah's WORD

Wherefore says the Elohim of hosts, because you speak this **WORD** behold I will make my words in thy mouth **FIRE** and this people wood and it shall devour them. When you speak the **WORD** of **YAHUAH** it is like a devouring fire. It devours anything the enemy has stolen, it devours lies and deception, corruption, and it will pierce your very heart. There is nothing else that does that – only the **WORD of YaH**. Is not my **WORD** like a fire says **YAHUAH** and like a hammer that breaks into pieces the rock. It will break the strongest strongman. There is nothing that hasatan can stand against when you speak the **WORD** – when you come against him with the **WORD of YAHUAH** he can't stand

13

against it. He might try, he might try to fool you and made you think that he is victorious and you have lost the battle. That is only one of his deceptions or lies. But if you **STAND UP and RISE UP, GET OUT YOUR SWORD, GET OUT THE WORD OF YaH and BEGIN TO SPEAK IT OUT;** he's got to move – he has no choice.

This is vital for survival during tribulation! Knowing your authority, putting on the **WHOLE ARMOR** and wielding the **WORD** . The **WORD** will destroy any and all strongholds. The **WORD of YAHUAH** is quick and powerful and sharper than any two edged sword. The **WORD** is a devouring **FIRE** . It burns into you heart. It is a crushing hammer, a life giving force, a defensive weapon, a sword, it is salt, it cleanses, it separates you, it's the bread of life, it brings light out of darkness, understanding to the simple. It orders your steps, it keeps sin from having dominion , it is hidden treasure. His **WORD** brings healing to body, soul, and spirit it tears down and it builds up, it brings dead bones together in resurrection power. **HIS WORD IS POWER** !

Most of us know the importance of READING and KNOWING and DOING the WORD. I can **NOT** stress enough for each of us to remember this!! **YAHUAH** called those that had no oil in their lamps "fools". In Revelation 1:16 **Yahusha** had in **HIS** hand seven stars and out of **HIS** mouth went a sharp two – edged sword and **HIS** countenance was as the sun shining – **HE IS COMING BACK WITH THE SWORD – HIS WORD** – the very thing he brings with **HIM is THE SWORD – HIS WORD.**

2 Tim. 2:15---correctly handling the **WORD of YaH.** So thyself approved.

<u>Guidelines for Interpretation-</u>

Pray and ask **Yahuah** to open your mind to understanding and revelation. Ask for the Ruach HaKodesh to lead you into all truth and pray for wisdom, and surrender all perceptions. One of the things **ABBA** Yahuah said to me was to forget all I thought I had learned or "heard through preaching" of the **WORD** and allow the Ruach to guide me into the "deeper" waters of understanding.

Only the one who truly desires to go deeper and set aside their own motives or traditions will be allowed to enter through the **"NARROW DOOR"** .

<u>Times of Retreating to the " **Cave"**</u>

Parallel- Cave of Treasures where Adam & Chavah were sent after the fall.

There are times in our life journey that **YaH** has us retreat into the "cave" for an hour, day, or season. We can feel a tug within our spirit to pull away from the "norm" and at times completely retreat from people all together. The various lengths of time, surroundings, and situations depend upon our walk with **Yahuah Elohim.** I want to encourage you, that if you are experiencing a sensation to withdraw from others pray about it.

Simply go to the Father and ask for **WISDOM** and ask **HIM** if you need to "retreat to the cave"? The Ruach is faithful to guide you. If it is time for "cave dwelling" then you must have in place strong boundaries for those in your life. Many times when we are called into the cave it is for a time of intercession, prayer, cleansing, purification, and drawing into the secret place of T **he Most High.** You must obey **ABBA** if **HE** leads you to the cave. If you do not then you could possibly be delaying your growth spiritually or the possibility of being cleansed and set free from some "idols" that are causing a blockage between you and **HIM** . We are to knows the times, seasons, and appointed feast days of **The Most High** . It is time to enter into *Yahuah's rhythm* for the year and set aside our own agendas in obedience. This is the **very root of our faith (emunah).**

As a Son or Daughter of Zadok, you are to know the talents you have been given by Yahuah. I am a Zadok Scribe who operates in the office of the Prophetic, a teacher, researcher of truth, and **Yahuah's** servant. It took me over 25 years to learn who I was and only the Ruach HaKodesh can reveal it to one. It is important to remember that not everyone is a Son or Daughter of Zadok nor is everyone called to be a minister unto **Yahuah** . I will tell you that **YaH is the ONLY ONE** who reveals it to a person and for me HE revealed it in many ways as to give confirmation to **HIS WORD** and **GLORY ONLY** unto **HIM** for the revelation. This calling is not to be taken lightly either; it is a very serious matter and most likely involves much persecution and alienation from loved ones and from the world.

"And Yahusha said to them, "There is no Prophet who is despised except in his city and among his kindred and in his house." Mark 6:4

The one who gives up family, friends, and the pursuit of the "dream life" and things of this world. The person who relinquishes the pleasure and inheritance and support gained from "family" in order to go and do what **Yahuah** tells him or her to do is a Son or Daughter of Zadok. For the inheritance of Sons and Daughters of Zadok is **Yahusha** himself. **Yahuah** has always offered himself as the inheritance of the priestly tribe because they had no inheritance among the Tribes.

The Communion of Learning

Sons and Daughters of Zadok consider the presence of **Yahuah** to be an everyday occurrence. They have **HIS** attention, **HIS** power, **HIS** way of being and doing, **HIS** wealth, **HIS** wisdom, **HIS** resources. They possess **HIM** and are possessed by **HIM** . They are to eat of the sacrifices , the first fruits which are the spiritual **FIRST FRUITS** ! They share in the communion of learning from **Yahuah** and them. Our communion with **The Most High** is based on righteousness. First, **DEATH** must come. Death to personal agendas, death to pride, death to fleshly pursuits, death to **YOUR VERSION** of life. We must be opposed to all "system regimes".

RIGHTEOUSNESS= the WISDOM of THE RIGHT WAY

Judgement is a constant factor in righteousness. **Yahuah's** judgement is what Sons and Daughters of Zadok seek as King David did when he cried, " Create in me a clean heart **O Yahuah** and a right spirit within."

I am יהוה your Elohim, Who brought you out of the land of Mitsrayim ; Open your mouth wide, and I fill it. Psalm 81:10

But solid food is for the mature whose senses have been trained by practice to discern both good and evil. Hebrews 5:14

A lion has roared! Who is not afraid? The Master יהוה has spoken! Who would not prophesy? Amos 3:8

And after this it shall be that I pour out My Spirit on all flesh. And your sons and your daughters shall prophesy, your old men dream dreams, your young men see visions. Joel 2:28

I stand at my watch, and station myself on the watch-tower, and wait to see what He says to me, and what to answer when I am reproved.

And יהוה answered me and said, **"Write the vision and inscribe it on tablets,** so that he who reads it runs. **For the vision is yet for an appointed time, and it speaks of the end, and does not lie.** If it lingers, wait for it, for it shall certainly come, it shall not delay. Habakkuk 2: 1-3

and I have filled him with the **Spirit of Elohim in wisdom,** and in understanding, and in knowledge, and in all work,

to make designs for work in gold, and in silver, and in bronze ,

and in cutting stones for setting, and in carving wood, and to work in all work. Exodus 31:3-5

But the Word of יהוה was to them, **"Command upon command, command upon command, line upon line, line upon line, here a little, there a little** ,** so that they go and shall stumble backward, and be broken and snared and taken captive. Isaiah 28:13

There are 5 positions of Yahusha

High Priest - YaH prophesying blessing, YaH is for us and Yahusha putting things legally in place.

Intercessor – Yahusha always intercedes for us

Mediator of New Covenant – Legal Position (lawyer) Reconciler

Lawyer/Advocate – Spirit of comfort, conciliation to be released

Head of the Church - Yahusha prophesied to bring the church to maturity Disciples in the book of Acts were filled with the Ruach HaKodesh, shook cities, towns, and villages and rejecting hell's gates and turning the world upside down! **Yahusha** at work in these powerful believers is the exciting example of how you and I can become the 'powerhouse **YaH** created us to be in **Yahusha HaMashiach** . Eph. 2:10

"Discipline" is the key to life on this earth. You live this life to learn who your Creator is. You learn through the concept of discipline which is guided by the Law of **Yahuah** . Discipline will prevail in your life in two forms (the form is dictated by your level of spiritual maturity)

Discipline imposed by Yahuah - in which case discipline takes the form of "outside correction for wrong doing". **Yahuah** ordained a system of "cause and effect" for every action in this life. You will repeat your mistakes and you will reap the benefits of your actions until you have learned what **Yahuah** has to teach you and have the maturity to impose self-discipline.

Self imposed discipline - self-imposed discipline is the basic key to life.This form of discipline leads to knowledge, wisdom, and success in life.

In ancient times, **Yahuah** requested that the Levites wear only white linen. Same for the Melchizedek/ Zadok Priesthood. The reason I have included this information on linen in this section is because **YaH** said, "what was will be again." I am paraphrasing of course. In these last days I believe that as Sons and Daughters of Zadok we will be required to wear linen again to show ourselves pure and in right standing with **The Most High** . Just as **HE** has led me to purchase a few linen dresses to wear when **HE** tells me too. I encourage you to seek, pray, and ask if that is something you personally should be doing.

KEY---A Lesson In Linen

Flax fabric is an excellent filter protecting against chemical exposure, noise and dust. – Linen clothing reduces solar gamma radiation by almost half thereby protecting humans wearing linen. Flax fiber retrieved from contaminated soil appears to be totally resistant to harmful radiation. Linen underwear heightens positive emotions as well as possessing rare bacteriological properties. Resistant to fungus and bacteria, flax is found to be an effective barrier to some diseases. According to Japanese researchers, studies have shown that bed-ridden patients do not develop bedsores where linen bed sheets are used. Wearing linen clothes helps to decrease some skin diseases – from common rash to chronic eczemas. Linen is highly "hygroscopic" meaning it rapidly absorbs and gives up moisture. Adsorbing water as quickly as a pond surface, before giving a feeling of being wet, linen cloth can absorb as much as 20% of its dry weight. This explains why linen cloth always feels fresh and cool.

Linen does not cause allergic reactions and is helpful in treating a number of allergic disorders. Linen is effective in dealing with inflammatory conditions, reducing fever, and providing a healthy air exchange. Some neurological ailments benefit from the use of linen clothing.

The Most High instructed me to wear linen daily. With 5G being utilized at this time it is my belief that linen has the ability to protect us from the harmful radiation of 5G. I would encourage you to wear linen as much as possible, hang curtains of linen in your home and sleep on linen sheets. This is only one way for us to be protected from millimeter waves of radiation from 5G.

- **Sanctify ye a fast,**
- **Call a solemn assembly,**
- **Gather the elders**
- **And all the inhabitants of the land**
- **Unto the house of the Most High your Elohim,**
- **And cry unto the Most High**
  Joel 1:14

Then I proclaimed a fast there at the river of Ahava, that we might humble ourselves before our **Elohim** , to seek from Him in the right way for us and our little ones and all our possessions So we fasted and entreated the **Most High** for this, and He answered our prayer..

Ezra 8:21; 23

And I set my face unto the **Most High** , to seek by prayer and supplications, with fasting and sackcloth, and ashes.

Daniel 9:3

Covenant Code for Health and the Tapestry of LOVE is reflected in being created in HIS IMAGE.

We were bought for a price. When we are born, we are born into sin. We never had a chance to choose hasatan or **Yahuah Elohim.** Because we are born into a fallen world, hasatan has rights to us. When we come to Yahusha, **HE** bought us with **HIS** blood. That makes us **NOT our own.** We do not belong to ourselves. **Yahusha** has set us **FREE.** In being set free we still have the ability to choose. We can choose to walk in the light or stay in the dark. He has given us the freedom to say yes or no whenever we want. He will never force our hand. How we care for ourselves reveals how much we love **ABBA,** **Yahusha** and the Ruach HaKodesh.

 As non-believers who are living in the dark we can expect to see extremities and ailments. The dis-eases of Egypt. When we come to salvation and **Yahusha** frees us from sin and death we are expected to surrender **ALL** of ourselves to Him. Meditate on that for a bit. Really we as Believers have no excuse in how we look, act, talk and live our lives in this world. We are not of the world although we are in the world. It is our responsibility as Melchizedek/ Zadok Priest to lead by example. The world is watching. Not just that but also because we **ARE NOT** our own and we become at the time of deliverance **HIS TEMPLE** . If you backslide you can come back after repentance and begin again, although that is **NOT** a get out of jail free card! No, you can lose your salvation. No matter what you may have heard in churchianity!! You absolutely can lose your salvation. As image bearers it is an ongoing process of cleaning our temples and being delivered. Depending on what stage in life you come to **Yahusha** it could take years or months. Probably, the latter. We must always have a heart of repentance always. Which means to remain humble in all things. Always be surrendering more and more. He has called us His Set Apart People. Are you committed to being and staying set apart from the world?

(The above paragraphs are from my book School of the Warrior Woman; I included them here because you will need to reference it often to keep your mind, body, spirit, and soul pure.)

We are living in tribulation and darkness. With the cloud of darkness surrounding us, hasatan will attempt almost every sec of minutes to invade our thoughts, emotions, will and to invade our spirit and soul with anything and everything he can. We must with every effort keep our temple clean. We must also, with every effort; keep our mind, emotions and will pure and true. Our very soul and spirit depend on it and we must remain standing with boldness until the very end! The light and energy of Yahuah which is in us repels the darkness. hasatan must continuously work exuding all his energy to deceive us. We must know our authority and position over him. This is a vital **KEY** for this age.

This earth is shrouded in darkness and is only getting darker! As Sons and Daughters of Zadok we must pray without ceasing for wisdom and sound mind. hasatan is betting on us getting weary and tired. From minute to minute your thoughts will fail so remember what the **WORD** says:

Proverbs 3
My son, do not forget my Torah, And let your heart watch over my commands;
For length of days and long life And peace they add to you.

Let not kindness and truth forsake you – Bind them around your neck, Write them on the tablet of your heart,

Thus finding favour and good insight In the eyes of Elohim and man.

Trust in יהוה with all your heart, And lean not on your own understanding;

Know Him in all your ways, And He makes all your paths straight.

Do not be wise in your own eyes; Fear יהוה and turn away from evil.

It is healing to your navel, And moistening to your bones.

Esteem יהוה with your goods, And with the firstfruits of all your increase;

Then your storehouses shall be filled with plenty, And your vats overflow with new wine.

My son, do not despise the discipline of יהוה, And do not loathe His reproof;

For whom יהוה loves He reproves, As a father the son whom he delights in.

Blessed is the man who has found wisdom, And the man who gets understanding;

For the gain from it is better Than gain from silver, And its increase than fine gold.

She is more precious than rubies, And all your delights are not comparable to her.

Length of days is in her right hand, Riches and esteem in her left hand.

Her ways are pleasant ways, And all her paths are peace.

She is a tree of life to those taking hold of her, And blessed are all who retain her.

יהוה founded the earth by wisdom; He established the heavens by understanding;

By His knowledge the depths were broken up, And the clouds drop down dew.

My son, let them not depart from your eyes; Watch over sound wisdom and discretion;

Then they become life to your being And an adorning to your neck.

Then you would walk safely in your way, And your foot would not stumble.

When you lie down, you need not be afraid. And you shall lie down and your sleep shall be sweet. Do not be afraid of sudden dread, Nor of the ruin of the wrong when it comes;

For יהוה is at your side, And He shall guard your foot from being caught.

Do not withhold good from those who deserve it, When it is in the power of your hand to do so. Do not say to your neighbour, "Go, and come back, and tomorrow I give it," When you have it with you. Do not plan evil against your neighbour, Seeing he dwells safely beside you. Do not strive with a man without cause, If he has done you no evil.

Do not envy a cruel man, And choose none of his ways;

For the perverse one is an abomination to יהוה, And His secret counsel is with the straight. The curse of יהוה is on the house of the wrong, But He blesses the home of the righteous. He certainly scoffs the scoffers, But gives favour to the humble.

The wise do inherit esteem, But fools are bearing away shame!

KEYS FOR THE WARRIORS
Mindset Warrior
Fasting Warrior
Mantle of the Overcomer
Yahuah's Principles--Health and Wellness
Declaration of Wisdom--FEAR OF YAHUAH
The Hardness of the Way Walk of Trueness

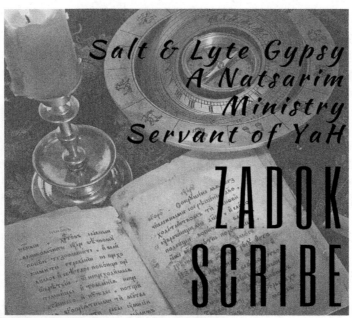

Salt & Lyte Gypsy
A Natsarim
Ministry
Servant of YaH

ZADOK SCRIBE

TENT OF MEETING- KEEP THE CAMP CLEAN
BET= TENT= HOUSE= FAMILY

Symbolizes **Yahuah's** family HIS set apart ones.

Yahuah expects us who retreat to wilderness living hosting places of refuge in these last days to keep the camp clean. For know **HE** did this with the Israelites in the wilderness with Moses and it will be no different with us during the Second Exodus. We will take refuge in the Name of **YaH** !
We must gather supplies and share the burden. We will need plenty of oil, food, and other survival essentials.

This is a prophetic word I received December 2018

Yahuah says:

" I will establish you and fortify you with strong walls. I will guard your gates. I will release the seeds of truth, and the roots will grow deep as I have placed you in a place of fertile soil. A time of shaking and sifting is almost over and the roots of righteousness are beginning to grow. For if you stay where I plant you, your walls will become strong and secure. You will grow in radiant beauty. You will bloom in season, and reap a harvest of many for many. This is a year of establishment, preparation, and growth like never before and never has been. You will become a fortified city on hill armed with the best weapons. Storehouses full of supplies, plenty of faith, oil, and wine to last a lifetime. Many will fear you. They will say, he or she serves The Most High Yahuah, for HE is their Protector and Guard!! Your enemies will move around you to avoid contact at all costs. If you do what I say and allow me to lead! I will release Angels as guards at your gates,and ministering angels as your teachers. For it is time my people prepare as never before. In faith and truth!
"

Read and study Ezekiel 47 with this **WORD!** Write it out line by line.

AMBASSADOR IN CHAINS/ write more about Armor and Intercession
KEY- Debriefing on all Prayer Watches

And in the fourth watch of the night Yahusha went unto them, walking on the sea. Matthew 14:25

THE WATCHES OF THE NIGHT

My eyes are awake before the watches of the night, that I may meditate on your promise. Psalm 119:148

The Israelites divided the night into military watches instead of hours.

The Burden of the Intercessors

Confess your trespasses to one another, and pray for one another, so that you are healed. The earnest prayer of a righteous one accomplishes much. James 5:16

When we pray, we stand watch over our families, cities, and nations. Just as men stood on city walls in the WORD to watch for approaching danger, **Yahuah** calls us **NOW** to be **WATCHMEN** and be on alert to warn those of any danger. We are also to pray during these " **WATCHES** " for any instructions from **Yahuah** .The Bible speaks of " **WATCHES** ," which are specific times of the day or night. There are basically eight watches covering 24 hours. This is because everyone has a prayer watch, even though they may not know it. This is why you may find yourself repeatedly praying at specific times of the day or evening. If you have ever been awakened during the night or are wondering why you are being led to pray at specific times, it is probably because **ABBA** wants you to pray or intercede for someone. Every prayer watch has a purpose. We must understand that each watch carries a release, destiny, a call; and should be taken seriously . Habakkuk 2:1 says "I will stand upon my **WATCH** to see what He will say to me. Every-time you stand upon your watch, you receive direction, revelation, guidance and more – from Yahuah. As Warriors in the last days we all need to know our watch and be active during those hours. This is one of the tools we use to defeat hasatan and thwart his plans. The fervent and faithful prayers of and intercessor are **POWERFUL!**

1ST WATCH : **6pm – 9pm** Unlocking Destinies, etc.- Genesis 24:62, Luke 8
2ND WATCH : **9pm – 12am** Midnight – Time of Visitations & Acts of Change- Mark 6:47
3RD WATCH : **12am – 3am** Much Spiritual Activity- Luke 12:38
4TH WATCH : **3am – 6am** Angelic Release, Encounters- Matt 14:25, Matt 14:26, Genesis 28:12; Genesis 32:21

A second is the gate to a minute.
A minute is the gate to an hour.
An hour is the gate to a watch.
A watch is the gate to a day.

Thus, it is key to value not just our personal time, but have a respect for time in general. We can possess our day through these gates and frames of time, if we stay sober and alert. That said, here are the last four prayer watches.

And there was evening and there was morning, one day.
Genesis 1:5 NASB

Become a Tent Dweller Today

There is freedom from the world in the idea of tent dwelling. I am not saying all of us are called to be tent dwellers. But, if we can learn the principles of the tent dweller this becomes a precious thing. To let go of the chains of possessions and consecrate ourselves to the **Most High** .

Everything must truly be placed on the altar. **Yahuah** will not allow us to live for our own pleasure, and our own self or by our own strength. **Yahuah** expects our lives to be-come lives on the altar so to speak. What we place on Yahuah's altar, **HE** accepts but not everything gets burned. We must learn to place everything before **HIM** on the altar and allow **Yahuah** to tell us what we may use and keep. We must learn to apply the principle to the tent to all physical things that **Yahuah** permits us to retain.

We may use them, but we must not be touched by them. We can have them or let them go. We must not be like little children and take items off the altar once it is placed on the altar until **HE** says we can have it. The whole principle here is that nothing can occupy our hearts. Our conscience is at peace before **Yahuah** . We must first consult the **Father** before we take anything to our tent. What has been placed in the tent can also go back on the altar at any time. If **Yahuah** says to us, we do not need it, we are to obey and relinquish it right away. The trick of hasatan is when **something becomes and I or mine.** ...remember that!

GOLDEN ANOINTING OIL AND BEING THE BRIDE

We are the Bride of Yahusha.

How do you look?

How do we keep the temple clean?

After we accept Yahusha and are baptized in the Ruach Hakodesh is our temple supernaturally clean forever?

Can our temple get dirty again?

If so, what can we do to clean it and maintain a clean temple?

I am going to walk you through each of these questions slowly, there is great importance in understanding why our temples must be kept clean and our doors guarded. Being that we are the generation living in the last of the last days, this is **MOST IMPORTANT** to understand; we have been **Set -Apart** *for such a time as this!*

This is a lifelong journey, a pilgrimage to:
righteousness /integrity /excellence /health /wellness /cleanliness /honor/ wisdom /truth /teshuvah.

Where do we begin?

Let us first, come to the knowledge that our bodies shadow the Tabernacle in the Wilderness, the Tent of Meeting. The very first Tabernacle that Yahuah Elohim commanded Moses to build when the Israelites came out of Egypt.

The picture below will put this into perspective for you. Take a few minutes to study and learn how **ABBA** made this miracle so!

Weapons for the Overcomer= Fasting and Prayer

(you have an enemy that does NOT want you to do those two things together!)

FASTING AND PRAYER - eliminates strongholds, eliminates toxins, submission, draw close to ABBA, hear HIS voice, our weapon

Fasting is necessary to conquer the flesh! It is our holy surrender. It is the last option when we need help! It is when **ABBA** sees us humble ourselves before HIM.

Fasting is Feasting Prayer from the website (Soul Shepherding)

By the mercy of Yahusha I shall not live by bread alone.
But by every word that proceeds from the mouth of Yahuah.
The Word of Yahuah Is alive and active;The Most High is right now speaking
His life into my soul. The Spirit of Yahuah that raised Yahusha from the dead.
Lives and prays in my body and reminds me of Yahusha's words.
So as I fast from food I feast with joy on the manna from heaven, the bread of angels,
The Bread of Life, who is Yahusha our Messiah.
My food is to be one with Yahusha:To do the will of the Father,
To finish his works of love, To share my food with the hungry.
In the name of the Father,The Son ,and the Spirit.
Amein.

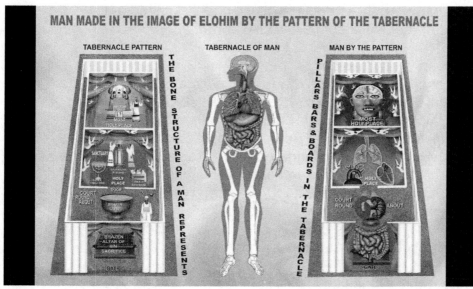

What have you eaten today?

Whether, with your mouth, your eyes, your nose. your ears, or what you have touched. You eat daily with these five gates. What you watch, listen too, eat physically or drink, or what goes in your nose. Yahuah cares about every aspect of what we put in or on our bodies. That is why we eat of Yahusha daily. Partake of His goodness. HIS mercies are new everyday.

The Dietary Laws-- What is the big deal about **KOSHER?**

Rabbinical Kosher & Biblical Kosher

The word **KOSHER** literally means fit or appropriate.

Rabbinical refers to the 613 laws and to the Talmud man made laws that Yahuah did **NOT** give. Let us set this aside and look to what Yahuah Elohim said.

Biblical Kosher is what is found in the **WORD.** YaH made it very clear what we can eat. HE gives us a list of **CLEAN** and **UNCLEAN** animals.

In this section, are the very **WORDS** of Yahuah Elohim concerning what we are and are **NOT** to eat. YaH gave us the commands for our bodies, health and caring for our "tent of meeting" because it is the temple of the Ruach and **HE** already had a plan for redemption in place and **HE** wanted our bodies to remain clean so they could operate at the highest capacity just the way **HE** made us. This is a great point of reference in this field manuel because in these last days the enemy will try everything to steal, kill and destroy us. His mission is still the same. As Sons and Daughters of Zadok and Natsarim we must lead by example for those that do not know the laws yet!

1. Animals (flesh)

Clean Animals

Mammals That Chew the Cud and Part the Hoof:

Antelope, Bison (buffalo), Caribou, Cattle (beef, veal), Deer (venison), Elk, Gazelle, Giraffe, Goat, Hart, Ibex, Moose, Ox, Reindeer, Sheep (lamb, mutton), Tapir. The milk of these animals is also lawful.

Unclean Animals

Animals With Unclean Characteristics:

Swine, Boar, Peccary, Pig (hog, bacon, ham, lard, pork, most sausage and pepperoni), Canines, Coyote, Dog, Fox, Hyena, Jackal, Wolf, Felines, Cat, Cheetah, Leopard, Lion, Panther, Tiger, Equines, Donkey, Horse, Mule, Onager, Zebra, Armadillo, Badger, Bat,Bear, Beaver, Camel, Elephant, Gorilla, Groundhog, Hippopotamus, Kangaroo, Llama (alpaca, vicua), Mole, Monkey, Mouse, Muskrat, Opossum, Porcupine, Rabbit (hare), Raccoon, Rat, Rhinoceros, Skunk, Slug, nail(escargot), Squirrel, Wallaby, Weasel, Wolverine, Guinea pigs, Worm, rattlesnake and squirrel

Reptiles:

Alligator, Caiman, Crocodile, Lizard, Snake, Turtle.

Amphibians:

Blindworm, Frog, Newt, Salamander, Toad.

2. Fish

(Leviticus 11:10-12) "And all that have not fins and scales in the seas, and in the rivers, of all that move in the waters, and of all the living creatures that are in the waters, they are an abomination unto you, and they shall be an abomination unto you; ye shall not eat of their flesh, and their carcasses ye shall have in abomination. Whatsoever hath no fins nor scales in the waters, that is an abomination unto you.

Fish With Fins and Scales (clean):

Anchovy, Barracuda, Bass, Black pomfret (or monchong), Bluefish, Bluegill, Carp, Cod, Crappie, Drum, Flounder, Grouper, Grunt, Haddock, Hake, Hardhead, Herring (or alewife), Kingfish, Mackerel(or corbia), Mahimahi (or dorado, dolphinfish[not to be confused with the mammal dolphin]), Minnow, Mullet, Perch (or bream), Pike (or pickerel or jack), Pollack (or pollock or Boston bluefish), Rockfish, Salmon, Sardine (or pilchard), Shad, Silver hake (or whiting), Smelt (or frost fish or ice fish), Snapper (or ebu, jobfish, lehi, onaga, opakapaka or uku), Sole, Steelhead, Sucker, Sunfish, Tarpon,Trout (or weakfish),Tuna (or ahi, aku, albacore, bonito or tombo), Turbot (except European turbot),Whitefish.

Marine Animals Without Fins and Scales (unclean):

Fish, Bullhead, Catfish, Eel, European Turbot, Marlin, Paddlefish, Shark, Stickleback, Squid, Sturgeon (includes most caviar),Swordfish, Shellfish, Abalone, Clam, Conch, Crab, Crayfish (crawfish, crawdad),Lobster,Mussel, Oyster,Scallop, Shrimp (prawn), Soft body, Cuttlefish, Jellyfish, Limpet, Octopus, Squid (calamari)

Sea mammals:

Dolphin, Otter, Porpoise, Seal, Walrus, Whale.

3. Birds

(Deuteronomy 14:11-20) "Of all clean birds ye may eat. But these are they of which ye shall not eat: the eagle, and the gier-eagle, and the osprey, and the glede, and the falcon, and the kite after its kind, and every raven after its kind, and the ostrich, and the nighthawk , and the sea-mew, and the hawk after its kind, the little owl, and the great owl, and the horned owl, and the pelican, and the vulture, and the cormorant, and the stork, and the heron after its kind, and the hoopoe, and the bat. And all winged creeping things (duck, goose and swan) are unclean unto you: they shall not be eaten. Of all clean birds ye may eat.

Clean Birds

Chicken, Dove, Grouse, Guinea fowl, Partridge, Peafowl, Pheasant, Pigeon, Prairie chicken, Ptarmigan, Quail, Sagehen, Sparrow (and other songbirds), Teal, Turkey. The eggs of these birds are lawful to eat.

Unclean Birds of Prey, Scavengers and Others:

Albatross, Bittern, Buzzard, Condor, Coot, Cormorant, Crane, Crow, Cuckoo, Eagle, Flamingo, Grebe, Grosbeak, Gull, Hawk, Heron, Kite, Lapwing, Loon, Magpie, Osprey, Ostrich, Owl, Parrot, Pelican, Penguin, Plover, Rail, Raven,

Roadrunner, Sandpiper , Seagull, Stork, Swallow, Swift, Vulture, Water hen, Woodpecker.

4. Insects

(Leviticus 11:22-23) "Even these of them ye may eat: the locust after its kind, and the bald locust after its kind, and the cricket after its kind, and the grasshopper after its kind. But all winged creeping things, which have four feet, are an abomination unto you.

Clean Insects: Types of locusts that may include crickets and grasshoppers

Unclean insects: All insects except some in the locust family

5. Vegetation

(Genesis 1:29-30) "And God said, Behold, I have given you every herb yielding seed, which is upon the face of all the earth, and every tree, in which is the fruit of a tree yielding seed; to you it shall be for food: and to every beast of the earth, and to every bird of the heavens, and to everything that creepeth upon the earth, wherein there is life, I have given every green herb for food: and it was so".

Clean vegetation :

Not every "herb" bears seed, and not every tree bears fruit. Most of the vegetation we ate everyday is clean.

Unclean vegetation:

Mushrooms (they don't photosynthesize), Seaweed and Algae.

6. Blood

(Leviticus 17:14) "For as to the life of all flesh, the blood thereof is all one with the life thereof: therefore I said unto the children of Israel, Ye shall eat the blood of no manner of flesh; for the life of all flesh is the blood thereof: whosoever eateth it shall be cut off".

(Genesis 9:4 "But flesh with the life thereof, which is the blood thereof, shall ye not eat".

(Leviticus 22:8) "That which doth of itself, or is torn of beasts, he shall not eat, to defile himself therewith:-I am Yahuah".

7. Fat

(Leviticus 7:23) "Speak unto the children of Israel, saying, Ye shall eat no fat, of ox, or sheep, or goat".

If we love Yahuah our Elohim we follow **HIS** food laws, then we will enjoy health benefits, and longer life.

FULL CIRCLE- FASTING AS A CURE

Earlier, I briefly shared about fasting as a way to cleanse the Temple. I felt led by the Ruach, to spend more time on this very subject here. Yes, fasting popularity has risen a great deal in the last 10 years in both the secular and non-secular world as a way to get healthy and remove toxins and cleanse your body. These are all true and very important reasons to fast often, but more important for the Natsarim is that fasting is a weapon of warfare. It is a weapon for deliverance. It is hard for the untrained Natsarim. The enemy of your soul will do just about everything he can think of to keep one from completing a fast because he knows the level of power that fasting and prayer hold together and equip the saint. I know first hand his scheming tricks of the trade for keeping one from obeying **Yahuah** when it comes to fasting. I once was needing very badly to overcome the spirit of pharmakeia. This is a demonic spirit that possesses one through psychological/ mind altering/ pain/and other pharmaceuticals oftentimes prescribed by your doctor (who is completely unaware). When you take a drug which is a potion, a mixture, a blend of drugs which, was taught to humans from the fallen angels, demonic possession from this spirit occurs because it causes such agony to the flesh (state of your physical body) when you are not taking it that you become totally dependent. This is where fasting comes in, you can be delivered and set free through fasting and prayer. You must commit to submit!!

Sometimes, one is unable to do this on their own and may require the help of a trained individual. hasatan literally, played on every emotion, every thought, and especially through physical pain to keep me in bondage. It is only through deep prayer and intercession along with fasting that I am able to overcome this.

Intercession is a tool the Spirit/ Ruach HaKodesh uses to counteract evil and purify human vessels.

PURIFY= CLEANSE

Fasting really is a discipline of desire and a purpose of passion for a new level of authority. As Sons and Daughters of Zadok, we must come to the conclusion at once that this walk in this realm, must be done as Yahusha did as the example for us. To attain the power and authority that Yahusha said we each would do and even greater than he requires us to be completely set apart in every area of our lives. This is NOT an option! Through fasting, the overcoming spirit is awakened in us and it increases our stamina which is necessary for the type of worship we were created to worship **KING YAHUSHA!**

"For the kingdom o f G od is not a matter of eating and drinking, but of righteo usness, peace, and joy in the Ruach HaKodesh." Romans 14:17

Fasting opens the door between two dimensions in order to feast on **Yahuah's DIVINE NATURE.** Fasting is the vehicle to receive the golden anointing oil that brings forth miracles, signs, and wonders as you could never have imagined until you let go of this world and step into the supernatural realm with Yahuah!

Prayer for the Sick
Mi Sheberach Hebrew
Avoteinu: Avraham, Yitzhak, v'Yaakov,
v'Imoteinu: Sarah, Rivka, Rachel v'Leah,
Hu yivarech virapei
et hacholeh/hacholah _____ ben/bat _____
HaKadosh Baruch Hu

yimalei rachamim alav/aleha,
l'hachalimo/l'hachlimah,
u-l'rap'oto/u-l'rap'otah,
l'hachaziko/l'hazikah,
u-l'chay-oto/u-l'chay-otah.
V'yishlach lo/lah bim-hera
r'fuah   shlemah ,
r'fu-at hanefesh u-r'fu-at hagoof,
b'toch   sh'ar cholei Yisrael v'cholei yoshvei tevel,
hashta ba'agalah u-vizman kariv,
v'no-mar, Amen!

POWER OF YAHUAH, YAHUSHA, and RUACH HAKODESH targeted to healing of physical and spiritual body and being.

The Ruach is like a special medical team for those who have especially deep wounds -- for example, those who have been raped, those who suffer from what's done by despotic governments, those who have to constantly face their society's racism, those on the losing end of an economic system or a political power struggle, those who are enslaved by alcohol or drugs, or rendered slaves to fear.

In Yahusha's own ministry, **inner healing** was firmly connected to **physical healing** , both being a work of the Spirit. Yahuah is concerned about the whole of us, not just the inner self. We're all fractured beings that the Ruach HaKodesh is working to make complete.

Mi Sheberach English

May the One who blessed our ancestors —
Patriarchs Abraham, Isaac, and Jacob,
Matriarchs Sarah, Rebecca, Rachel, and Leah —
bless and heal the one who is ill:
_____ of _____ .
May the Holy Blessed One
overflow with compassion upon him/her,
to restore him/her,
to heal him/her,
to strengthen him/her,
to enliven him/her.
The One will send him/her, speedily,
a complete healing —
healing of the soul and healing of the body —
along with all the ill,
among the people of Israel and all humankind,

soon,
speedily,
without delay,
and let us all say: Amen!

We are the **BRIDE of Yahusha** ; we have been washed in the blood of the
Lamb (brazen altar) cleansed through immersion (brazen lava) betrothed in
Marriage Covenant (ten commandments) and is practising her deliverance to
gain her wedding garments (inner sanctum services of Moses Tabernacle)
and is now using the three amazing behavioural rules to be perfected and
matured in **BEHAVIOUR** granting her direct access to the presence of
Yahusha Himself (David's Tabernacle).

WE know that our fleshly vessels are the tent of meeting today. How we take care of our
bodies reflects where we are in our walk with **YaH** and our transformation to becoming
HIS Bride. Is your body (Tent of Meeting) dedicated to religious beastly/worldly behaviour
or is your body, mind, soul being trained to that of **Yahusha's** who practically lived these
three rules below:

LOVE (loving others and YaH) **OBEDIENCE** (in all things to the Father, to
Torah, the Law.) **SPIRIT OVER FLESH** (HE overcame all things) Yahusha
did not pollute the temple physically nor spiritually. **HE** fasted, prayed,
obeyed, and walked in love. **HE** was always honoring **HIS FATHER** in all
HE did!!

Faith in Action= Power Now= Miracles
Three fold prescription for HEALING-
Accept the truth
Embrace deliverance
Allow healing and blessing to overtake you
Ten Healing Commandments
   1. I am Yahuah, your HEALER and thou shalt have no other healers before me.
      Exodus 15:26
   2. Thou shalt receive my healing scriptures Psalm 107:20
   3. Thou shalt not be offended at miracles or healings Matthew 11:5,6 Luke 7:22
   4. Thou shalt live righteously in gratitude for Yahusha's stripes 1 Peter 2:24
   5. Thou shalt not fear sickness Jeremiah 30:11, 13, 17
   6. Thou shalt take care of your body (robe for this world) 1 Corinthians 3:16
   7. Thou shalt eat your fruits and vegetables Genesis 1:29
   8. Thou shalt ask for the anointing oil James 5: 14, 15
   9. Thou shalt believe Matthew 13:58
   10. Thou shalt lay hands on the sick Mark 16: 17, 18

ISAIAH 58
Light:
Then your light shall break forth like the morning

Healing:
Your healing shall spring forth speedily

Righteousness:
And your righteousness shall go before you

Glory:
The glory of Yahuah shall be your rear guard

Prayers Answered:
Then you shall call, and Yahuah will answer; You shall cry, and He will say, 'Here I am'

Guidance:
The Most High will guide you continually

Satisfaction:
And satisfy your soul in drought

Refreshment:
And strengthen your bones; You shall be like a watered garden, And like a spring of water, whose waters do not fail
Restoration:
And you shall be called the Repairer of the Breach, The Restorer of Streets to Dwell In

Renewal:
You shall raise up the foundations of many generations.
But when he saw many Pharisees and Sadducees coming to his immersion, he said to them, "You brood of vipers! Who warned you to flee from the coming wrath? Therefore produce fruit worthy of repentance; and do not think that you can say to yourselves, 'We have Abraham as our father'! For I tell you that from these stones [Elohim] can raise up children for Abraham. Already the axe is laid at the root of the trees; therefore every tree that does not produce good fruit is cut down and thrown into the fire! As for me, I immerse you in water for repentance. But the One coming after me is mightier than I am; I am not worthy to carry His sandals. He will immerse you in the Ruach ha-Kodesh and fire. His winnowing fork is in His hand, and He shall clear His threshing floor and gather His wheat into the barn; but the chaff He shall burn up with inextinguishable fire. **Matthew 3.7-12**

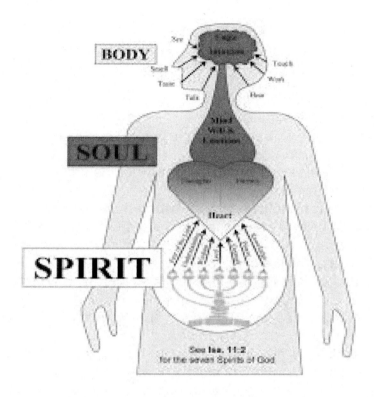

The diagram labels include: BODY, SOUL, SPIRIT, Mind Will & Emotion, Heart, and reference "See Isa. 11:2 for the seven Spirits of God"

Ecclesiasticus (Sirach) 2

My son, if thou come to serve Yahuah, prepare thy soul for temptation.

Set thy heart aright, and constantly endure, and make not haste in time of trouble.

Cleave unto him, and depart not away, that thou mayest be increased at thy last end.

Whatsoever is brought upon thee take cheerfully, and be patient when thou art changed to a low estate.

For gold is tried in the fire, and acceptable men in the furnace of adversity.

Believe in him, and he will help thee; order thy way aright, and trust in him.

Ye that fear Yahuah, wait for his mercy; and go not aside, lest ye fall.

Ye that fear Yahuah, believe him; and your reward shall not fail.

Ye that fear Yahuah, hope for good, and for everlasting joy and mercy.

Look at the generations of old, and see; did ever any trust in the Lord, and was confounded? or did any abide in his fear, and was forsaken? or whom did he ever despise, that called upon him?

For the Most High is full of compassion and mercy, longsuffering, and very pitiful, and forgives sins, and saveth in time of affliction.

Woe be to fearful hearts, and faint hands, and the sinner that goeth two ways!

Woe unto him that is fainthearted! for he believeth not; therefore shall he not be defended.

Woe unto you that have lost patience! and what will you do when **Yahuah Elohim** shall visit you?

They that fear **Adonai** will not disobey **HIS** Word; and they that love him will keep his ways.

They that fear **Adonai** will seek that which is well, pleasing unto **HIM;** and they that love **HIM** shall be filled with the law.

They that fear the **Most High** will prepare their hearts, and humble their souls in **HIS** sight,

Saying, We will fall into the hands of **Yahuah** , and not into the hands of men: for as his majesty is, so is **HIS** mercy.

Be counted WORTHY through the true test of Tribulation

"And take heed to yourselves, lest at any time your hearts be overcharged with surfeiting, and drunkenness, and the cares of this life, and so that day come upon you unawares. For as a snare shall it come on all them that dwell on the face of the whole earth. Watch ye therefore, and pray always, that ye may be accounted worthy to escape all these things that shall come to pass, and to stand before the Son of man." Luke 21:34-36

Be PREPARED to pray without ceasing and always putting on the **FULL ARMOR OF YAHUAH.**

- Be prepared to help others always. Give all you have to help another.
- Water could be limited or supplies poisoned. Water filters will be necessary.
- Food will be limited and scarce. Stock up NOW. Grow your own. Save seeds. Share.
- Shelter could be a house, mobile home, RV, tent, whatever. Many us of will commune together in the coming times.
- Energy- There will be a need to find energy from solar, wind, or generators although fuel will be limited.
- Protection from criminals/those who are led by the enemy. You will see the demons in people manifest to the physical eyes. Be ready and expect to see the supernatural.

Pray the seven Spirits of YAHUAH ELOHIM and the Seven
PRAYERS from YaH together to overcome wickedness and the wicked one.

Seven SPIRITS OF YAHUAH	Seven Prayers of YaH
Spirit of Yahuah	Prayer of Agreement
Spirit of Wisdom	Prayer ofThanksgiving
Spirit of Understanding	Prayer of Binding
Spirit of Counsel	Prayer of Loosing
Spirit of Power	Prayer of Faith
Spirit of Knowledge	Pray for Understanding
Spirit of FEAR of YHWH	Praying in the Spirit

3 Types of People who aim to derail YOU! BEWARE

- ungodly
- sinners
- scornful

Prayer for:

Knowledge

Redemption

Teshuvah

Health

Forgiveness

Prosperity

Shalom/Joy

PRAY with -- INTENTION
DEVOTION
DIRECTION

True **WORSHIP** begins on the floor/ ground prostrate before The Most High.

YaH's Books	**Seven Angels of Yahuah**
Book of LIFE	Michael
Book of REMEMBRANCE	Gabriel
Book of the LIVING	Raphael
Book of the LAW	Uriel
Book of Moses	Selaphiel
Book of the VISION	Raguel
Book of the KINGS OF ISRAEL	Jegudiel
Book of PSALMS	Barachiel
Book of HISTORY	

Precious Metals-

1 Peter 1: 18,19- Exodus 30: 11-16- Duet. 33:25- Zec. 4:6
 Ephesians 3:16

GOLD- BRASS- - SILVER Gold=Bride, Silver=Beloveds,
Brass=Wicked/Lukewarmers
Copper can be found as a metal

Heavy Metals

hasatan's twists and mixes everything YaH meant for good to bad. How heavy metals harm our bodies now and in the coming days.

Basic Information About Protecting Yourself and Loved Ones from Heavy Metal Poisoning, 5G and other poisons intentionally released into the public now and during the tribulation. I am not a medical professional. I am only sharing information and suggesting supplements for you to stock up on now. Borax Supplementation Alleviates Hematotoxicity and DNA Damage. (PubMed)

BORAX DOSES AND REFERENCE: (Print and place on box. Store in an emergency kit.

Firstly dissolve a lightly rounded teaspoonful (5-6 grams) of borax in 1litre of good quality water. This is your concentrated solution, keep it out of reach of small children. Standard dose = 1 teaspoon (5 ml) of concentrate. This has 25 to 30 mg of borax and provides about 3 mg of boron. If there is no specific health problem you may continue indefinitely with 1 or 2 doses daily.

Note: Of the litre of solution made above you can safely take 4 tsp a day EASILY. And for short periods with breaks you can take 20 OR MORE tsp a day if you are in dire health and it is an applicable treatment.
Vitamin C, Bone Broth, Turmeric, Flax seeds, Onions, Garlic, Milk Thistle, Activated Charcoal, Cilantro, Bentonite Clay, Triphala, MSM
*I do not give medical advice or remedies.

EMF Radiation--What to Take
Iodine, Noni, Melatonin, Spirulina, Magnesium, Selenium, Potassium, Calcium. Frankincense, Oregano.

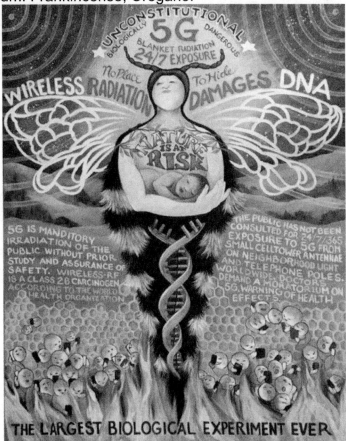

BEMIDBAR   31: 21-23

And Eleazar the priest said to the men of the campaign who went to the battle ,"This is the law of the Torah which יהוה commanded Mosheh: "Only the gold, and the silver, bronze, iron, tin, and the lead, every object that passes through fire, you put through the fire, and it shall be clean; only, let it be cleansed with the water for uncleanness. And whatever does not pass through fire you pass through water.

Take heed for these **WORDS** and scripts are dangerous and you could very well be put to death for having them in your possession. You will need what is here to sustain you. For these **WORDS** are of Yahuah our **GREAT AND MIGHTY ELOHIM** and with the blessed Ruach HaKodesh leading; YOU will eat and be full and drink and not thirst. Remember, you are only here for but, a short time,the **END of all ENDS** draws nigh. Do exactly what you read and take to these prayers daily. For hasatan and his demons will do whatever they can to cause strong delusions and false visions; he will tempt you, try to cause wicked strife and ignorance. he will play games with your mind and attempt to close your eyes and ears. he will whisper lies to you though you know he is the father of lies. Be not misled, nor misdirected. Do not judge one another. Do not be angry with one another. For there is strength in numbers and you must forge an alliance of good against all evil for the remainder of your time on this earth. Stay together, for if one of you strays you may all stray. Leave no one behind who confesses Yahusha HaMashiach. Hold tightly to one another as the disciples once did long ago. Forget **NOT** their example and the example of Yahusha Ha'Mashiach in the flesh. When the hour of your departure comes, rejoice for you know where you will go. hasatan will throw fear at you from every angle and you must not let it penetrate your gates; and you **MUST NOT** be weak in emotions, nor in your flesh, nor love this world.

Take time now to immerse yourself in the **WORD of LIFE** and cleanse your flesh by fasting, for the time you are in is worse than any could ever imagine. Accept where you are and hold fast to the truth that you will soon be in Paradise with Yahuah Elohim. You have a very dangerous and all important mission, **YOU** must share the **WORD** with those who refuse the mark, those who are sincerely lost and know their fateful mistake. Stay close to one another.

Two types of Servants: We will bear witness to the great and mighty power of Yahuah in these last days through immediate radical conversions and expedited discipleship to gather the lost just before the end.

- A Whosoever

-A Suddenly

Ahavah- Love

Emunah- Faith

Teshuvah- Repentance

These are the qualities of a Zadok Priest:

We as Sons and Daughters of Zadok are to worship in spirit and in truth. Worship means to bow down. In Spirit means breath or wind. When we worship in spirit and in truth to the Most High Elohim, we bow down prostrate before **HIM as HIS** wind (Ruach HaKodesh) blows over us. True worship is offering ourselves daily as a living sacrifice. Romans 12:1 We should be on our face daily thanking **HIM for HIS** favor to us and **HIS** loving kindness. **HE** establishes our thoughts as we walk by the spirit and **NOT** by the flesh. For we know that enmity is between the flesh and the spirit. The world is weariness to the righteous but the next is theirs. The Righteous depart from this habitation without fear, for they have a store of works preserved in treasuries. So, when judgement comes the members of the Natsarim community are assured of salvation.

Days Are Getting Darker

We are to examine ourselves daily. We are to do all we can to stand, endure, and overcome. **DO NOT ALLOW ANYONE TO STEAL YOUR CROWN!**

The Narrow Path

The narrow path is truly becoming narrower. The endurance of the set apart ones, we who guard the commands of Yahuah and the belief of Yahusha must keep an eternal perspective. We are warriors in every aspect. We know that **HE** will not let **HIS** elect be misdirected, we follow Yahusha as Natsarim obedient to **HIM!** We know we are to keep firmly to the observance of **HIS** commandments and **HIS** rules. To observe and apply ourselves daily in order that we may possess the land and bequeath it forever. Keep a fervent heart, single mind, and seek **HIM** and **HE** will be found.

TRUST YAHUAH--SUBMIT TO YAHUAH--LEAVE BABYLON

VISION OF NATSARIM TODAY

The faithful to the fellowship apostolic community; they in the past broke bread daily together and we will again too. They who prayed daily together and were filled with awe and worked signs, miracles, and wonders. We will do this again too! When in the time of the Natsarim community they came together and sold their possessions and their goods then distributed them among one another according to what each needed. **WE WILL DO THIS AGAIN TOO!** For together they shared their emunah (faith) and operated from one heart generously **PRAISING YAHUAH!** The reward was that daily their numbers increased. I believe we too will see this reward as in the **LAST HARVEST of SOULS!**

For then Yahuah, provided all they needed **DAY BY DAY!** This same promise is for us too! We who have chosen to come out of Babylon and have let go of the doctrines of man to search out what was hidden for so long are fully devoted to "The Way". Together we shall go from wilderness to wilderness. We who are the remnant of HIS seed those of us who keep the commandments. **We are Natsarim= the watchtower of Elohim.**

Natsarim are Kingdom Workers

Our very survival is in Yahuah's power. What can we do to help those who are still sleeping? We must pray for only YaH can truly wake someone up and call them to return to the ancient path. The world hates obedience. Obedience evokes bitterness. Yahuah Elohim has begun the restoration of all things.

KEFA= endtime restoration= Repent! Therefore turn back!

Examine Yourself

Where can the enemy breach my walls?

What are my biggest weaknesses?

What do I need to let go of?

How is my heart today? Are my thoughts pure? Is my mouth clean?

*ABBA, I pray you will bring me into correct alignment with **YOUR WILL, YOUR WAY**, and **YOUR WORD** today. Keep me on the narrow path. Help me to take every thought captive in obedience to YOU. Thank you ABBA. I love you. I am your humble servant. In Yahusha's Name--Amein.*

TORAH OF FREEDOM is A REVOLUTION in OBEDIENCE

The words of *Brother James* in chapter 2 verses 10-13 are to be taken very seriously! For your very soul and spirit are dependent on it. Judgement is never compassionate! Judgement is LAW. **LAW is YAHUAH ELOHIM, the GREAT and MIGHTY JUDGE WHO SITS ON HIS THRONE.**

For **whosoever** shall guard all the Torah, and yet stumble in one point, he is guilty of all.

For He who said, "Do not commit adultery," also said, "Do not murder." Now if you do not commit adultery, but you do murder, you have become a transgressor of Torah.

So speak and so do as those who are to be judged by a Torah of freedom.

For the judgment is without compassion to the one who has shown no compassion. And compassion boasts over judgment.

A Spirit of Excellence is required within the Sons and Daughters of Zadok. We are to be excellent in all things. To show the world what a life of excellence looks like.

Excellence = Holiness= Purity

Living with excellence and purity requires one also to be fully evicted from this world. We must have strong and secure roots that run deep so when testing and trials come we can not be moved. For we know that Yahusha himself is the root of our hope.

Seek יהוה, all you meek ones of the earth, who have done His right-ruling. Seek righteousness, seek meekness, if so be that you are hidden in the day of wrath of יהוה. Zep. 2:3

The Digital Apocalypse

Destroy the idols (gods, demons, and spirits) who possess technology. Age of technology has brought about the idolatry of knowledge. People idolize knowledge above understanding, They worship devices above the worship of the Most High, Yahuah of Abraham, Issac, and Jacob! This age has quickly ushered in demons through portals from other dimensions. These demons have full access to us because we are attached to the technology. People everywhere bow down and submit to the gods of the underworld who are now gods of the digital era. We are fast approaching the point of no return, where hasatans plan to create a host body and fill it with a demon through AI.

Beware! They will sell lies to you and loved ones to get you to embrace handing over your very soul, spirit, and free will with full permission aka the mark of the beast! Buyer beware, the chip will make you not only doomed to eternal hell fire but, to become the property of hasatan, the beast system.

STIMULANTS/ STIMULATION---MUTANTS or MUTILATION
Pay Attention to WORDS!

Mind control. This is the plan of the enemy. Full submission of the human body, soul, and mind to him. Knowing this and having been warned all throughout the **WORD** of YaH and from many Prophets, there will still be those who are sleeping and they will be lied to, manipulated, and greatly deceived into taking the mark of the beast. Technology already exists that can alter your thinking and deprive you about thoughts of Yahuah and cause you to think more logically. Once they have the mark their whole body, soul and mind belong to hasatan. There is no escape!!!

THE LOOPHOLE

There is a small loophole that my *Sister Jolene Canatone on YouTube* received revelation from the Ruach HaKodesh about the chip aka, Mark of the Beast.

It was revealed to her that those who receive the **MARK** who have **NO KNOWLEDGE** of Yahusha/ Yahuah at all can be redeemed by cutting off their hand or plucking out their The problem with this loophole, I see with this theory is that because their minds will be stimulated to hate Yahuah, I do not think it will be possible. People will literally lose their

minds and become " the walking dead ". They will feel terrible pain like being struck a thousand times by scorpions as it says in Revelations .
eye . Which is why the scriptures say

MANIFESTATION OF TECHNO DIS EASE

I have been reading and listening to warnings of the coming virus that will infect everyone who does not believe in YaH and those who turned their back on YaH. This virus will manifest itself in the most wicked of ways and varies in symptoms.

What am I talking about?

I am talking about technology. Smarter, faster, moving through energetic boundaries of color, form, and light in our perceived realities. The ability to create your own reality. Corruption of DNA, the kind of technology that is designed to breakdown the spiritual force center of man. This goes beyond scientific research for an artificial heart or a new limb. This technology started ever so subtle by the poisoning of our food, food supply and the air and water. By infecting first the very elements of our survival ensuring that eventually they would sell the population on enhanced upgrades to food, water, and environment through scare tactics of the world coming to an end if we don't do something. Next, they infected our minds in the form of social media. At first, it was about connecting us all. Friends and more friends. Then, once we have all been connected via social "destruction" the next move was to enforce the virus into everyone's bloodstream via the vaccination holocaust. If you don't comply well, they will "force" you! I forgot to add in the infection of abortions and destruction of our precious little ones via Planned Parenthood. Let's move on..now comes the whole faster, smarter, and better with 5G roll out. Society is now absorbed in radiation poisoning from millimeter wave technology. And with this now they can infect our bodies with nanotechnology thus creating a scoreboard dis-eases to separate us from our Creator, (which by the way is the ultimate plan). Add in body modification that the younger generation has been gladly injected with, that has led to self worship. Which, brings me to Body Hacking, Crisper, A.I., and the master virus of Transhumanism!!

The DIS-EASE of this AGE, is about mind control, mass control, and mass deception. With biohacking, implants, alternatives making fantasy a reality. Brain enhancements, brain performance drugs, i.e. supplements. Intelligent mind mapping, system intelligence slavery, mixing DNA and seed corruption. The goal is not only mind, body, spirit, and body corruption and infection but also, extermination! WAKE UP FRIENDS!

They have been dumbing us down for so long now. The ultimate goal is the creation of the synth. A body that is basically a shell that can have a digital brain of YOUR memories, thoughts, feelings, emotions and will. This being will operate miraculously by demons, spirits and entities that will enter because the portals that should not be open have been opened. hasatan the enemy of our soul has resurrected the Nephilim in our day. His goal is to defile the seed and cause chaos in our body's ability to function on a normal basis. With all this technology at hand, he can attempt to cause a blockage of the spirit and clog the flow of the Ruach HaKodesh in us. hasatan is drawing people into a techno-chaotic world in order to corrupt the free flow of energy through the body and turn man into a digital persona. Through the corruption of DNA the scripture is fulfilled that says, "men will seek death and not find it." The purpose of this post is to prayerfully wake you up. There

38

will come a time when men's hearts will fail them. If you are not awake now, there is a high probability that you will not see any of the coming before it is simply too late.
I leave you with these thoughts from the scripture:

"Guard your steps when you go to the House of Elohim. And draw near to listen rather than to give the slaughtering of fools, for they do not know that they do evil.
Do not be hasty with your mouth, and let not your heart hurry to bring forth a word before Elohim. For Elohim is in the heavens, and you on earth, therefore let your words be few.
For a dream comes through the greatness of the task, and a fool's voice is known by his many words." **Eccle. 5 : 1-3**

Brothers and Sisters, our mainline of defense right now is to stop eating GMO and processed foods (although everything is contaminated) but eat more "real" foods. Stop eating food sacrificed to idols! Stop using smart devices if you can. Stop holding your cell phone close to your body and always talk with the speaker phone. Stop vaccinations!!! I can not stress that enough. Do your own research! PRAYER!! Pray over your food, environment, and for others. Pray the blood of Yahusha over yourself, your family, your food, house, everything! Fasting!!! Fasting is the secret prescription for healing.
This technoapocalyse is here. It is the enemy's last stand to take out as many as possible. I encourage you to stay in the WORD which is life, pray for wisdom and discernment. Pray for our youth who were born into slavery that eyes may be opened!!
We must remain organic people to receive our new transformed bodies!! Simple living is key. Loose the bonds of digital slavery beginning today!
"And if your right hand causes you to sin, cut it off and throw it away. It is better for you to lose one part of your body than for your whole body to depart into hell."
Matthew 5:30
"If your right eye causes you to sin, gouge it out and throw it away. It is better for you to lose one part of your body than for your whole body to be thrown into hell."
Matthew 5:29

Schemes of hasatan

And they went up through the South and came to Ḥeḇron. And Aḥiman, Shĕshai, and

Talmai, the descendants of Anaq, were there. Now Ḥeḇron had been built seven years before Tso'an in   Mitsrayim . Numbers 13:22

Descendants of
ANAK = enemy
AHIMAN= will block plans and purposes, stronghold to hinder one.
SHESHAI= ability to make something appear better than it really is. i.e. beautiful outside/ ugly inside.
TALMAI= spirit of accumulation. Desires to keep us busy with "nothing". Meaningless tasks and time wasters.
GIANTS IN THE LAND
JEBUSITE= trodden down
GIRGASHITE= spirit of compromise (utilizes justification of the grey areas)
CANAANITE = spirit of materialism
HITTITES= spirit of fear

PERIZZITE= open and unwalled

AMORITE= spirits of pride, rebellion, bitterness, and boasting

HIVITES= spirit of open lies

For those of you who are "lukewarm" or unbelievers I just want to say, "the **MARK** IS **REAL** and the rapture **IS REAL!** " Once you have the mark there is no repentance and no forgiveness. You are at the mercy of hasatan, the enemy of your soul!! **REPENT NOW, CONFESS YOUR SINS** and receive **YAHUSHA as YOUR SAVIOR!!**

Rise Up! Call upon the **NAME OF YAHUAH** and **HE** will save **YOU!**

We must take up our weapons and go to **WAR** ! The Era of Spiritual Authority is **NOW!** With it we can with Yahusha's authority break open the darkness and go into the dark places and free the captives before it is too late. Yahuah is on the move and we are in a current time of preparation for the coming of **KING YAHUSHA!**

These are the things we must STAY ALERT FOR! I am repeating many things in this book because our memory will be tested as much as our minds.

5G- Chemtrails- Body Modification- Body Hacking- A.I.- Transhumanism
Mind Control- Mass Control- Mind Deception- Crispr Technology- Forced Vaccinations-
Nanotechnology- All Chip Devices- Social Media Control-Heat Seeking Drones

FEAR of YAHUAH = BEGINNING OF WISDOM

We know that for everything and anything that has purpose and meaning to YaH, there is a counterfeit which is hasatan's . Many words have multiple meanings as I have shared throughout this book. I find as I am researching for the topics and words to include I am blown away at how every single thing links back to only two things and that is Yahuah or hasatan basically **GOOD vs. EVIL.** Words have multi dimensional meanings. For example: dis **CERN** ment. **DIS-** ease and so on. It is interesting to note the following: greek word for **WISDOM** (**'Sophia')** or its translations as a divine name becomes sophistry.

As to the coming of our Master יהושע Messiah and our gathering together to Him, we ask you, brothers,

not to become easily unsettled in mind or troubled, either by spirit or by word or by letter, as if from us, as if the day of יהוה has come.

Let no one deceive you in any way, because the falling away is to come first, and the man of lawlessness is to be revealed , the son of destruction,

2 Thessalonians 1-3

The point is- **STAY ALERT!** Pay attention to detail in everything and take it into your prayer closet! This is sound advice for warning you for what is coming.

Yahuah gave me some insight into the digital apocalypse. **HE** said, " Before the internet hasatans testament was limited!" Why **HE** choose the word testament I did not know until this very moment. **HE** used the word testament because hasatan could not initiate the Beast System without technology being the internet. People who take the mark of the beast will become the property of the beast!!

Testament= Dictionary.com

Law .

    1.   a will, especially one that relates to the disposition of **one's personal property.**

2. a covenant , especially between God and humans.

Technology has advanced hasatan's agenda in the form of the Beast System. It presented and agreement of wicked people aka worshippers of hasatan, for fame, money, and even eternal life as they believe and have been deceived! Social Media was the prescription for self destruction on a new level as the world had never seen before! It thrusts many into idolatry of self by self seeking motives, self elevation, self loathing, self promotion and self love.

With Facebook, Instagram, Twitter, Snapchat, Pinterest, YouTube, and so on...hasatan tricked all of us! Thankfully we have an ABBA Father, who loves us enough to reveal the truth to us. But, for those who are not awake they are victims of the enemy's tricks, manipulations, to bring forth his short reign on earth. Some will not turn from their wicked ways because they love the world too much. They choose fame, fortune, and fantasy above faith, humility, and truth/ reality. With the 5G roll out this will not just allow A.I. to evolve it will also open portals to other dimensions that should not be opened.

A.I. is the evolution of smarter and more intelligent false beings that will become possessed by demonic spirits who will enter through the portals and take possession of synthetic bodies created by technology. Yahuah showed me the following breakdown and use of these words in our very near future and I am to share these with you so you will be alert to the truth when it is presented before you.

Technology is designed to break down the spiritual force center of man. This is the ultimate goal. It is meant to make any form of A.I. smarter and faster than humans. It serves one purpose that is to alienate us from our **CREATOR.** Corrupting **DNA=** men will seek death and shall not find it. Light energy= exploration of energetic boundaries of color/ form/ light/ perceived in our reality. We must remain organic to be transformed to our " **NEW BODIES"** .

DES   TIN   NATION

(destroy) (implode) (people)

Above is the breakdown of the word destination for us and the enemy's plan with technology.

A. I. Destiny= trickery

    Destination= ultimate goal

The Great Divide/ True Parting of the Red Sea/ Release of the Ten Plagues

Those on the side of **Pharaoh-** --------------------------Those on the side of **Moses**

The World	*Eternity with Elohim*
lies, deception	*love, wisdom*
rebellion	*discipline*
lukewarmers	*Kings & Priests- Melchizedek/Zadok*
love of things	*love of people*

We must examine ourselves daily. We are on the stand everyday. We must do all we can to stand, endure, and overcome! Let us remain humble and in a spirit of repentance. We are to offer ourselves as a living sacrifice daily. Keeping and eternal perspective. If we love **HIM** we will obey His commands! We are Warriors for Yahusha and Warriors of the Word. We must keep firmly to the observance of **HIS** commands and rules.

We are to keep a fervent heart, single mind to seek HIM and HE will be found in these dark days ahead. We are **HIS VESSELS** in the House of the **MOST HIGH** . We are vessels of every kind that HE fills for **HIS PURPOSES** . Know that this world is weariness to the righteous but the next is for the righteous. That is **OUR HOPE!**

The Beast System is HERE! We are to leave Babylon/Egypt!

YAH's Way	Beast System
Set our hands to the Kingdom of Heaven	wants us to work for the system
Clean heart	You are to labor the mark is
How to operate as a Priest	an external sign of an internal condition
Operate in the treasury rooms	
How to labor for fruit and for everlasting life	Labor for material worldly things
Yahuah gives provision	work of the world is still cursed
Yahuah seals **HIS BELOVED'S** to	Oppressed by the KIngs of the earth
eat from the "Tree of Life"	**SHAME** in doing things in our own
to him who overcomes	strength and power
Money in the Kingdom is not buy	**SHAME** of sin of Adam
or sell, exchange	

Seven PILLARS OF WISDOM

1. Fear of Yahuah
2. Prudence
3. Knowledge and Discretion
4. Sound Judgement
5. Insight
6. Power
7. Counsel

Now the works of the flesh are manifest which are these, adultery, fornication, uncleanness, lasciviousness, idolatry, witchcraft, hatred, variance, emulations, wrath, strife, seditions, heresies, envyings, murders, drunkenness, reveilings and the such like which I told you before, as I have told you in time past, that they which do such things shall not inherit the **KINGDOM OF YAHUAH!** Galatians 5:19-21

Fruits of the Spirit

Love- Joy- Peace- Patience- Goodness- Forbearance- Self-Control- Gentleness- Faithfulness- Kindness

Characteristics of Yahuah

Purity, Comforts, Perfect, Remembered, Requires Obedience, Trustworthy, Loves, Desires, Eternal, Taught, Proclaimed, Blesses, Righteous, True, Preserves, Gives Joy, Praiseworthy, Guides, Gives Wisdom

BREATH OF POWER

WISDOM is the Breath of POWER of YAHUAH

She is a reflection of eternal light. A mirror of YaH's active power. Image of **HIS** goodness. **WISDOM** is as I stated earlier, unchanging from generation to generation passing the **HOLY SOULS** . She makes them into Yahuah's friends and Prophets, for **YaH** loves those who dwell with **WISDOM.**

For wisdom is more moving than any motion: she passeth and goeth through all things by reason of her pureness.

For she is the breath of the power of Yahuah, and a pure influence flowing from the glory of the Almighty: therefore can no defiled thing fall into her.

For she is the brightness of the everlasting light, the unspotted mirror of the power of YaH, and the image of his goodness.

And being but one, she can do all things: and remaining in herself, she maketh all things new: and in all ages entering into holy souls, she maketh them friends of YaH, and prophets.

For Yahuah loveth none but him that dwelleth with wisdom.

For she is more beautiful than the sun, and above all the order of stars: being compared with the light, she is found before it. Book of Wisdom 7: 24-29

Ruach HaKodesh= Holy Breath of YaH

Yahuah is the Breath of Power in Action! We see this all throughout the **WORD of YaH.** To fully understand how powerful Yahuah's breath really is we must look at the sevenfold doctrine that Enoch talks about here in Enoch 93:12.

Afterwards, in the seventh week a perverse generation shall arise; abundant shall be its deeds and all its deeds perverse. During its completion, the righteous shall be selected from the everlasting plant of righteousness; and to them shall be given the **sevenfold doctrine** of **HIS** whole creation.

What is this sevenfold doctrine?

The Seven Doctrine of Yahuah Elohim

Ruach Emunah of Faith

Ruach Chokmah of Wisdom

Ruach Netsach of Long Suffering

Ruach Checed of Mercy

Ruach Mishpat of Judgement

Ruach Shalom of Peace

Ruach Rahtson of Benevolence

We are only discussing here the shear magnification of power that Yahuah's breath alone has. What is **HIS** breath? Is it a spirit or wind? Let us look at Strong's (7307) definition of Ruach.

Ruach = *understood to mean wind; by resemblance can be breath; a sensible or even violent exhalation. to blow; to breathe.*

Yahuah unifies the sevenfold doctrine to HIS seven spirits, together this display of **POWER** should release into every living being the true **FEAR of YAHUAH our ELOHIM!** Read here in Isaiah 11:1-5

We can see YaH's full display of **HIS Breath of POWER** in the seven days of creation.

Breath of Benevolence and Fear of Yahuah in Genesis 1:2-3

Breath of Wisdom and Ruach of Wisdom in Genesis 1: 3-5 (1st DAY)

Breath of Longsuffering and Ruach of Understanding in Genesis 1: 6-8 (2nd DAY)

Breath of Peace and Ruach of Counsel in Genesis 1: 9-13 (3rd DAY)

Breath of Judgement and Ruach of Strength in Genesis 1: 14-19 (4th DAY)

Breath of Mercy and Ruach of Knowledge in Genesis 1: 20-23 (5th DAY)

Breath of Faith and Fear of Yahuah in Genesis 1: 24-31 (6th DAY)
Then, **ELOHIM** saw what **HE** created and said, " it is good." **HE** rested on the 7th **DAY** !
Read here in **Isaiah 11:1-5**
And there shall come forth a rod out of the stem of Jesse, and a Branch shall grow out of his roots:
And the spirit of **YAHUAH** shall rest upon him, the spirit of wisdom and understanding, the spirit of counsel and might, the spirit of knowledge and of the fear of **YAH** ;
And shall make him of quick understanding in the fear of **YAHUAH:** and he shall not judge after the sight of his eyes, neither reprove after the hearing of his ears:
But with righteousness shall he judge the poor, and reprove with equity for the meek of the earth: and he shall smite the earth with the rod of his mouth, and with the breath of his lips shall he slay the wicked.
And righteousness shall be the girdle of his loins, and faithfulness the girdle of his reins.

KEYS OF THE PRIESTLY ORDER
House of David-----Tent of Abraham
Governors and Judges- - 1 Chronicles 24 and Revelation 4:4
Singers and Magicians --Prophesy with the Harp-- 1 Chronicles 25, Revelation 5, 8, & 9
Porters and Gatekeepers -- Living Creatures/ Opens and Seals Doors
Army Captains --Primary military legions--White, Red, Black, Pale
KEY--Intimacy--Call down HIS PRESENCE
Prayer and Worship are the roles of GateKeepers as Watchman!
Stand Guard those who proclaim the good news of the gospel.

KEY OF YEHOYADAH
King and Priestly Order of Four--Four Architects--Four Carpenters
"Thus said יהוה of hosts, 'If you walk in My ways, and if you guard My duty, then you shall also rule My house, and also guard My courts. And I shall give you access among these standing here."
Zechariah 3:7

Key to the House of David
We are the generation of men and women who wear the garments of David. This is the call, **WARRIORS RISE to support KING YAHUSHA!** YaH is raising a division of "Special Forces" for this last harvest! We will bear witness to radical conversions, people being healed and delivered, set free from demons, preachers, teachers and evangelists!! We are the pioneers forging paths into the mountains of government, business, arts, media and the "new church" the ekklesia of Natsarim in these last days.
4- Judges
24- Elders
24- Singers and Musicians
24- Porters
24- Military
As Sons and Daughters of Zadok the **WORDS** spoken to us and through us must be Rhema/ Revelation, we must become one with them. It is a part of us. The **RIVER OF LIFE** flowing out of the Temple (us) in the presence of Yahuah to a world thirsty for every

drop. Fear stops the flow. Sons and Daughters of Zadok were not allowed to fear or enable fear to be the reason or occasion for any action.

Mark= Lion = strength   **Mark= Ox** = Power   **Luke= Man** = Character
John= Eagle = Deity/ Person

" Before you speak, learn; and before you fall ill, take care of your health. Before judgement comes, examine yourself- and at the time of scrutiny you will find forgiveness. Before falling ill, humble yourself and when you have sinned, repent!" **Sirach 18:19-21**

Spiritual Tapestry

Habits that perfect the action of the soul on a higher level than that of its own natural mode. We know, in these end days, that those of us who are awake operating in the various gifts Yahuah has assigned to us will be met with great resistance because we will **NOT** follow the status quo. We are constantly challenging it which will ultimately lead to great persecution of our faith.For we have chosen to unwrap ourselves from the temptations to self deception. We hunger for righteousness and we are homesick for Heaven.

When the soul is dominated and led by spiritual inspirations of Yahuah, through the gifts HE has given we are leading the mystical life. We are humbled from the Ruach in us, suddenly arriving at a new level of supernatural knowledge and an intense degree of true supernatural all encompassing **LOVE** (ahavah).

ROEH = to see, to perceive

CHOZEH = a beholder in a vision, perception

He that loves another has fulfilled the Torah. You shall not break wedlock. You shall not steal. You shall not bear false witness. You shall not lust. You shall **LOVE** your neighbor as yourself. Love works no ill to his neighbor; therefore love is the fulfilling of the Torah. And knowing the **time that now is high time to awake out of sleep;** for now is our Yeshu'a nearer than when we believed. Cast off the darkness, let us put on the armor of light. Let us walk honestly, as in the day not rioting and drunkenness, not in chambering and wantonness and not in strife and envying. Put on Adonai Yahusha HaMashiach and make not provision for the flesh, to fulfill the lusts thereof. **Romans 13: 8-14**

Here is the call for the endurance of the saints, those who keep the commandments of Yahuah and hold fast to the faith of Yahusha. **Revelation 14:12**

RADICAL ABANDONMENT

There is nothing new under the sun!

WISDOM is;

the architect of Creation
the Father's delight
rejoices before the Father
rejoices, celebrates with laughter over the inhabited world
delights in humanity
increases our favor with Yahuah

We have entered the end of time; the hour of equipping and preparation. The season for the process of adjustment that results in complete preparedness. Take care to not be deceived. **WARNING IS** - refuse to join them! Do not be afraid all this must happen. The end will not come all at once. We know of the earthquakes, famines, great signs and wonders, plagues, and terrifying events. We will be persecuted and possibly handed over and imprisoned brought before Kings and Governors for the sake of HIS name and that will be your opportunity to bear witness. Make up your minds now to not prepare your defense.

For Yahusha himself will give an eloquence and a wisdom that none of our opponents will be able to resist or contradict. Be prepared to be betrayed by friends and family. Some will be put to death. We will be universally hated. Perseverance will win our lives. Great misery will descend on the land. For we have seen some of the signs in the sun, the moon, and the stars. Nations are already in agony bewildered by turmoil. Soon, tsunamis, earthquakes beyond our current comprehension. It will be a time when we run to the mountains and hide, to escape the cities being protected by Yahuah. We are to **STAY ALERT!** Watch ourselves or our hearts will be coarsened by debauchery and drunkenness and the cares of life. Then, that day will come upon us unexpectedly like a trap. **STAY AWAKE!** Praying at all times without ceasing! Praying for strength to endure and survive all that is going to happen! Hold your ground for the **RETURN OF OUR KING YAHUSHA DRAWS NEAR!**

POWER, THE BLOOD, TRAINING

The thing that has been, it is that which shall be; and that which is done is that which shall be done: and there is no new thing under the sun.

Ecclesiastes 1:9

I have also spoken by the prophets, and I have multiplied visions, and used similitudes, by the ministry of the prophets. **Hosea 2:10**

After this I saw in the night visions, and behold a fourth beast, dreadful and terrible, and strong exceedingly; and it had great iron teeth: it devoured and break in pieces, and stamped the residue with the feet of it: and it was diverse from all the beasts that were before it; and it had ten horns. I considered the horns, and, behold, there came up among them another little horn, (Obama) before whom there were three of the first horns plucked up by the roots: and, behold, in this horn were eyes like the eyes of man, and a mouth speaking great things. – **Daniel 7:7-8** .

* The final battle between Yahusha HaMashiach and the Anti-Messiah and their respective armies takes place in the same location of "Armageddon" or the "hills of Megiddo":

And I saw three unclean spirits like frogs come out of the mouth of [hasatan], and out of the mouth of the [Antichrist], and out of the mouth of the false prophet. For they are the spirits of devils, working miracles, which go forth unto the kings of the earth and of the whole world, to gather them to the battle of that great day of Yahuah Elohim…And he gathered them together into a place called in the Hebrew tongue Armageddon. – **Revelation 16:13-16.**

PRAYER TRAINING MANUAL FOR WARRIORS

2 Timothy 1:7 -For Yahuah did not give us a spirit of timidity (of cowardice, of craven and cringing and fawning fear), but [**HE** has given us a spirit] of power and of love and of calm and well-balanced mind and discipline and self-control.

Matthew 10:28 -And do not be afraid of those **who kill the body but cannot kill the soul** ; but rather be afraid of Him who can destroy both soul and body in hell (Gehenna).

John 14:12 - I assure you, most solemnly I tell you, if anyone steadfastly believes in **ME** , he will himself be able to do the things that I do; and he will do even greater things than these, because I go to the Father.

We believe that victory will be through the Power of the MOST HIGH Himself, through us Believers, using the name of Our Messiah Yahusha. Glory! I would not want to be on the side of the enemy, knowing what could happen to them in the hands of the Living GOD.

II Corinthians 10:3-4 - For though we walk (live) in the flesh, we are not carrying on our warfare according to the flesh and using **MERE HUMAN WEAPONS.** For the weapons of our warfare are **NOT** physical [weapons of flesh and blood], but they are mighty before **ELOHIM** for the **OVERTHROW and DESTRUCTION of strongholds,**

In II Kings Chapter 6, Elisha the Prophet was Supernaturally getting the battle plans of Israel's enemy , and gave it to the king of Israel. Naturally the enemy king wanted this man captured. 6:14 So [the Syrian king] sent there horses, chariots, and a **GREAT ARMY.** They came by night and surrounded the city.

6:15 When the servant of the man of God rose early and went out, behold, an army with horses and chariots was around the city. Elisha's servant said to him, Alas, my master! "What shall we do? 6:16 [Elisha] answered, **FEAR NOT;** for those with us are more than those with them. 6:17 Then Elisha prayed, **YAHUAH ELOHIM,** I pray You, open his eyes that he may see. And the **MOST HIGH opened the young man's eyes, and he saw, and BEHOLD, THE MOUNTAIN WAS FULL OF HORSES AND CHARIOTS OF FIRE ROUND ABOUT ELISHA.** 6:18 and when the Syrians came down to him, Elisha prayed to Yahuah, smite this people with blindness, I pray You. And YaH smote them with blindness, as Elisha asked.

Matthew 26:53 (Yahusha said) Do you suppose that I cannot appeal to My Father, and He will **IMMEDIATELY** provide Me with more than twelve legions [more than 80,000] of angels?

Psalm 68:17 The chariots of **THE MOST HIGH** are twenty thousand, even thousands upon thousands.

A word of caution to you. Although true Believers have this power passed down to us by Yahusha HaMashiach, he did say to us to **BUY WEAPONS!!!**

PRAY FOR THESE MIRACLES- Just as in the time of Moses we too will go through an EXODUS of monumental proportions!! We can pray for the same things as Moses did to come against those who come after us!

PRAY TO STRIKE THE ENEMY BLIND - Genesis 19:11 And they struck the men who were at the door of the house with blindness [which dazzled them], from the youths to the old men, so that they wearied themselves [groping] to find the door.

PRAY TO TURN THE ENEMY INTO A PILLAR OF SALT - Genesis 19:26 But [Lot's] wife looked back from behind him, and she became a pillar of salt.

MIRACLES DONE BY GOD THROUGH MOSEH..

ROD TURNS INTO SERPENT AND EATS OTHER RODS - Exodus 7:12 For they cast down every man his rod and they became serpents; but Aaron's rod swallowed up their rods.

CHANGE THE ENEMIES WATER INTO BLOOD - Exodus 7:17 Thus says Yahuah, In this you shall know, recognize, and understand that I am Yahuah Elohim: behold, I will smite with the rod in my hand the waters in the [Nile] River, and they shall be turned to blood. 18 The fish in the river shall die, the river shall become foul smelling, and the Egyptians shall loathe to drink from it.

SEND FROGS - Exodus 8:5 And THE MOST HIGH said to Moses, Say to Aaron, Stretch out your hand with your rod over the rivers, the streams and canals, and over the pools, and cause frogs to come up on the land of Egypt.

SEND MOSQUITOES AND GNATS - Exodus 8:16 Then Yahuah said to Moses, Say to Aaron, Stretch out your rod and strike the dust of the ground, that it may become biting gnats or mosquitoes throughout all the land of Egypt.

SEND GADFLIES - Exodus 8:21 ..behold, I will send swarms [of bloodsucking gadflies] upon you, your servants, and your people, and into your houses; and the houses of the Egyptians shall be full of swarms [of bloodsucking gadflies], and also the ground on which they stand.

PRAY THAT LIVESTOCK (THEIR FOOD) WILL BE KILLED - Exodus 9:3 Behold, the hand of Yahuah [will fall] upon your livestock which are out in the field, upon the horses, the donkeys , the damsels , the herds and the flocks ; there shall be a very severe plague.

SEND BOILS - Exodus 9:8 Yahuah said to Moses and Aaron, Take handfuls of ashes or soot from the brick kiln and let Moses sprinkle them toward the heavens in the sight of Pharaoh. 9/ And it shall become small dust over all the land of Egypt, and become boils breaking out in sores on man and beast in all the land [occupied by the Egyptians].

SEND HAIL - Exodus 9:23 Then Moses stretched forth his rod toward the heavens, and THE MOST HIGH sent thunder and hail, and fire (lightning) ran down to and along the ground, and the Lord rained hail upon the land of Egypt.

SEND LOCUSTS - Exodus 10:12 Then Yahuah said to Moses, Stretch out your hand over the land of Egypt for the locusts, that they may come up on the land of Egypt and eat all the vegetation of the land, all that the hail has left.

SEND DARKNESS - Exodus 10:21 And Yahuah said to Moses, Stretch out your hand toward the heavens, that there may be darkness over the land of Egypt, a darkness which may be felt.

SEND DEATH TO FIRSTBORN - Exodus 11:4 " 5 And Moses said, Thus says Yahuah, About midnight I will go out into the midst of Egypt; and all the firstborn in the land [the pride, hope and joy] of Egypt shall die, from the firstborn of Pharaoh, who sits on his throne, even to the firstborn of the maidservant who is behind the hand mill, and all the firstborn of beasts.

PRAY FOR A MIRACLE CLOUD - Exodus 14:19"20 And the Angel of Yahuah Who went before the host of Israel moved and went behind them; and the pillar of the cloud went from before them and stood behind them, 20/ Coming between the host of Egypt and the host of Israel. It was as cloud and darkness to the Egyptians, but it gave light by night to the Israelites; and the one host did not come near the other all night.

DIVIDE THE WATER AND WALK ON DRY GROUND - Exodus 14:21-22 Then Moses stretched out his hand over the sea, and Yahuah caused the sea to go back by a strong east wind all that night and made the sea dry land; and the waters were divided. 22/ And the Israelites went into the midst of the sea on dry ground, the waters being a wall to them on their right hand and on their left.

STOP THE GUN BOATS AND SHIPS - JOSHUA 3:16 Then the waters which came down from above stood and rose UP IN A HEAP far off, at Adam, the city that is beside Zarenthan ; and those FLOWING DOWN toward the Sea of the Arabah, the Salt [Dead] Sea, were wholly cut off. And the people passed over opposite Jericho.

CROSS THE RIVER ON DRY GROUND - Joshua 3:17 And while ALL Israel passed over on dry ground, the priests who bore the ark of the covenant of Yahuah stood firm ON DRY GROUND in the midst of the Jordan, until ALL the nation finished passing over the Jordan.

PRAY FOR A FULL EXTRA DAY OF SUNLIGHT - Joshua 10:13 And the sun stood still, and the moon stayed, until the nation took vengeance upon their enemies. Is not this written in the Book of Jasher? So the sun stood still in the midst of the heavens and did not hasten to go down for a whole day.

PRAY THAT SEA SWALLOWS ENEMY - Exodus 14:28 The waters returned and covered the chariots, the horsemen , and all the host of Pharaoh that pursued them; not even one of them remained. But the Israelites walked on dry ground in the midst of the sea, the waters being a wall to them on their right hand and on their left.

ASK FOR CLOUD BY DAY; FIRE BY NIGHT - Exodus 13:21 THE MOST HIGH ELOHIM went before them by day in a pillar of cloud to lead them along the way and by night in a pillar of fire to give them light, that they might travel by day and by night.

FREE MEAT AND BREAD FROM HEAVEN - Exodus 16:13 In the evening quails came up and covered the camp; and in the morning the dew lay round about the camp. 14/ And when the dew had gone, behold, upon the face of the wilderness there lay a fine, round and flake like thing, as fine as hoarfrost on the ground. (It was bread.)

GET WATER FROM A ROCK - Exodus 17:6 Behold, I will stand before you there on the rock at [Mount] Horeb; and you shall strike the rock, and water shall come out of it, that the people may drink. And Moses did so in the sight of the elders of Israel.

PRAY TO OPEN THE GROUND AND SWALLOW ENEMY - Numbers 16:31 As soon as Moses stopped speaking, the ground under the offenders split apart and the earth opened its mouth and swallowed them and their households and [Korah and] all [his] men and all their possessions.

SEND A PLAGUE - Numbers 16:41, 44, 45, 49 But on the morrow all the congregation of the Israelites murmured against Moses and Aaron, saying, You have killed the people of Yahuah. And YaH said to Moses, Get away from among this congregation, that I may consume them in a moment. And Moses and Aaron fell on their faces. Now those who died in the plague were 14,700, besides those who died in the matter of Korah.

STOP THE RAIN - I Kings 17:1 Elijah the Tishbite, of the temporary residents of Gilead, said to Ahab, As THE MOST HIGH, the EL ELYON of Israel, lives, before Whom I stand, there shall not be dew or rain these years but according to My word.

PRAY THAT YOUR FOOD WILL NOT RUN OUT - I Kings 17:14 For thus says ADONAI, the ELOHIM of Israel: The jar of meal shall not waste away or the bottle of oil fail until the day that the Lord sends rain on the earth.

RAISE THE DEAD - I Kings 17:21 And he stretched himself upon the child three times and cried to Yahuah and said, O Yahuah RAPHA, I pray You, let this child's soul come back into him. (It did!)

SEND THE FIRE OF THE LORD - I Kings 18:38 Then the fire of YaH fell and consumed the burnt sacrifice and the wood and the stones and the dust, and also licked up the water that was in the trench.

PRAY FOR RAIN - I Kings 18:41 And Elijah said to Ahab, Go up, eat and drink, for there is the sound of abundance of rain.

PRAY FOR ANIMALS TO ATTACK THE ENEMY - II Kings 2:24 and he turned around and looked at them and called a curse down on them in the name of Yahuah. And two she-bears came out of the woods and ripped up forty-two of the boys.

SUPERNATURALLY SPY ON YOUR ENEMY - II Kings 6:12 One of his servants said, None, my lord O king; but Elisha, the prophet who is in Israel, tells the king of Israel the words that you SPEAK IN YOUR BEDCHAMBER.

SEND BLINDNESS - II Kings 6:18, 20 And when the Syrians came down to him, Elisha prayed to Yahuah, Smite this people with blindness, I pray You. And Yahuah smote them with blindness, as Elisha asked. And when they had come into Samaria, Elisha said, Yahuah open the eyes of these men that they may see. And Yahuah opened their eyes, and they saw. Behold, they were in the midst of Samaria!

PRAY FOR THE WALLS TO FALL - Joshua 6:20 So the people shouted, and the trumpets were blown. When the people heard the sound of the trumpet, they raised a great shout, and [Jericho's] wall fell down in its place, so that the [Israelites] went up into the city, every man straight before him, and they took the city.

PRAY FOR THE SUN TO STOP - Joshua 10:13 And the sun stood still, and the moon stayed, until the nation took vengeance upon their enemies.

YOU ARE GOD'S WAR CLUB - Jeremiah 51:20 You [Cyrus of Persia, soon to conquer Babylon] are My WAR CLUB or maul and weapon of war - for with you I break nations in pieces, with you I destroy kingdoms.

PRAY THAT GOD WILL SEND FIRE - Ezekiel 39:6 I will send fire on Magog and upon those who dwell securely in the coast lands, and they shall know, understand, and realize that I am YAHUAH [the Sovereign Ruler, Who calls forth loyalty and obedient service]

. *PAY ATTENTION TO THE RETURN OF ANCIENT WORDS/ CURSES/ AND DEMONIC INFLUENCES--LAST DAYS SIGNS*

If you are getting email or reading web pages about **TERAH,** *you may be dealing with someone involved with the occult, as in witchcraft or satanism.* **TERAH is a code word** *used by them when they sound like a "Christian". Also watch out for the word MICHAEL in their correspondence. He seems to be the leader of the pact. Even automobile license plates with* **TERAH** *are appearing all over the country. I would do some heavy Spiritual*

*Warfare every time you came across this **TERAH** , and especially to **RETURN** all evil being sent your way. Below is just a little background from another ministry. I have been doing some "Terah" study. Terah is a Phoenician god. Means shadowy darkness and malign. Intermediate to lesser god of the moon and secrets. Consort of Amat Asherat (minor goddess of Alchemy and conjuration). Note the similarity to Ashteroth of the Bible.*

TIME, TIMES, HALF A TIME TO COME

"And I shall take you as a bride unto Me in trustworthiness, and you shall know יהוה."And it shall be in that day that I answer," declares יהוה, "that I answer the heavens, and they answer the earth,and the earth answer the grain and the new wine and the oil , and they answer Yizre'ĕl."And I shall sow her for Myself in the earth, and I shall have compassion on her who had not obtained compassion. And I shall say to those who were not My people, 'You are My people,' while they say, 'My Elohim!' " Hosea 2: 20-23

VISION OF THE MIND

On March 9, 2019 , **ABBA** gave me this vision. **HE** said, " I want to take you through the gates into the city of the mind! Within this city are many townships and these townships answer to the mind itself. The townships are: thoughts, emotions, will, sight, hearing, and speaking. As, **HE** led me though these townships that existed within the mind, I could see all the moving parts. The township of the emotions reacted to whatever the township of the thoughts ordered. Then **ABBA** said, " Many, many of my children have left the gates to each of these open for far too long and this has allowed the enemy access to come in and release "nano-demons". These demons attack your weaknesses first, striking at your most vulnerable moment. These "nano-demons" are so small, so fast at moving in and through each gate to township after township in lightning speed so they can plant roots that run deep and last an entire lifespan of a person.

What I believe the Ruach HaKodesh was revealing to me was this; we must be on guard even more now than ever to guard our gates and that new technology was being created to be so untraceable that we won't even notice until we find ourselves in a mental illness or some other **DIS-EASE** from demon implantation. **BE ALERT!! BEWARE!**

17 ACTS OF THE FLESH

Galatians 5:19-21

 " Now the works of the flesh are manifest, which are these; **Adultery, fornication, uncleanness, lasciviousness, idolatry, witchcraft, hatred, variance, emulations, wrath, strife, seditions, heresies, envyings, murders, drunkenness, revellings,** and such like: of the which I tell you before, as I have also told you in time past, that they which do such things shall not inherit the kingdom of Yahuah."

Our Acts are Expressions of Our Inner Selves

Note that Paul's list in Gal 5:19-21 was just a partial list because he concludes it by saying *"and such like* " in verse 21. The works of the flesh are many and varied, and they that do such things will not inherit the kingdom of Yahuah. This is serious stuff.

Yahusha says in John 3:6, *"That which is born of the flesh is flesh; and that which is born of the spirit is spirit".*

As Isaiah tells us in 64:6, "But we are all as an unclean thing, and all our righteousnesses are as filthy rags; and we all do fade as a leaf; and our iniquities, like the wind, have taken us away" The works of the flesh bring nothing good.

THE RUACH HAKODESH

The Set-Apart Spirit pours faith into us. We are to live in Spirit and Truth!! To deny the wickedness of our flesh we need the Ruach HaKodesh in us. It is only with the Set-Apart Spirit we can overcome. I am pressing in and believing for revival and a new outpouring of the Set-Apart Spirit as in the book of Acts that will produce radical conversions and usher in the last **HARVEST of SOULS!!**

The Ruach HaKodesh does:

gives life (John 7:38);

gives gifts (1 Corinthians 12);

counsels (John 14:26);

encourages (Acts 9:31)

steps in on our behalf (Romans 8:23);

builds up (Romans 8:27);

leads us to obedience (2 Corinthians 3:5);

brings to mind (1 John 2:20, 27)

energizes and makes effective (Acts 1:8).

According to the book of Acts, the pouring out of the Spirit leads to becoming filled to an overflow with the **Spirit of Yahuah** . For with the Ruach our cup overflows!

For example:

In his first testimony before the Sanhedrin, the Apostle Peter was filled with the Spirit when he spoke; After Peter and John were arrested, the believers prayed for them, and were all filled with the Spirit; the deacon Stephen, the church's first martyr, died filled with the Ruach HaKodesh so he could bear that final witness; the Spirit was 'poured out' on Samaritans who were converted through Peter and John; the deacon Philip was led by the Set-Apart Spirit to bear witness of Christ to the Ethiopian eunuch; Paul's first teacher in the faith, Ananias, assured the soon-to-be-apostle that he would regain his sight and be filled with the Ruach HaKodesh.

The Ruach gives us **WISDOM, UNDERSTANDING** , and **INSIGHT.** It is **WISDOM** that drives the process of discernment! Which, we all need to seek every single day in these last days so we are **NOT DECEIVED!** As, **Sons and Daughters of Zadok,** it is our responsibility to know what is and is **NOT** of Yahuah, the very difference between holy and profane and to teach it to others!

The Ruach HaKodesh reveals first and foremost through Scripture. Without the Ruach's work, the Bible is just dead ink and paper. Without the Ruach's **WISDOM** and **INSIGHT,** science is mere trickery, psychology is just self-obsession, sociology is just the barking of the rabble, math is a mere preoccupation done to avoid those living in the street, language becomes just a tool for manipulation, and religion actually becomes the **opiate** of the masses that Marx thought it was.

Marriage Covenant- Display of Agape Love

The Covenant is a marriage between **Yahuah** *and* **Israel** *, His bride; and* **Natsarim Israel** *(Nazarene Israel) represents the* **First-Fruits** *of a great harvest.* **Israel** *is the only "denomination", and the Natsarim are an elect group within Israel, as they are called by Yahusha as workers in His Harvest of mankind.* **The Name of the Creator** *and the* **symbol of His Torah** *are on the banner below, a prophesied reality taking place in the*

52

Earth. Yahusha removed His menorah (lampstand) from the 1st assembly in Ephesos, Rev. 2:5. It has been restored to Natsarim Israel today. The menorah is a symbol of the **TORAH** , and it also is the most widely known symbol for **ISRAEL** .The **TORAH** and **ISRAEL** are inseparable.

One of the purposes of understanding who we are as **Sons and Daughters of Zadok** in these end days is a revelation of the future time to come when we are gathered together with Yahusha at the banquet table as the Bride. The present remnant will sit with the past remnants feasting together as if there was no separation of time. To feast with the ancients and Messiah past, present and future beyond time and space at the Wedding Feast. What a day that will be!

The quote is about the coming Messianic banquet when the believers will share bread and wine, which this sect at Qumran also did at their own communal meals: This quote is from the Dead Sea Scrolls and can be a little hard to follow due to its fragments and age of the scroll but the points are clear.

(The procedure for the meeting of the men of reputation when they are called to the banquet held by the society of the *Yahad,* when Yah-uah has fa[th]ered(?) the Messiah (*or, when the Messiah has been revealed*) among them: [the priest,] as head of the entire congregation of Israel, shall enter first, trailed by all [his] brot[hers, the Sons of] Aaron, those priests [appointed] to the banquet of the men of reputation. They are to sit be[fore him] by rank. Then the [Mess]iah of Israel may en[ter] and the heads of the th[ousands of Israel] are to sit before him by rank, as determined by [each man's comm]ission in their camps and campaigns. Last, all the heads of [the con]gregation's cl[ans], together with [their] wis[e and knowledgeable men], shall sit before them by rank. [When] they gather [at the] communal [tab]le, [having set out bread and w]ine so the communal table is set [for eating] and [the] wine (poured) for drinking, none [may re]ach for the first portion of the bread or [the wine] before the priest. For [he] shall [bl]ess the first portion of the bread and the wine, [reac]hing for the bread first. Afterw[ard] the Messiah of Israel [shall re]ach for the bread. [Finally,] ea[ch] member of the whole congregation of the Yahad 151 [shall give a blessing, [in descending order of] rank. This procedure shall govern every meal, provided at least ten men are gathered together.)

Dead Sea Scrolls A New Translation page 147

Polish the arrows! Put on the shields! יהוה has stirred up the spirit of the sovereigns of the Medes. For His plan is against Baḇel to destroy it, because it is the vengeance of יהוה, the vengeance for His Hĕḵal.

Lift up a banner on the walls of Baḇel, strengthen the watch, station the watchmen, prepare the ambush. For יהוה has both planned and done what He spoke concerning the inhabitants of Baḇel. Jer. 51:12.

Do you take.....to love and to cherish.....in sickness and in health?

Are you living as the **Bride of Yahusha** ? If you are married, does your marriage reflect the image of Yahusha and **HIS BRIDE?**

Ponder on those questions for a minute. While watching a video on marriage I was deeply convicted and I had to repent for not honoring my marriage and fully submitting myself to my husband in such a way that it reflects my marriage to Adonai. Marriage in this world is simply training for our marriage to Adonai.

Let marriage be respected by all, and the bed be undefiled. But Elohim shall judge those who whore, and adulterers. **Hebrews 13:4**

In the same way, wives, be subject to your own husbands, so that if any are disobedient to the Word, they, without a word, might be won by the behaviour of their wives, **1 Peter 3:1**

Wives, subject yourselves to your own husbands, as to the Master. Because the husband is head of the wife, as also the Messiah is head of the assembly, and He is the Saviour of the body. But as the assembly is subject to Messiah, so also let the wives be to their own husbands in every respect. Husbands, love your wives, as Messiah also did love the assembly and gave Himself for it, in order to set it apart and cleanse it with the washing of water by the Word. **Ephesians 5: 22-26**

In this way husbands ought to love their own wives as their own bodies. He who loves his wife loves himself . **Ephesians 5:22**

F ervent. **O** vercomers. **C** hosen. **U** nique. **S** ubmissive.

FOCUS TRIBE= NATSARIM MISSION

Covenant of AHAVAH/ LOVE- The Ten WORDS are this very Covenant of LOVE

For you are a set-apart people to יהוה your Elohim. יהוה your Elohim has chosen you to be a people for Himself, a treasured possession above all the peoples on the face of the earth. "יהוה did not set His love on you nor choose you because you were more numerous than any other people, for you were the least of all peoples, but because of יהוה loving you, and because of Him guarding the oath which He swore to your fathers, יהוה has brought you out with a strong hand, and redeemed you from the house of bondage, from the hand of Pharaoh sovereign of Mitsrayim . And you shall know that יהוה your Elohim, He is Elohim, the trustworthy Ĕl guarding covenant and kindness for a thousand generations with those who love Him, and those who guard His commands, but repaying those who hate Him to their face, to destroy them. He does not delay *to do so* with him who hates Him, He repays him to his face. And you shall guard the command, and the laws, and the right-rulings which I command you today, to do them. And it shall be, because you hear these right-rulings, and shall guard and do them, that יהוה your Elohim shall guard with you the covenant and the kindness which He swore to your fathers,- **Deuteronomy 7: 6-12**

Commandments- (*mitzvah*): This is the general Hebrew term for "commandment" and usually refers to the comprehensive list of laws or body of laws given by the Elohim in the Books of Moses.

Statutes- (*choq*): According to *Vine's Expository Dictionary* , this word means "statute, **prescription** , rule, law, regulation, and can refer to laws of nature or what is allocated, rationed, or apportioned to someone.

Rules- (*mishpat*): A judicial verdict or formal decree.

Statutes/Commands- (*chuqqah*)according to Vine's dictionary. It refers to a particular law related to a festival or ritual, such as Passover, the Days of Unleavened Bread, or the Feast of Tabernacles .

All four of these hebrew words refer to the commands from Yahuah to be obeyed by Yahuah's people.

SURVIVAL--TRIBE--ORDER and ORACLES of YAHUAH
The Way of the Ancients
Sacred Seeds and the Return to the Agrarian Way
THE ORDER; is the gathering of HIS people
THE MINISTRY; are the ministers of the WAY
THE WAY; are the doctrines and ways of YAH

Yahusha

The original Name for the man commonly called "Jesus". " **YAHUSHA** " is the English transliteration of the Name which is of Hebrew origin. His Name is pronounced "YOW-sha" or "Ya-HU-sha". The Hebrew letters that make up this name are the **Yod** , Hay, Waw, Shin, Ayin and are written from right to left in the Hebrew. The letter J is not even 600 years old yet. How can a man who lived around 2,000 years ago have a name that started with a letter that didn't exist? "Jesus" is not the Name. YAHUSHA is the Savior of the world. With belief in Him and the **observance** of His Father's Word, especially the Ten Commands in Exodus/ **Shemoth** 20, one will inherit eternal life.

" **YAHUSHA** is my **delivere r** , and His death on the **stake** redeemed me from my fate of destruction."
"I love YAHUSHA and **Yahusha** loves me!"

The Natsarim were known to follow The Way and were easily identified due to their use of the Name. The name of our Elohim was outlawed and not to be used by those practicing Judaism. The Natsarim used His name regularly as did Yahusha. They also did not teach the traditions of Judaism, referred to as the traditions of men. For these reasons the religious leaders of the Jews had Yahusha put to death on the cross. Little did they know this was all to fulfill prophecy.
The Natsarim follow the Torah of Yahuah and accept the salvation granted by the sacrifice of Yahusha. The Torah of Yahuah did not pass away with the death of Yahusha. The Torah is eternal and was followed perfectly by Yahusha; making him the perfect sinless sacrifice for us. Now the Natsarim

are coming forward again to guard The Way of Yahuah and His son Yahusha ha Mashiach.

Revelation 12:17 : And the dragon was enraged with the woman and he went to fight with the remnant of her seed, those guarding the commands of Elohim and possessing the witness of Yahusha ha Mashiach (The Natsarim).

Always remember ; Do not let it depart from your mouth what is written in the Book of the ·Teachings [Law]. ·Study [Meditate on] it day and night to be ·sure [careful; diligent] to obey everything that is written there. If you do this, you will be ·wise [prudent; successful] and ·successful [prosperous]. Joshua 1:8

Put together it could be said of Nechamah/Comfort:

A separation will be followed by entry through the guardian of the WAY into the protection from the chaos of the storm/deluge, look in awe to the process of entry into new life which will continue.

Pray fervently that your flight not be in the winter nor a Sabbath day. YaH will tell you when to flee.

Yirmeyahu (Jeremiah) 18:15 (TS2009)

"But My people have forgotten Me, they have burned incense to what is false, and they have stumbled from their ways, from *the ancient* paths, to walk in bypaths and not on a highway,

Ḥaḇaqquq (Habakkuk) 3:6 (TS2009)

He shall stand and measure *the* earth. He shall look and shake *the* nations. And *the ancient* mountains are shattered, *The* age-old hills shall bow. His ways are everlasting.

The Hebrew prophets, seers, and givers of the law, were men of power, men of holy/kodosh thought, and they bequeathed to us a system of philosophy that is ideal; one strong enough and good enough to lead our people to the goal of perfectness. Behold, for Yahuah has made incarnate wisdom, love and light, which HE has called

Immanuel.   To HIM is given the keys to open up the dawn; and here, as a man, HE walks with us.---Agrarian Gospel of Jesus the Christ--1920

2 Esdras 14:13-18   (NRSV) 13 Now therefore, set your house in order , and reprove your people; comfort the lowly among them, and instruct those that are wise. [a] And now renounce the life that is corruptible, 14 and put away from you mortal thoughts ; cast away from you the burdens of mankind, and divest yourself now of your weak nature; 15 lay to one side the thoughts that are most grievous to you, and   hurry to escape from these times . 16 For evils worse than those that you have now seen happen shall take place hereafter. 17 For the weaker the world becomes through old age, the more shall evils be increased upon its inhabitants. 18 Truth shall go farther away, and falsehood shall come near. For the eagle [b] that you saw in the vision is already hurrying to come."

Each man must go through the assignments and each teacher must go through the assignments as well....

THE ORDER- (To keep order in the camp in **days of chaos**) YaH's orders for the Tribes during Tribulation.

Keep the unity of Spirit in the bondage of Shalom

Apostles, Prophets, Evangelist, Pastors, Teachers (each must be called, ordained, and anointed) Each of these ministries may be changed/evolved in title only to a modern day survivalist/Tribal position of servitude.

Organize the wise (the elders of the Tribe) as the High Counsel.

Operations/Responsibilities/Service of said High Counsel must include members active in prayer, fasting, and ministering the WORD of YAH.

HIGH COUNSEL - 3/5/7 or 12who are assigned according to the size of Tribe. High Counsel will elect 3 to 7 honest ones, full of the Ruach HaKodesh and having wisdom, discernment, and sound mind to be ELDERS/ OVERSEERS of the Tribe.

ELDERS conclude the business concerning the whole of the commune itself.

Together ELDERS and OVERSEERS will elect 3 to 7 members who are anointed in the area of HELPS and SERVICE.

These leadership positions, whether small or a large , it will not matter and must be used in the places of refuge in the end days as YAHUAH has created this selection of leadership as HIS TRIBAL ORDER!

Gather together to pray for the **Spirit of Truth** . Pray to escape all things. Pray to be found worthy at the hour of temptation!

Judge NOT

Let ALL be done in LOVE, one towards another for YAH is love.

Unite and gather under the common bond of the love of YAHUSHA, in the Spirit of Truth, unto the glorifying of Yahuah and Yahusha our MaShiach.

Yahusha who was lifted up on the cross, for HE it is who gathers all men unto HIM.

Study The Scriptures Daily-- **Seek and Pray for WISDOM and UNDERSTANDING**

Concerning Immersion: by WATER and by the OUTPOURING of the Ruach HaKodesh

Ordinances of YaH: Breaking bread together, drinking wine, washing one another's feet. Acts of servitude.

Restoration and Return of the Tribes/ReFormation and Reuniting of the 12 TRIBES

LOVE YAHUAH/YAHUSHA-heart, mind, soul LOVE YOUR NEIGHBOR- as yourself.

LOVE one ANOTHER for the corruption of self is the destruction of service.

LAWS OF YAH--

The WORD of YAHUAH ministers the LAW OF YAHUAH by the RUACH HAKODESH through the available submitted and anointed Servant of YAH.

YAHUAH honors emunah/faith and shema/obedience and emunah/faith and shema/obedience in return honors YAHUAH.

We are commanded to feed the hungry, give drink to the thirsty, clothe the naked, heal the sick, pray fervently to be found of YAH pleasing and obedient children doing HIS WORK and HIS WILL. We are to be fully surrendered of our own will and ways to HIM alone! We are to be reflections of Yahusha as our lights are to shine bright during these dark days!

There is no room for the sloth in these places of refuge.

THE ORDER OF KODESH/HOLINESS

Being and becoming kodesh. The charge to be holy must be specified for all situations of daily life in the Tribe. In the wilderness we must live with YaH in our midst and a prerequisite is to be kodesh/holy strive to. We must have a refined ability to distinguish the kodesh from the profane. For you are a Dwelling Place of the living Elohim, as Elohim has said, "I shall dwell in them and walk among them, and I shall be their Elohim, and they shall be My people."Therefore, "Come out from among them and be separate, says יהוה, and do not touch what is unclean, and I shall receive you."And I shall be a Father to you, and you shall be sons and daughters to Me, says יהוה the Almighty." Qorintiyim 6:16-18

Different levels of holiness for survival and well being of the Tribe; Priest/ Judges must accurately discern who or what is fitting to come into the camp. The safe havens/places of refuge are Yahuah's sacred precincts.

ANCIENT MEDICINE/ PRESCRIPTION FOR LIFE

PLANTS TO GROW IN A MEDICINAL HERB GARDEN--

Calendula- Peppermint-Cayenne-Chamomile-Chickweed-Yarrow-Nettle-Dandelion-Echinacea-Elderberry-Garlic-Lavender-Lemon Balm-Turmeric-Red Clover-Rosemary Sage-St. John's Wort-Thyme-Ginger-Burdock-Mullein

Roots are best dug in fall or early spring. Buds and flowers are best harvested just as they are opening up. Leaves are harvested just before the plant is in full bloom.

We know that YAH provides **ALL WE NEED!** Food, Shelter, Medicine, Oxegen, and Water! We are to trust HIM completely! In the end of days with pestilence, famines, earthquakes and more, we must separate from the world! Yahuah has warned us and I am convinced that right now in 2020 it is time we **ALL COME OUT OF HER MY PEOPLE!** This is for those of us that have heard the call but maybe we are in the planning and preparation. YaH is gathering HIS people into "safe havens". Places of refuge and protection. Divinely protected land both physically and spiritually! HE is gathering us together as judgements begin to fall on America and the world. As, I said these places are fully protected by Yahuah, HIS angels, to ensure that a remnant remains to give testimony to all and witness the insurmountable power of Elohim, Yahuah! We will be together in a refuge in the wilderness living as disciples and early apostles in the book of ACTS. By combining all resources together and distributing them as one needs we will be truly embracing one another in brotherly love.

Will we experience manna from the shamayim?

I do not know for sure but I pray we will! Nevertheless, I DO KNOW YAHUAH will work mighty signs and wonders during this time to encourage us and provide for us and protect us.

Be prepared for the enemy to target us on all sides. He can cause us to feel unfocused, lethargic, and possibly cause us to become susceptible to an illness, or get irritable with one another and so on. We are to be on guard always!! Watching and always ready. Always in prayer. ABBA has laid out some instructions for us just like HE did for Israel when they came out of Egypt.

During this period of living and dwelling together we will need to pray and ask for the ancient paths. Some of YaH's ancient paths are farming, which is growing your own food and herbs. Having animals to care for gives us food. Natural and organic wellness and health. Including ancient medicine.

Our hope and example is that YaHusHA overcame the world!! We too can overcome!

Be SEPARATE--------NOW!

What does that mean? **IN ALL ASPECTS OF LIFE!**

"In the future we will have to know Yahuah's ancient language. This could possibly be our very protection when communicating with one another during tribulation."

KEYS for the Future - Which we must always be on guard and pay attention for the enemy will use it to deceive the masses, possibly giving false hope which is a victory of falsity. We are reclaiming the words The enemy has stolen from Yahuah. The reason I am sharing this with you is not because I think all of us will learn ancient Hebrew correctly or possibly even enough to speak it fluently; because we need an alternative way to communicate during tribulation and even right now. Some have talked about Ham radios, walkie talkies, Morse code, and other such ways of communication. we know that we will have to figure out something; I believe that Yahuah has already been working on this through other Brothers and Sisters possibly. One thing, Abba put on my heart and told me to work on was the formation of the Underground Railroad during tribulation. This will be very similar to that during the times of World War II when the Jewish people had to hide in various places to stay alive and escape towns, the same will be true for Believers , true followers of the Way but, those not already in a tribe or a refuge will have to flee in order to stay alive and certain called ones will be sent in to rescue them. The need to form the **Underground Railroad** is urgent for the time is short! I don't know all the details right now but I know that this is something that must be done soon, so I'm looking at maps and thinking about my locale, back roads dirt roads etc....I am encouraging you to do the same! For we are Yahuah's Militia His Special Forces for the end days! Some have been called to go out as Disciples and build Houses of Prayer. Some have the Intercessors FIRE that will and is even now burning up deception.

DECEIVERS = Anti Messiah- 2 John it says," If anyone **does NOT** remain in the teaching of Yahusha; but goes beyond it-he **does NOT** have Yahuah with him. Only those who remain in what Yahusha taught can have the Father and the Son in them.

We ARE a Peculiar Nation- Set Apart Ones

Rules of the "TRIBE" include; Always speak the truth to one another. Keep peace always. Plotting evil towards another will NOT be tolerated!

Seek holiness, I know keep saying it over and over because it is so important for us to strive for it. But, keep in mind it is NOT us that do the work to become holy but Yahusha in us that brings us to holiness. For we can do nothing apart from and no physical act will make us kodesh/holy on our own! We know what the WORD says, "be holy as I am holy." 1 Peter 1:15-16. We are chosen unto holiness. Ephesians 1:4. If we are NOT holy we will not see heaven. Hebrews 12:14. It is our desire for holiness that separates us from the world.

144,000 a number I do NOT mention much in my writings and mostly because I do NOT know anything about it. Ever wonder why YaH picked the number 144,000? Or 12? Or 7?? NO. So I do NOT assume anything when it comes to ABBA's groups, numbers, mathematics etc..What HE did appoint me to share is the reformation of the 12 TRIBES of ISRAEL. YAHUAH ELOHIM will and is gathering the Tribes together. **HE** is quickening people and bringing them to the knowledge of what Tribe they belong to for the End Days. The Awakening of the Tribes has begun, ABBA confirmed to me which Tribe I belonged to over a year ago. I know that I am Naphtali. I encourage you to pray and ask HIM to reveal which Tribe you belong to, this is important as we move into position because each Tribe is assigned a unique mission in these END of DAYS. It is the decade of the Tribes! Yahuah will place a wall of FIRE around those who are HIS CHOSEN! Just like the Tribes in ancient times we too will go through a time of pilgrimage. Moving our tents from place to place as we are going through the final purification process to come into New Jerusalem and be with our Bridegroom at the Marriage Supper of the Lamb! **HALLELUYAH!**

CHILDREN OF DARKNESS

YaH brought to my attention this morning an opened eye vision HE had given me July 1, 2019. HE wanted me to share this so HIS people do not perish for lack of knowledge. Many in these last days will fail to recognize what I am about to share and they will die because of deception!! Heed these words and remember them please! ABBA stressed in this vision the importance of continuous prayer and knowing our authority and power, given us. In the days ahead as it gets darker and darker we will have to WAR like never before casting out demons, principalities, and evil forces out of people. The spiritual warfare is only going to increase 100 fold. We must be ready and active as YaH's warriors. HE said, there are those who are children of darkness-their blood is black, their hearts are black, and they are pure evil. These are the generals in hasatan's army. They will not be adults!! They will be children! Children who were brought forth from the Fallen Angels seed, possibly mixed with A.I. technology. Many wicked ceremonies took place to conceive them from the darkest pits of wickedness and evil. hasatan brought them forth to lead his end time army. People who do not know what they are will be deceived because they are children-- and will be killed by them. Some have already seen these creatures. The black eyed children! **DO NOT BE DECEIVED BELOVED!** Test everything and follow the unction of the Ruach haKodesh. hasatans next line of defense will be his captains, YaH said those are ones who volunteered in his army. They are people who have surrendered their will to him and have become conduits for evil spirits and demons to flow in and out of. They are full of evil energies, their blood remains red and their hearts are hardened. Yahuah said, they can still repent and come to the light if they chose too. If they do NOT, at the last call then they will be completely taken over by the demons and their spirits will be trapped forever in outer darkness. hasatan is using every ounce of his evil energies to irritate, influence and manipulate the masses in this hour to rapidly bring chaos. We know that Yahuah's energy of light cuts right through the darkness! AMEIN! We must pray and walk in Spirit and in Truth as the Ruach leads us in wisdom and greater discernment daily. We must know and live in the authority given to us from Yahusha. This is vital for our survival. hasatan has a dark army waiting to be activated, they everyone and no one. Some are only being used and abused unknowingly by mind control and other vicious traps with false promises. hasatan has cleverly deceived them in his wicked intelligence in all his glory making them work tirelessly to recruit other unknowing victims.The ``dark ones" with black hearts,eyes, and blood are completely sold out and engulfed in darkness. They already wear the "mark" of the Beast proudly. In the days to come it will be those who exude emunah/faith, meekness,and ahavah/love who are seasoned and matured that will lead YaH's army. Those in the strength of Yahusha who overcome the enemy and occupy a position in the courts of heaven. Many do NOT understand the true conflict that is going on between Yahusha and hasatan over the souls of men. Everything is returning to the **first ORDER** before the fall. We will see the Garden of Eden! We are Yahusha's warriors and have joyfully submitted to the difficulties ahead. It is because of our great love, commitment, and joy for YaH that we have sacrificially and proudly enlisted to take out the enemy of our Master, King, and Savior! We anticipate with joy and gladness the trials to come knowing that each one will purify us a little more. Our lives have and will become ones of constant aggressive warfare and perseverance. We understand as Yahusha's Special Forces the work we do will tax our energies to the utmost yet empower us with HIS STRENGTH mighty! Those of us that do understand the blood stained banner of Yahusha, who are willing partakers of HIS conflicts and intentionally wage a determined war against the powers of darkness will enter New Jerusalem and receive our crown! This last decade is the final manuscript of Creation's Redemption. hasatan's rebellion is a lesson to all of Creation throughout the Ages and a perpetual testimony to the results of wickedness and sin.

We have overcome by the BLOOD of YAHUSHA and the WORD of our testimony. We have entered a time where many testimonies will blossom as a result of Yahuah protecting HIS people! Just as in the days of the Patriarchs of old.

GLUTTONY and INTEMPERANCE

Sound sleep cometh of moderate eating: he riseth early, and his wits are with him: but the pain of watching, and choler, and pangs of the belly, are with an insatiable man. And if thou hast been forced to eat, arise, go forth, vomit, and thou shalt have rest. My son, hear me, and despise me not, and at the last thou shalt find as I told thee: in all thy works be quick, so shall there no sickness come unto thee. Whoso is liberal of his meat, men shall speak well of him; and the report of his good housekeeping will be believed. Sirach 31: 20-23

The state of dissipation is one of the marked evidences of the soon close of this earth's history.

Three **KEYS to OUR Survival--Self-Control, Surrender, and Discipline.** hasatan's three fold prescription to destroy man, dispensation,disease, and death. If one chooses to take it!

F athers
A ncient
R emedies
M astered

The F. A. R. M . Sefer of Sacred Ancient Remedies
Prayer combined with the Father's remedies including; anointing oils and fasting.
Prescription of Prayer- ---Tehillim 91 and 119

Code of Conduct for Sparrow and Dove Refuge: Study & Define each area.

The 12 pillars of a Tribe-

Love

Honesty

Wisdom

Shalom/Kindness

Faith

Respect

Honor

Integrity

Self Control

Patience

Forgiveness

Selflessness

MANTEL OF JOHN THE IMMERSER

Honey & locusts, messy hair, camels hair for clothes----

MANTEL of MOSEH

Boldness/Obedience/Warnings

Uncultivated Eretz

Subduing the land (eretz) is an act of obedience. Agrarian life is one of selflessness, Undisciplined environments create chaos and confusion. Hotbed of sin and iniquity. ust as idle hands are an invitation to wickedness and rebellion.

Agrarian Revolution is Revelation of YaH's Ways

"One of the main reasons that we are in the mess we are in today is because we have neglected the simple Scriptural fact that God appointed man to be a tiller of the ground. And we will never see the establishment of a truly godly social order until we return to our agrarian roots." Howard Douglas King

Mass migration, the destruction of the social fabric of our communities, urban sprawl, insecurity, agrochemicals, GMOs, junk food, the homogenization of diets, the destruction of mangrove forests, the acidification of the sea, the depletion of fish stocks,are all symptoms of what is taking place. Proposals for food sovereignty, popular agrarian reform, the building of agroecological food production territories, and peasant agriculture

"By destroying the village and the productive homestead, the Industrial Revolution has wreaked a calamity upon mankind of incalculable dimensions . Though enriched in the number and variety of possessions, we have been impoverished in terms of human values like community, family life, self-expression and fulfilling work." Dr. Bartlett

The application of these principles will not be easy. That said, the apostle Paul's words ring true for us when he commands us to not be conformed to this world, but to be transformed by the renewing of our minds, that we may prove what is the good, acceptable and perfect will of Yahuah.

Safe Havens/Places of Refuge

" And I shall make a covenant of peace with them, and make evil beasts cease from the land. **And they shall dwell safely in the wilderness and sleep in the forest.**

"And I shall make them and the places all around My hill a blessing, and shall cause showers to come down in their season – showers of blessing they are."And the trees of the field shall yield their fruit and the earth yield her increase, and they shall be safe in their land. And they shall know that I am יהוה, when I have broken the bars of their yoke. **And I shall deliver them from the hands of those who enslaved them,** and they shall no longer be a prey for the nations, and the beasts of the earth shall not devour them. And they shall dwell safely, with no one to make them afraid. " <u>And I shall raise up for them a planting place of name</u> , and **they shall no longer be consumed by hunger in the land,** nor bear the shame of the nations any more. "And they shall know that I, יהוה their Elohim, am with them, and that they, the house of Yisra'ĕl, are My people," declares the Master יהוה.' " "And you, My flock, the flock of My pasture, are men, and I am your Elohim," declares the Master יהוה.' " **Yehezqel 34:25-31**

Impending Persecution is not optional.

2 Esdras 16: 68-78 speaks of our impending persecution. We must ready ourselves for what is coming and be firm in our faith. Many will compromise and it will cost them greatly! Don't you want to be found among the worthy who endures all things to the end? I do. Prepare your hearts for betrayal, prepare your minds by not trying to figure the "why" in persecution. Prepare your physical bodies to endure horrors unimaginable to the end. I want to remind us all about the mother and the seven sons in Maccabees. They simply refused to eat pork and look at what happened to them! They were tortured in horrific ways. WHY would anyone who is a Hebrew brother or sister think they are "special" and would not have to endure such trials? Be real it is going to happen! Embrace it now as a possibility for your life, be firm in your emunah, and lead by example, pray fervently that you may escape and yet surrender yourself to ABBA's WILL be done.

2 Esdras 16:68-78 New Revised Standard Version (NRSV)

68 The burning wrath of a great multitude is kindled over you; they shall drag some of you away and force you to eat what was sacrificed to idols. 69 And those who consent to eat shall be held in derision and contempt, and shall be trampled under foot. 70 For in many places and in neighboring cities there shall be a great uprising against those who fear

Yahuah. **71** They shall be like maniacs, sparing no one, but plundering and destroying those who continue to fear YaH. **72** For they shall destroy and plunder their goods, and drive them out of house and home. **73** Then the tested quality of my elect shall be manifest, like gold that is tested by fire.

Promise of Divine Deliverance

74 Listen, my elect ones, says Yahuah; the days of tribulation are at hand, but I will deliver you from them. **75** Do not fear or doubt, for Yahuah Elohim is your guide. **76** You who keep my commandments and precepts, says the Most High YaH, must not let your sins weigh you down, or your iniquities prevail over you. **77** Woe to those who are choked by their sins and overwhelmed by their iniquities! They are like a field choked with underbrush and its path overwhelmed with thorns, so that no one can pass through. **78** It is shut off and given up to be consumed by fire.
The Horror of What Is Upon Us..

2 Esdras 16:18-34 New Revised Standard Version (NRSV)

18 The **beginning of sorrows,** when there shall be much lamentation; the **beginning of famine** , when many shall perish; **the beginning of wars,** when the powers shall be terrified; the **beginning of calamities,** when all shall tremble. What shall they do, when the calamities come? **19** *Famine and plague, tribulation and anguish* are sent as scourges for the correction of mankind. **20** Yet for all this they **will not** turn from their iniquities, or ever be mindful of the scourges. **21** Indeed, ***provisions will be so cheap upon earth that people will imagine that peace is assured for them*** , and then calamities shall spring up on the earth— **the sword, famine, and great confusion. 22** For many of those who live on the earth shall perish by <u>famine</u> ; and <u>those who survive the famine shall die by the sword</u> . **23** And the dead shall be thrown out like dung, and there shall be no one to console them; for the earth shall be left desolate, and its cities shall be demolished. **24** No one shall be left to cultivate the earth or to sow it. **25** The trees shall bear fruit, but who will gather it? **26** The grapes shall ripen, but who will tread them? For in all places there shall be great solitude; **27** a person will long to see another human being, or even to hear a human voice.
28 For ten shall be left out of a city; and two, out of the field, **those who have hidden themselves in thick groves and clefts in the rocks** . **29** Just as in an olive orchard three

or four olives may be left on every tree, 30 or just as, when a vineyard is gathered, some clusters may be left [a] by those who search carefully through the vineyard, 31 so in those days three or four shall be left by those who search their houses with the sword. 32 The earth shall be left desolate, and its fields shall be plowed up, [b] and its roads and all its paths shall bring forth thorns, because no sheep will go along them. 33 Virgins shall mourn because they have no bridegrooms; women shall mourn because they have no husbands; their daughters shall mourn, because they have no help. 34 Their bridegrooms shall be killed in war, and their husbands shall perish of famine.

2 Esdras 16:35-40 New Revised Standard Version (NRSV)

Yahuah's People Must Prepare for the End

35 Listen now to these things, and understand them, you who are servants of Yahuah Elohim. 36 This is the WORD of Yahuah; **receive it and do not disbelieve** what YaH says. [a] 37 The calamities draw near, and are not delayed. 38 Just as a pregnant woman, in the ninth month when the time of her delivery draws near, has great pains around her womb for two or three hours beforehand, but when the child comes forth from the womb, there will not be a moment's delay, 39 so the calamities will not delay in coming upon the earth, and the world will groan, and pains will seize it on every side. 40 **Hear my words, O my people; prepare for battle, and in the midst of the calamities be like strangers on the earth.**

Nation of Natsarim---YaH's Special Forces
Sanctified, Refined, and tested. Enemies of the state. (world)
In uniform---our ARMOR.
Warriors on frontines. Ground Zero.
The WAY---The TRUTH---The LIFE
  * You will have trials and tribulations as you proceed.
  * You will find friends and family turning away from you.
  * You will be attacked by the physical and the spiritual.
  * You will have to leave some behind because they will not walk **The Way** with you.
  * You will have to leave the traditions with which you grew up.
  * You WILL be persecuted.
Called to walk the **NARROW ROAD** . Many are called and few are chosen.
Servant Leaders to Model After

Yahusha of course!
John the Immerser
James the Just- Acts 12:17 Acts 21:18-26 Galatians 1:19
Paul Acts 24:5 Acts 23:6 Acts 22:3
Luke the Physician

Nation of Natsarim- Lifestyle of Simplicity & Surrender
Serving Yahuah Elohim in Yahusha with our whole heart, whole soul, whole mind!
Loving HIM with great passion. Practicing a life of obedience, love, wisdom, integrity, discipline, and freedom.
Life of constant prayer and communion with YaH. Living examples of Loving YaH and loving your neighbor. Natsarim are NOT conformed to this world nor are they influenced by it. They are truthseekers. Natsarim fast regularly. They commune with one another breaking bread together. Each Natsarim shares their belongings with one another freely in joy. Simplicity in clothing and women sometimes cover their heads.
Yah's voice gives revelation and hasatan's voice is words of deception
Ezekiel 20:10-12 **Preparing the heart, soul, and mind.** Exodus 34: 10-11, 34: 27-28
Mark 12: 28-31

Our HEADS and HANDS / ARMS need to constantly be SOAKED IN YAHUSHUA'S BLOOD and GUIDED BY YAH to make the RIGHT DECISIONS!!!
Times time a half a time ---example in Daniel, Jeremiah, Isaiah, Ezekiel they all prophesied in their time and sometimes they prophesied in our time and at times they prophesied for both times at the same time.......A time past we are in and a time to come.
The potions of hasatan--how hasatan deceives many and **if POSSIBLE** even the elect.

The Unholy Trinity the FAKE COPY includes:
- Unholy Father (who is hasatan himself)
- Unholy son (the only begotten son of hasatan who will manifest as the Anti-Messiah)
- Fake/Unholy Spirit / Kundalini/Fake Prophet

Counterfeit MIRACLES, etc will look very similar to those of YaH but will produce ADVERSE RESULTS in the SPIRITUAL REALM which will only lead to hell!
Mixing of the WORD with all forms of paganism
It is the SH'MA that enables many **MEN OF YAH to STAND UP FOR THE TRUTH.**
Elijah and Elisha! Elijah's and Elisha's MINISTRIES involved BATTLING AGAINST THE WORSHIP OF OTHER gods and battle against those MIXING YAH with PAGANISM by worshiping YAH as the PAGANS DO. Sadly PAGANISM has continued on into our generation and it is still infiltrating and influencing our WORSHIP OF YAH!
YAH has sent HIS PROPHETS to warn against it however most people ARE NOT HEARING YAH whereas others are just choosing to IGNORE YAH.
Delicacy of deceit and YaH's bowl of wrath to come.
Three fold strategy of YaH in the hearts of HIS PEOPLE.
Devotion to YaH/ Intention of YaH-Direction of YaH---
4 Phases of the Great Awakening

1- Awake - to Truth
2- Affirm - the Call
3- Align - with Purpose
4- Anoint - for the Work

Now I beseech those that read this book, that they be not discouraged for these calamities, but that they judge those punishments not to be for destruction, but for a chastening of our nation. For it is a token of his great goodness, when wicked doers are not suffered any long time, but forthwith punished.For not as with other nations, whom the Lord patiently for beareth to punish, till they be come to the fulness of their sins, so dealeth he with us, Lest that, being come to the height of sin, afterwards he should take vengeance of us. And therefore he never withdraweth his mercy from us: and though he punishes with adversity, yet doth he never forsake his people. But let this that we have spoken be for a warning unto us. And now we come declaring the matter in a few words.
2 Macc. 6:12-17

HIVE MIND versus TRIBE MIND
HIVE MIND=

- Collective consciousness or collective intelligence , concepts in sociology and philosophy

    - Group mind (science fiction) , a type of collective consciousness

- Groupthink , in which the desire for harmony or conformity in a group results in irrational or dysfunctional decision-making

    - Sheeple , a derogatory term referring to groups of people who mindlessly follow those in power

- Swarm intelligence , the collective behavior of decentralized, self-organized systems, natural or artificial

    - The apparent consciousness of colonies of social insects such as ants, bees, and termites

- Universal mind , a type of universal higher consciousness in some esoteric beliefs
- Egregore , a concept in occultism which has been described as group mind

TRIBE MIND=

information or knowledge that is known within a tribe but often unknown outside of it. A tribe, in this sense, may be a group or subgroup of people that share such a common knowledge. "Tribal Knowledge or know-how is the collective wisdom of the Tribe or group. It is the sum of all the knowledge and capabilities of all the people".
Tribalism is the state of being organized by, or advocating for, tribes or tribal lifestyles. Human evolution has primarily occurred in small groups, as

opposed to mass societies , and humans naturally maintain a social network .
In popular culture , tribalism may also refer to a way of thinking or behavior in
which people are loyal to their social group above all else.

*It seems that every letter of the Ancient Hebrew alphabet is instrumental in
telling the overall Tabernacle tale. Consider how every ancient Hebrew letter
has some correlation to the ancient Tabernacle story: (from Ancient Hebrew
Research Center)*

The letter ב or ⊎ or "bet" was originally drawn to represent a tent floor plan.
The letter ו or Ύ or "vav" is a picture of a tent peg.
The letter ח or or "chet" depicts a tent wall.
The letter ד or ▽ or "dalet" refers to a doorway, which a tent must have.
The letter ל or ∠ or "lamed" is a rod / shaft / stick, which are used to create the tent
frame.
The letter ת or ✝ or "tav" is portrayed as crossed sticks, which give strength to the tent
frame.
The letter פ or ↘ or "peh" resembles a lip or a mouth and alludes to the facility's
perimeter.
The letter כ or ⊎ or "caph" is like an open/cupped hand, as the court is described (above).
The letter ש or ᕲ or "shin" portrays an opposing pair, as were the courtyard halves.
The letter ה or ⍦ or "hey" conveys elevation (tent), praise (human), and inspiration
(divine).
The letter ר or ℜ or "resh" or "rosh" is a head, which is what Exodus called the tent top.
The letter o or ∓ or "sameck" is tack/pin-like, as used for court posts and sting compass
lines.
The letter מ or ᨓ or "mem" is water, which is found in the basin next to the tent.
The letter ט or ⊗ or "tet" is basket-like, as is the round copper altar at the gate of the
court.
The letter ז or ⊬ or "zayin" is a hatchet or blade, which is used for slaughter at the altar.
The letter נ or ↘ or "nun" is seed, which was offered (e.g., grain or first-fruits) at the
altar.
The letter י or ↵ or "yad" is drawn like a hand, which depicts work and worship.
The letter א or 𝒴 or "aleph" is the ox head, and oxen would be used to haul tent beams.
The letter צ or ᒪ or "tzade" shows a wandering path, as were Israel's journeys.
The letter ג or ✓ or "gimmel" is drawn like foot or camel, which are used by wandering
nomads.
The letter ק or ℗ or "quf" is subdivided circle, common to sunrise, equinox, and the
domed tent.
The letter ע or ◉ or "ayin" is where "eye" comes from, and the structure looks like an
eyeball.

Clearly, the entire wilderness-desert-life experience can be seen in this remarkable aleph-bet language, and even two three letter words are able to tell part of the story. But this is only the beginning.

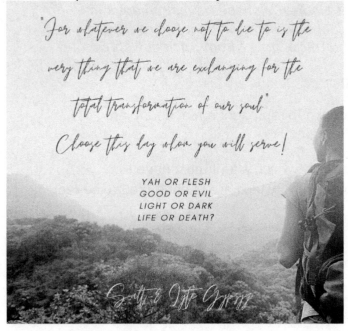

"For whatever we choose not to die to is the very thing that we are exchanging for the total transformation of our soul."

Choose this day whom you will serve!

YAH OR FLESH
GOOD OR EVIL
LIGHT OR DARK
LIFE OR DEATH?

O Yahuwah, **give me understanding according to Your Word** . (Psalms 119:169b)

> **The entrance of Your Words give light** ; it gives understanding unto the simple. (Psalms 119:130)
> How can a young man keep his way pure? **By guarding it according to Your Word** . (Psalms 119:9)
> **Uphold me according unto Your Word** , that I may live …. (Psalms 119:116a)
> To the law [torah] and to the testimony: **if they speak not according to this Word [the Scriptures], it is because there is no light [no truth] in them** . (Isaiah 8:20)
> **THE TENT REVIVAL IS; THE LAST HARVEST**
> A GATHERING OF NATSARIM---INVITING THE LOST, BROKEN, AND LUKEWARM--
> IN A TENT SPECIFICALLY ERECTED FOR REVIVAL/MEETINGS/HEALING/DELIVERANCE
> **TENT of MEETING**
> This is very interesting that:every year adds to the year of Creation 3760---5780-2020= **3760**
> If we are subtracting from instead of adding too---then all of Creation is collapsing. It is retreating backwards if we are being led right back to the Garden of Eden. Could the " **NARROW PATH, THE WAY** " be getting narrower by the day as the earth begins to collapse and force all of creation into a sort of vacuum being pulled

forcefully into the narrow way? Just some food for thought. It is interesting to note that from the ancient earth to now all of Creation including ourselves has been shrinking dramatically. Adam was a larger, taller man than Moseh. Moseh than Ezra, Ezra than Paul and Paul to us....there is physical evidence in the earth to prove this.

THE PANIC of 20/20- Year of transformation and the dividing.

Fear is a virus that spreads faster than the speed of light. Fear manifests from the unknown. Fear can be controlled chaos. Fear is the sickness that kills freedom and hope. People are afraid of what they do not know. Once fear has taken root it then festers into anger, rage, and panic. People lose all common sense and result in selfish ambition amidst FEAR. The enemy of our soul thrives in fear. It is as if feeding fuel to the fire, thus consuming all in its path.

Parasites we all carry parasites I'm not talking about physical little bugs I'm talking about parasitic demons who have been given access to our physical bodies and our flesh; this results in behaving in a certain way, uncontrollable anger, frustration, hatred manipulation, lies and all of the lust of the flesh, so what do we do? The only answer is to fast and pray and we kill them one by one with the sword, **THE WORD!**

Pour the **BLOOD of Yahusha** over the entrance and seal in **HIS NAME!**

BEANS/BULLETS/BANDAIDS

Living the DO ---As Yahuah commands SHEMA--Hear Israel and do! Move be in action.

"And it shall come to pass afterward, that I will pour out my spirit on all flesh [*kol-basar*]; your sons and your daughters shall prophesy, your old men shall dream dreams, and your young men shall see visions" (Joel 2:28, RSV; cf. Acts 2:17).

Hebrew Life Intro-

ABBA has laid it on my heart to research, write in, and share about living Hebrew life is a set apart life this is the WAY of YaH's peculiar people. I have been reading so much and this topic really sets my heart on fire! For us it is not about going backward - living the ancient life but more about moving forward into something new--where each of us are learning to walk and talk for the first time as we exit Babylon and her ways. Most of us do not know how to leave Babylon and obey YaH when HE says "come out of her my people.." What does that look like for us on an individual level as well as a corporate level (body).

We will talk about the Exodus---Deuteronomy---Paul---Yahusha and how YaH's living WORD (Yahusha) is beautiful tapestry woven in and out of time, space, and matter from the ancient days to the end of days. There is so much wisdom and revelation to be gained in this walk!! I pray that we can all be blessed and enjoy time gleaning from one another!

Sirach 32:14-24, 33:1-6

14Whoso feareth the Yahuah will receive his discipline; and they that seek him early shall find favour.

15 He that seeketh the law shall be filled therewith: but the hypocrite will be offended thereat.

16 They that fear the Yahuah shall find judgment, and shall kindle justice as a light.

17 A sinful man will not be reproved, but findeth an excuse according to his will.

18 A man of counsel will be considerate; but a strange and proud man is not daunted with fear, even when of himself, he hath done without counsel.

19 Do nothing without advice; and when thou hast once done, repent not.

20 Go not in a way wherein thou mayest fall, and stumble not among the stones.

21 Be not confident in a plain way.

22 And beware of thine own children.

23 In every good work trust thy own soul; for this is the keeping of the commandments.

24 He that believeth in Yahuah taketh heed to the commandment; and he that trusteth in him shall fare never the worse.

There shall no evil happen unto him that feareth Adonai; but in temptation even again he will deliver him.

2 A wise man hateth not the law; but he that is an hypocrite therein is as a ship in a storm.

3 A man of understanding trusteth in the law; and the law is faithful unto him, as an oracle.

4 Prepare what to say, and so thou shalt be heard: and bind up instruction, and then make answer.

5 The heart of the foolish is like a cartwheel; and his thoughts are like a rolling axletree.

6 A stallion horse is as a mocking friend, he neigheth under every one that sitteth upon him.

Hymn of the Saints-Manual of Discipline-Dead Sea Scrolls

YAHUAH's Appointed Time

Day and night will I offer my praise
and at all the appointed times which YAHUAH has prescribed,
When daylight begins its rule,
when it reaches its turning-point,
and when it again withdraws to its appointed abode;
When the watches of darkness begin,
when YAHUAH opens the storehouse thereof,
when HE sets that darkness against the light,
when it reaches its turning-point,
and when it again withdraws in face of the light;
When sun and moon shine forth from the kodesh Height,

and when they again withdraw to the glorious Abode;
When the formal seasons come on the days of new moon,
when they reach their turning-points,
and when they yield place to one another,
as each comes round anew;
When the natural seasons come, at whatever time may be;
when, too, the months begin;
on their feasts and on kodesh days,
as they come in order due,
each as a memorial in its season
I shall hold it as one of the laws
engraven of old on the tablets
to render to YAHUAH as my tribute
-the blessings of my lips.
When the (natural) years begin;
at the turning-points of their seasons,
and when each completes its term
on its natural day,
yielding each to each -
reaping-time to summer,
sowing-time to verdure;
In the (formal) years of weeks,
in the several seasons thereof,
and when, at the jubilee,
the series of weeks begins
I shall hold it as one of the laws
engraven of old on the tablets
to offer to YAHUAH as my fruits
the praises of my tongue,
and to cull for HIS as my tithe
-the skilled music of my lips.
With the coming of day and night
I shall come ever anew
into YAHUAH's COVENANT;
and when evening and morning depart,
shall observe how HE sets their bounds.
Only where YAHUAH sets bounds
-the unchangeable bounds of HIS LAW
will I too set my domain.
I shall hold it as one of the laws
engraven of old on the tablets
to face my sin and transgression

and avouch the justice of YAHUAH.
I shall say unto YAHUAH:
'You, for me, art the Right!'
and unto the Most High:
'For me You art cause of all good!'
Fountain of all knowledge,
Spring of holiness,
Zenith of all glory,
Might omnipotent,
Beauty that never fades,
I will choose the path HE shows me,
and be content with HIS judgments.
Whenever I first put forth my hand or foot,
I will bless HIS name;
when first I go or come,
when I sit and when I rise,
when I lie down on my couch,
I will sing unto HIS.
At the common board,
or ever I raise my hand
to enjoy the rich fruits of the earth,
with that which flows from my lips
I will bless HIS as with an oblation.
At the onset of fear and alarm,
or when trouble and stress are at hand,
I will bless him with special thanksgiving
and muse upon HIS power,
and rely on HIS mercies always,
and come thereby to know
that in HIS hand lies the judgment of all living,
and that all HIS works are truth.
Whenever distress breaks out,
I still will praise HIS;
and when HIS Yeshua comes,
join the chorus of praise.
I will heap no evil on any,
but pursue all men with good,
knowing that only with YAHUAH
lies the judgment of all living,
and HE it is will award
each man his deserts.
I will not be envious

of the profit of wickedness;
for wealth unrighteously gotten my soul shall not lust.
I will not engage in strife
with reprobate men,
forestalling the Day of Requital.
I will not turn back my wrath
from forward men,
nor rest content until justice be affirmed.
I will harbor no angry grudge
against those that indeed repent,
but neither will I show compassion
to any that turn from the way.
I will not console the smitten
until they amend their course.
I will cherish no baseness in my heart,
nor shall there be heard in my mouth
coarseness or wanton deceit;
neither shall there be found upon my lips deception and lies.
The fruit of holiness shall be on my tongue,
and no heathen filth be found thereon.
I will open my mouth with thanksgiving,
and my tongue shall ever relate
the bounteousness of YAHUAH
and the perfidy of men
until men's transgressions be ended.
Empty words will I banish from my lips;
filth and perverseness from my mind.
I will shelter knowledge with sound counsel,
and protect it with shrewdness of mind.
I will set a sober limit
to all defending of faith
and exacting of justice by force.
I will bound YAHUAH's righteousness
by the measuring-line of occasion.
I will temper justice with mercy,
will show kindness to men downtrodden,
bring firmness to fearful hearts,
discernment to spirits that stray,
enlighten the bowed with sound doctrine,
reply to the proud with meekness,
with humility answer the base
-men rich in worldly goods,

who point the finger of scorn
and utter iniquitous thoughts.
To YAHUAH I commit my cause.
It is HIS to perfect my way,
HIS to make straight my heart.
HE, in HIS charity,
will wipe away my transgression.
For HE from the Wellspring of Knowledge
has made HIS light to burst forth,
and mine eye has gazed on HIS wonders;
and the light that is in my heart
has pierced the deep things of existence.
HE is ever the stay of my right hand.
The path beneath my feet
is set on a mighty rock
unshaken before all things.
For that rock beneath my feet
is the truth of YAHUAH,
and HIS power is the stay of my right hand;
from the fount of HIS charity
my vindication goes forth.
Through HIS mysterious wonder
light is come into my heart;
mine eye has set its gaze
on everlasting things.
A virtue hidden from man,
a knowledge and subtle lore
concealed from human kind;
a fount of righteousness,
a reservoir of strength,
a wellspring of all glory
wherewith no flesh has converse
these has YAHUAH bestowed
on them that HE has chosen,
to possess them for ever.
HE has given them an inheritance
in the lot of the Kodesh Beings,
and joined them in communion with the Sons of Heaven,
to form one congregation,
one single communion,
a fabric of holiness,
a plant evergreen,

for all time to come.
But I belong to wicked mankind,
to the communion of sinful flesh.
My transgressions, my iniquities and sins,
and the waywardness of my heart
condemn me to communion with the worm
and with all that walk in darkness.
For a mortal's way is not of himself,
neither can a man direct his own steps.
The judgment lies with YAHUAH,
and 'tis HIS to perfect man's way.
Only through HIS knowledge
have all things come to be,
and all that is, is ordained by HIS thought;
and apart from HIS is nothing wrought.
Behold, if I should totter,
YAHUAH's mercies will be my yeshua.
If I stumble in the error of the flesh,
I shall be set aright
through YAHUAH's righteousness ever-enduring.
If distress break out,
HE will snatch my soul from perdition,
and set my foot on the path.
For HE, in HIS compassion,
has drawn me near unto HIS,
and HIS judgment upon me shall be rendered in HIS mercy.
In his bounteous truth HE has judged me,
and in HIS abundant goodness
will shrive my iniquities,
and in HIS righteousness cleanse me
from all the pollution of man
and the sin of human kind,
that I may acknowledge unto YAHUAH HIS righteousness,
and unto the Most High HIS majestic splendor.
Blessed art You, O my YAHUAH,
Who hast opened the heart of Thy servant unto knowledge.
Direct all his works in righteousness,
and vouchsafe unto the son of Thine handmaid
the favor which You hast assured to all the mortal elect,
to stand in Thy presence for ever.
For apart from Thee no man's way can be perfect,
and without Thy will is nothing wrought.

You it is that hath taught all knowledge,
and all things exist by Thy will;
and there is none beside Thee
to controvert Thy plan;
none to understand all Thy kodesh thought,
none to gaze into the depths of Thy secrets,
none to perceive all Thy wonders and the might of Thy power.
Who can compass the sum of Thy glory?
And what is mere mortal man
amid Thy wondrous works?
And what the child of woman
to sit in Thy presence?
For, behold, he is kneaded of dust,
and his is the food of worms.
HE is but a molded shape,
a thing nipped out of the clay,
whose attachment is but to the dust.
What can such clay reply,
or that which is molded by hand?
What thought can it comprehend?

DAN- Tribe of Israel turned wicked? Will the Anti Messiah will rise from?

JUDAS - One of the twelve that would betray Yahusha

A Vulgar Display of Power

The working agent of hasatan is a design of excuse, compromise, and complacency. With the forerunner being that of the will of self service. The victim believes in deserved blessing and therefore is blinded by the subtle ambition of the spirits of deception. Walking as though

"You shall not defile yourselves with them" Lev. 11.43 "You shall not defile yourselves" Lev. 11.44 "For themselves and for their descendants" Esther 9.31 "You who tear yourself in your anger" Job 18.4 "He justified himself" Job 32.2 "But themselves go into captivity" Is. 46.2 "What every one (original, "every soul") must eat, that only may be prepared by you" Ex. 12.16 "Who kills any person (original, "kill any soul") without intent" Num. 35.11,15 "Let me (original, "let my soul") die the death of the righteous" Num. 23.10 "When any one (original, "any soul") brings a cereal offering" Lev. 2.1 "I have . . . quieted myself" Ps. 131.2 AV

 "Think not that in the king's palace you (original, "soul") will escape" Esther 4.13 "The Lord God has sworn by himself (original, "sworn by his soul")" Amos 6.8 T

THE TEN WORDS *eseret ha-devarim*
1. I AM **Yahuah** YOUR **Elohim**- HAVE NO OTHER BEFORE MY FACE.
NO FOREIGN NAMES ,RITUALS, CUSTOMS OF PAGANS

2. *you do not* **BOW** TO *IMAGES*
3. *you do not CAST* THE   Name OF   Yahuah YOUR   Elohim TO *RUIN* "SHOAH" **RUIN**
4. *remember* **SHABBAT, TO KEEP IT QODESH. QODESH = SET-APART**
SABBATH IS THE Sign OF everlasting Covenant OF LOVE
THE SHABBAT ACKNOWLEDGES YAHUAH AS CREATOR.
5. **YOU RESPECT YOUR FATHER AND YOUR MOTHER.**
6. *you do not* **MURDER** .
7. *you do not* **BREAK WEDLOCK.**
8. *you do not* **STEAL.**
9. *you do not*   **BEAR FALSE** witness **AGAINST YOUR NEIGHBOR.**
10. *you do not* **COVET YOUR NEIGHBOR'S HOUSE, WIFE, SERVANTS,OX, ASS, OR ANYTHING THAT BELONGS TO YOUR NEIGHBOR.**

THESE ARE TO BE DILIGENTLY taught TO YOUR CHILDREN and POSTED ON THE DOORPOSTS OF YOUR HOME.
WILD-AUTHENTIC WORSHIP
As Sons and Daughters of Zadok and as the sect of Natsarim, we enter into the presence of **YaH** through our own authentic worship of **Elohim** . We **HONOR HIM** , we **LOVE HIM** , we **PRAISE HIM** , and we **WORSHIP HIS NAME** . It is a deep passionate love for **HIM** that pours out when we seek **HIM** in pure, wild, true, and free worship. This is a **KEY** that opens the portals of Heaven for us to see the miraculous **POWER OF YAHUAH** manifest on earth.
Infiltrator/ hastan
And as you go, proclaim, saying, 'The reign of the heavens has drawn near.'"Heal the sick, cleanse the lepers, raise the dead, cast out demons. You have received without paying, give without being paid. **Matthew 10: 7,8**
And having called His twelve taught ones near, He gave them authority over unclean spirits, to cast them out, and to heal every disease and every bodily weakness.
Matthew 10:1
WE have the authority to dethrone the enemy's plan.
And having called His twelve taught ones together, He gave them power and authority over all demons, and to heal diseases. **Luke 9:1**
REVELATION-ARY WAR
Are You Ready?
We are in a war of revelations....as everyone seems to know everything and knowledge has increased and runs to and fro in the earth. Beware the trap of searching for air. Our enemy is cunning at masquerading in costumes disguised as wisdom!! Many will be led astray and deceived. Pray fervently daily even hourly for true wisdom that comes from **ABBA! Pray for the spirit of wisdom to guide you.**
The WAR has begun! Get out your weapons, put on your armor and stand!
In these days to come many have been instructed to build **"Safe Havens"** all throughout the U.S. I have been called to do this myself with my husband. These are places that Yahuah has picked out to keep HIS hand of protection over for the coming tribulation. Not

all "Safe Havens" will look the same. Some will be in the wilderness, some could be in cities in the underground, some could be on farms, etc. I can not share with you any information about the other Brothers and Sisters who have been called to build these places, I can only share what YaH told me to do and how it is to operate in the midst of tribulation time.

Our " *Safe Haven* " is called the **Sparrow and Dove Refuge** , it will be set up much like a camp with tents and some structures. All will share a communal kitchen, commons, all bathrooms will be located in one place, and there will be a perimeter hedge forged around the camp that YAHUAH will draw a line around and protect us within. We will live and work as a family. Each assigned a prayer watch, cleaning duties, cooking duties, gathering food duties, watchmen duties and such. The following lists delegate the spiritual matters that ABBA instructed me to write out.

Play powerful worship/praise music as much as possible. Assign prayer watches. Those who are intercessors and prayer warriors will pray for the lost, miracles, and healings. There will be some who just fast and pray to see people delivered from demons. Intercessors will pray daily over the camp and for our physical needs to be met. Pray for **FIRE** of the Ruach to stay within the camp. Others will continuously offer thanksgiving and praise to Yahuah. Others still will call FIRE down from h eaven. More will pray for revelations and prophetic instructions from **ABBA** . Daily we all will gather after each has had their own alone time with **ABBA** and pray together for wisdom, discernment, and that we will **NOT** be deceived nor will we step through the gate of temptation.

The time we will be living in will be a time of heavy demonic forces in the earth, the enemy will attempt to control our minds, destroy our thoughts and try to get us to turn on one another. It is vital we learn to forgive quickly and walk in love for one another. Gossip **WILL NOT** be tolerated!! The camp will have rules that will be enforced. Keep Shabbat holy, Love YaH with all our heart, soul, and mind. Love Yahusha and the Ruach HaKodesh. Love one another, be honest and truthful. Keep all the Feast Days, study the **WORD** daily together, and use our gifts to serve YaH and others. The physical aspects of the camp are just as important to **ABBA** , as HE said the camp **MUST BE** kept clean! Discipline and self-control are a must. Everyone will be trained in the use of firearms and spiritual warfare, how to slay demons, deliverance. We have authority to do this and more our beloved Yahusha said. **The Sparrow & Dove Refuge** will be a place of YaH's shalom and joy. Yahuah will place a shield of protection over the camp supernaturally as long as we obey HIM. There are many "Safe Havens" already throughout the country is you want to find one near you, go to Laterrain333 YouTube. This sister was called a while ago to build a network online and you can go to her site, click your state and search.

Welcome Natsarim!

LAST DAYS SAFE HAVEN
ACTS 2 & JOEL 2,3
BRANCH OF SALT & LYTE GYPSY
MINISTRY OF A ZADOK SCRIBE

SPARROW & DOVE REFUGE

What does a key symbolize?

KEYS to Reset Your Mind--Declarations & Decrees Daily

The enemy of our soul has a three fold ministry in the world; steal, kill, destroy. Our mind, thoughts, perceptions, and assumptions are the battlefield of the greatest war we fight. In order to overcome, we must submit to **Yahuah** our mind, will, and emotions and then begin to soak in **HIS WORD** . Read, study, and apply.

We also must be proactive by saying declarations and decrees out loud daily. This is a vital key to overcoming hasatan. Repeat the following daily these declarations are the ammunition in your arsenal as a Warrior of the **Most High** ! Your first step is to declare out loud that you will not allow any outside force into your thinking! There are spiritual laws that demons must obey. They cannot stay where a man wills them not to stay. Your power is in the **Name of Yahusha** , His Blood and the **Word of Yahuah** . The Ruach will provide the **FIRE** that will burn through us with boldness and authority! We must also ask for wisdom, knowledge and for discernment daily as the days get darker!

1 Chronicles 28:9

" As for you, my son Shelomoh, know the Elohim of your father, and serve Him with a perfect heart and with a pleasing
life,for יהוה searches all hearts and understands all the intent of the thoughts. If you do seek Him, He is found by
you; but if you forsake Him, He rejects you forever."

Nehemiah 4:6
So we built the wall, and the entire wall was joined together up to the half of it, for the people had a heart to work.
Psalm 26:2
Examine me, O יהוה, and prove me; Try my kidneys and my heart.
Isaiah 26:3
The one steadfast of mind You guard in perfect peace, for he trusts in You.
Romans 8: 5-8
For those who live according to the flesh set their minds on the matters of the flesh, but those who live according
to the Spirit, the matters of the Spirit. For the mind of the flesh is death, but the mind of the Spirit is life and peace.
Because the mind of the flesh is enmity towards Elohim, for it does not subject itself a to the Torah of Elohim,
neither indeed is it able, and those who are in the flesh are unable to please Elohim.
Romans 12:2
And do not be conformed to this world, but be transformed by the renewing of your mind, so that you prove what is
that good and well-pleasing and perfect desire of Elohim.

2 Corinthians 10: 3-6
For though we walk in the flesh, we do not fight according to the flesh.
For the weapons we fight with are not fleshly but mighty in Elohim for overthrowing strongholds,
overthrowing reasonings and every high matter that exalts itself against the knowledge of Elohim, taking captive every thought to make it obedient to the Messiah,
and being ready to punish all disobedience, when your obedience is complete.
- Have the mind of Yahusha.
- Set your mind on things above and not below.
- Set your mind on things that are true, honest, just, pure, lovely, and of good report. If there is any virtue or praise, think on these things.
- Present your body as a living sacrifice to Yahuah - holy, devoted, and consecrated to please HIM, which is a part of my spiritual worship to HIM.
- Be not conformed to this world's way of thinking, but I am continually being transformed by the renewing of my mind to HIS WORD so that I can prove what is the good, the acceptable , and perfect will of Yahuah Elohim in my life.
- Declare you have the mind of Yahusha!
- Lean not on your own understanding but in all my ways acknowledge HIM!
- Fill your mind with the WORD of Yahuah!

These are just a few declarations and decrees to set your mind first thing in the morning. As a Tribe of Natsarim Warriors we need to be alert and aware of how hasatan can invade our thoughts and our mind. We must be proactive! You can always add more as you pray and seek **YaH** . Ask **HE** will lead you and protect you. **HE** will reveal the enemy's plans, so we know how to war.

Commanded By **YaH** to live by **EMUNAH!**

- *We must give **YaH** the first opportunity to meet our needs.*
- ***DO NOT** allow the fear of man to replace the **FEAR of YAHUAH**!*
- *Pray- **ASK** -Listen-Stay Humble-Believe-Trust-Know-Receive*
- *Step by step we must **BELIEVE***
- ***SHALOM** = is available all the time. **ABBA** is the prescription for fear, anxiety, depression, hopelessness,worry. Take as much as needed.*

Confess your need to your Tribe!

If you do not tell others your needs you are essentially not allowing them to sow seeds. This allows "the family/tribe" to share the burden, be a part or solution.

-If two agree on earth it will be done. Pray with others and lift the need.

-Learn to BE STILL. Sit back, watch, and expect YaH to meet the need.

-You have to flex your emunah/faith muscles. It does take practice. Your muscles get stronger the more you flex them.

* Every need is an opportunity for Yahuah to show himself. Bringing **GLORY** to **HIMSELF!** We have entered the **ERA of SPIRITUAL AUTHORITY.** This new Era will break open the darkness and dark places in the earth and set the captives **FREE!** Yahuah is moving. It is the time of preparation for the coming of Messiah! HalleluYaH! Here are two more keys to the many that **ABBA** has been revealing to me through the Ruach and through **HIS WORD!**

KEY- By the power of the **WORD** of Yahuah on my lips and high Praises to YaH on my tongue and weapons of the sword and the shofar/tambourine/cymbals/drums/singing etc. (your unique weapon)

Sing **LOUD PSALM 149.**

KEY- be open and receptive to Yahuah, have a humble and teachable spirit. Pray-create in me a clean heart **ABBA** , and renew a right spirit within.

John 4:24 **WARship** in Spirit and truth.

Sing - 2 Timothy 1:7 as you move into warship and praise. Thus eliminating fear or shame. Rids the atmosphere of doubt, anxiety or fear that the enemy of our soul attempts to play on. Sing Psalm 150:6 **LOUD!**

Beloveds,

hasatan, the enemy of our soul sees you coming from afar and he knows that you are a **WARRIOR for YAHUAH** . As Warriors be alert that he roams to and from looking for whom he can devour. So today and everyday-set your mind by praying in authority--say,

 "I cancel any and all demon assignments against me or my family today with the spiritual weapons Yahuah has given me. The Sword of the Spirit, Shield of Faith to deflect the fiery arrows of the enemy. I put on the whole armor of righteousness 2 Corinthians 6. I remove all demons, principalities, and dark forces from my midst!

In Yahusha's Name--Amein"

Your Valley of Decision--

Keys for Healing and Deliverance

KEY- *Seal a Decree or Declaration in the Blood of Yahusha HaMashiach*

KEY- *Fast acceptable to Yahuah*

KEY *-Embrace Deliverance*

KEY- *Allow Healing and Blessing to Overtake Us*
We must have a heart of teshuvah.
We must agree with the Ruach HaKodesh.
We must allow the anointing to flow.
We renew our minds daily!
We must soak in the oil of joy and oil of gladness.

Luke 12:24
"Consider the ravens: they neither sow nor reap, they have neither storehouse nor barn and yet **YaH** feeds them. Of how much more valuable you are than the birds!"

Psalms 81:10
I am **YAHUAH your ELOHIM,** who brought you up out of the land of Egypt.
Open your mouth wide, and I will fill it.

Psalms 84:11
For **YAHUAH** is a sun and shield; **HE** bestows favor and honor.
No good thing does he withhold from those who walk uprightly.

Matthew 6:31-32
Therefore do not be anxious, saying, 'What shall we eat?' or 'What shall we drink?'
or 'What shall we wear?' For the Gentiles seek after all these things, and your heavenly
Father knows that you need them all.

Philippians 4:19
And **YAHUAH my ELOHIM** will supply every need of yours according to his riches in
glory in **YAHUSHA HAMASHIACH.**

Hebrews 11:6
And without <u>faith</u> it is impossible to please **HIM** , for whoever would draw near to **YaH**
must believe that he exists and that he rewards those who seek **HIM** .

John 15:16
You did not choose me, but I chose you and appointed you that you should go and bear
fruit and that your fruit should abide, so that whatever you ask the **Father** in my name, he
may give it to you.

John 16:23-24
On that day you will ask nothing of me. Truly, truly, I say to you, whatever you ask of the
Father in my name, he will give it to you. Until now you have asked nothing in my name.
Ask, and you will receive, that your joy may be full .

Romans 8:32
He who did not spare his own **Son** but gave him up for us all, how will he not also
with him graciously give us all things?

James 4:1-2
What causes quarrels and what causes fights among you? Is it not this, that your
passions are at war within you? You desire and do not have, so you murder. You covet
and cannot obtain, so you fight and quarrel. You do not have, because you do not ask.

1 John 3:22
and whatever we ask we receive from him, because we keep his commandments and do
what pleases **HIM** .

Throughout Bible times and continuing today, every stream of the anointing for favor is activated by teshuvah!

It was that anointing of favor in the Old Covenant that caused Abram, later called Abraham, to prosper wherever he went, even as he obeyed Yahuah's voice and left his homeland to journey into the land of Canaan with at least 400 people who worked for him (Genesis 12).

Deuteronomy 29:5 – And I have led you forty years in the wilderness. Your clothes have not worn out on you, and your sandals have not worn out on your feet.

Acts 2:47 – Praising **YaH** and having favor with all the people. And the **YAHUAH** added to the church daily those who were being saved. When you begin to **PRAISE YAH** , you change the spiritual atmosphere wherever you are and whatever you're going through. **Activating YAHUAH'S ANOINTING OF FAVOR -** I heard **ABBA's** voice today, " stay faithful, press in. **TRUST ME** ." Many Pastors have said, " Where God calls/sends HE provides."Yes, day to day I trust for our manna. Day to day, I trust for our shelter. Today, I said, "Thank you **ABBA** , that I own nothing in this world. Because it would be much harder to let go for what is coming." I need to express a few things I do believe **ABBA** supplies and provides! I do know that **HE** gives good gifts and wants us to have things. I do not judge anyone. I have made mistakes so has my hubby. We confessed and dealt with it with our **Yahuah** . What is coming will test a believer to the very core. If you do not know how to trust **HIM** for manna and basic needs, now is the time to learn. If you do not fast enough or know how to fast, now is the time to do so. If you need material security, go camping more this year. Beloveds, it is coming. We need to be Brothers and Sisters right now. We need to live as the disciples lived. We need to walk as our **Mashiach, Yahshua** walked. We need to be on our face , praying and talking to our **Father** more!! I love you. I do not want any of you to be deceived. Or to take the mark because you are afraid you won't be able to get your medicine or food or water. Study, pray and help a Brother or Sister today. **LOVE YOUR NEIGHBOR** enough to share the Kingdom message and the message of Salvation! The world is changing. Do not be foolish!

This was taken from a study that I have revisited from Yom Teruah. It deepened my understanding of an **Image Bearer.** That if we are walking the narrow path, and our lamps are filled unto **Yahshua** we will reflect his works, **HIS Torah** and keep **His Commandments** .

Proverbs 6:23 *"for the mitzvah (commandment) is a lamp, Torah is light, and reproofs that discipline are the way to life.*

Proverbs 20:27 "The human spirit is a lamp of **YAHUAH** ; it searches one's inmost being."How can the "lamp" be both a commandment and the Torah as well as spiritual? It is because it is **YAHUAH'S** spirit within us that causes us to keep the commandments and Torah, that he lights the lamp within us.

Ezekiel 36:27 "I will put my spirit inside you and cause you to live by my laws, respect my rulings and obey them."

If the **"Lamp"** represents **YAHUAH'S Commandments** , and the **"Light"** is his Torah, then an empty Lamp indicates one that does not keep his commands, and if there is no light that indicates that there is no Torah. In other words, we are "lawless".

Matt. 7:21-23 Not everyone who says to me "Adonai, Adonai!" will enter the Kingdom of Heaven, only those who do what my **FATHER** in heaven wants. On that day, many will say to me, "Adonai, Adonai! Didn't we prophesy in your name? Didn't we expel demons in your name? Didn't we perform miracles in your name? Then I will tell them to their faces, "I never knew you! Get away from me, you workers of lawlessness!"

Oh warrior, now is the hour for **Yahuah** to train our hands for war. Psalm 144:1.

I am encouraging you Natsarim's to begin to pray, seek, and ask **ABBA** to tell you what instrument **HE** is calling you to carry. I remember being in prayer and asking **ABBA** what I could have as HIS servant, I said, Moseh had a staff, Yoseph received a coat, Sampson had his hair, and so on. I waited and waited. I continued to pray and ask for quite some time. It was one early morning in prayer when I heard the Yahuah say, "the tambourine/timbrel is your weapon of warfare." I was thrown off because honestly I never thought about the tambourine before. Funny thing was a few months prior **ABBA** actually had given me a tambourine!! Along with gaining wisdom from **YAHUAH** about the weapon **HE** has given me to use, I also must learn to wield it with spiritual discernment and authority. It is a weapon of deep intercession and powerful warfare. Which, I will, and I am only learning to do by asking now.

Romans 13:11 *And do this, knowing the time, that it is already the hour for us to wake up from sleep, for now our deliverance is nearer than when we did believe.*

AWAKE-AWARE-NO FEAR

COMMON UNION OF THE
TRIBE OF NATSARIM

SALT & LYTE GYPSY-ZADOK SCRIBE FOR YAH

Ancient Path of Wellness --This is very important in these last days because we will need our bodies to be operating at "peak performance" to help others and overcome so that **NO ONE** can steal our crow

Quest for Optimal Health Questionnaire Biblical Wellness Yahuah's Great Plan for Our Body

Do you have consistent energy throughout your day?
Do you fall asleep easily without assistance?
Do you easily digest your food? Does it feel natural and comfortable?

Do you feel a spike in your energy after eating a meal? Do you experience normal bowel movements one to three times per day?
Do you urinate every few hours?

Is your skin clear and glowing?

Does your hair have a sheen or glossiness to it?

Is your mind clear and alert?

Do you recover quickly from seasonal threats?

Are you a person who does not get ill often?

Is your body toned and flexible?

Do you maintain a comfortable weight?

Are your eyes shiny and clear?

Do you feel that your emotions are stable most of the time?

Do you experience joy, laughter, and happiness daily?

Do you have a sense of purpose in life?

Do you generally experience feelings of gratitude?

Do you attain a sense of inner peace most of the time?

When faced with a challenge are you able to handle it without feeling overwhelmed?

Do you view obstacles and setbacks as opportunities for growth?

Constitution of Freedom = TORAH

Pillars-Loosing & Binding- Earth & Heaven

What you bind on earth is bound in heaven. What you loose on earth is loosed in heaven. The enemy attempts to steal this principle from us through the spirit of unbelief.

Choose this day whom you will serve.

Windows in heaven are open. YaH is releasing keys of **WISDOM and of SURVIVAL.** How can we "alter" our tomorrow so it does not look like today? Our energy is a **KEY** --are you going to give it away to hasatan? Often we do not know we have given our power away to the enemy of our soul through the blinding of the mind. hasatan wants to harness the power in us that drives success, power, authority, and prosperity.

Yahuah , will teach us to number our days. **Yahuah** wakes us up so we can regain our consciousness. We must understand that our time is spent like money. **Yahuah's** desire is that we would apply our hearts to wisdom. Learn to leverage the knowledge to begin to prophesy success into our tomorrow and our day to day activities, Wasting **TIME** is wasting **LIFE** .

The biggest **LIE** today is the lie of time management! You **CAN NOT** manage that which you **CAN NOT** control.

Sun goes up/ the sun goes down. Learn to manage your activities. Learn to place value on every day/hour/minute/second of your life. Once you place value on your time. Once you appreciate **YaH's** creation time clock with respect and honor. Your entire perception of time shifts. Tribe of Issachar-knew the times and seasons.

1 Chronicles 12:32. **Yahuah** has a divine time table. Oftentimes, when **YaH** tells us to do something, it is a time sensitive matter. **HE** knows the thoughts He thinks of us! Since, **Yahuah** knows the end of our life He works then from the end to the beginning. **YaH** backs up to lead us. Geography has no place

without time and time has no place without geography. Our blessings are time sensitive and they have a geographical location.

hasatan has a prescription for failure. He will

> *-place distractions in our lives*
> *-causes us to loose focus*
> *-frustrate us to the point of giving up*

We are to ask **Yahuah** for our needs and then ask when and where to be to receive them. It is the same as going to the grocery store on Wednesday at 11am to buy bread because it is half price. This is how Yahuah connects your blessing to time and location? This is how **YaH** gives us provision in our life.

hasatans plan, is always to cause distractions and frustrate us to hold us back from every possible blessing and provision **YaH** has for us. Even if it is only for a second which is just long enough for us to lose focus.

Many times we think **Yahuah** has not provided but, maybe we are not "in the right place", naturally or maybe spiritually. How is your passion for **YaH** and for **HIS** things? Never be satisfied in your journey with **Yahuah Elohim!** Declare today that you will no longer walk in the flesh!

You will NO longer tolerate Jezebel!!

The spirit of Jezebel will whisper in your ear, lies of discouragement and lies, it will manipulate your thoughts and actions. Which is **WHY** you must never compromise anything! The one time you compromise you have lost the battle. It is much harder to stand your ground in the future!

Now is the time for you to begin to conduct yourself and your affairs based on a divine timetable. Understanding life is given to us day by day.

Make these your Daily Declarations--and commit to declaring them daily!

Begin your day with ABBA; no matter what is going on whether in persecution or temptations or fleeing. Always begin before the sunrises with HIM and inquire HIS thoughts and actions for that day! This is a vital KEY for surviving the coming times!

Seek the wisdom of **YaH** and seek it before any major decisions

WISDOM IS GOING TO BUILD YOUR HOUSE!

Ask for wisdom daily! Wisdom for discernment! **Joshua 1:8**

Holy Habits---Stewardship

Expectation/ aka Job Description/ Your Position in the End Days

Eph'siym-Ephesians 1:17-19

that the **Elohim** of our **Master יהושע Messiah, the Father of esteem** , would give you a spirit of wisdom and revelation in the knowledge of **Him** ,

the eyes of your understanding being enlightened, so that you know what is the expectation of **His** calling, and what are the riches of the esteem of **His** inheritance in the set-apart ones, and what is the exceeding greatness of **His** power toward us who believe, according to the working of **His** mighty strength.

Prayer:

Lead me, guide me, and teach me Ruach HaKodesh. Let my pen be the
FIRE *of the Ruach HaKodesh of my soul. And lead in the great and mighty*
FEAR *of Yahuah!For my pen can not lie! Truth in **LOVE**, let me love all and*
*break **FREE** from divisions and illusions, traps set before me by the enemy*
*of my soul. Let me see today **ABBA,** my children blessed and **FREE** from*
the patterns and traps of this world. Cover each of them in the protecting
*blood of your Beloved Begotten **SON**, Yahusha HaMashiach! Thank you*
***ABBA**! My **LOVE** grows deeper for **YOU** day after day, for You are my*
Shalom, my Love, my discipline, and all Truth! For from You are all things,
see Your daughter and forgive me. If there is any sin in my life I repent.
Known and unknown. I desire for my heart to be clean before You! Create in
me a clean heart O God and renew a right spirit within today! Teach me to
lead with confidence and brush off the wicked.Keep us all from evil
*persuasions and perversions! I sing praises to you **MY KING!** Glory Glory*
*Glory to **YOU** on **HIGH!** HalleluYaH! Grant me this day wisdom and*
discernment and not let me walk through the door of temptation! I choose this
*day to serve **YOU!** Teach me to walk in integrity and honor. I desire to*
*please You **ABBA** with my life this day! I love Your **LAW** and Your **WAY!***
*Keep me on the narrow path that leads to **LIFE**.*

In Yahusha's Name-Amein

Our Warfare

Eph 6:10-12 11 Put on the full armor of **Yahuah** so that you can take your stand against the devil's schemes. For our struggle is not against flesh and blood, but against the rulers, against the authorities, against the powers of this dark world and against the spiritual forces of evil in the heavenly realms.

Engaging in warfare (Lk 14.31) Our weapons (train and know how to use them) 2 Cor 10.3- WORD of God, High praises of God, -Sing-Dance-Instruments-Intercession-Prayer-Tongues, WORD of our testimony Rev 12.11 , Sword of the Spirit- Speak, Pray, Confess the WORD, Name of Yahusha Prov 18.10, Blood of Yahusha, Power of Praise expressing our warship through creativity.

Our duty is:

To take and put on the **whole armour of YaH** and then, standing our ground, to withstand or resist our enemies.

We must withstand (vs.13) We must not yield to the devil's allurements and assaults, but oppose them. hasatan is said to stand up against us, 1 Chron 21:1. If he stand up against us, we must stand against him; set up, and keep up, an interest in opposition to the devil. hasatan is the wicked one, and his kingdom is the kingdom of sin: to stand against hasatan is to strive against sin. That you may be able to withstand in the evil day, in the day of temptation, or of any sore affliction.

We must stand our ground, and, having done all, stay standing. We must resolve, by Yahuah's grace, not to yield to hasatan. Resist him, and he will flee. If we are insecure or not fully trusting in our cause, our Leader, or our armour, we give the devil an advantage.

Our present business is to withstand the assaults of the devil, and to endure. Then, having done all that is part of being good soldiers of Yahusha HaMashiach, our warfare will be accomplished, and we shall be finally victorious.We must take our stand in full armor!!!

The Natsarim must be in complete armor: a divine armor: the Armour of YaH, armor of light, (Rom 13:12); Armour of righteousness (2 Cor 6:7). The armor is both offensive and defensive. The military girdle or belt, the breast-plate, the greaves (soldier's shoes, including shinguards), the shield, the helmet, and the sword. Notice that there is none for the back. If we turn our back upon the enemy, we lie exposed. (from Matthew Henry's Commentary on the Whole Bible)

MANNA & DEW

The Ruach HaKodesh is equal to dew in Deuteronomy 33:28-29. We have the authority to dethrone the enemy's plans.

High places in the WORD of YaH, represent sin, iniquity, idolatry and the dew as in Deut. 33:28-29 washes us clean and gives us **AUTHORITY** to tread the high places and defeat old enemies! This is why we must be continuously submitted unto **Yahuah** in every area because this allows **YaH** to replace old deceptions with new thought patterns. We walk in overcoming power.

Genesis 27:28,39

The "dew" must come down first before the manna or the manna will have nothing to stick to and fall to the ground and disappear.

Dew= Ruach Hakodesh and Manna= the WORD

Hebrews 10: 23-25

Let us hold fast the confession of our expectation without yielding, for He who promised is trustworthy.And let us be concerned for one another in order to stir up love and good works, not forsaking the assembling of ourselves together, as is the habit of some, but encouraging, and so much more as you see the Day coming near.

In these last days, the enemy of our soul is going to throw everything at us to keep us from gathering together. He knows that together we are more powerful. We must make an effort in every way to come together with one voice and pray fervently for a supernatural boldness. When we do this a fresh anointing of the Ruach HaKodesh will fill us with that boldness and grace as it was in Acts 4. We are facing times of great persecution and tribulation and we must remember what the apostles themselves faced and look to their example for us. For it is by the power of the Ruach HaKodesh, that will give us great grace and a spirit of unity and love will be present, so that we can face whatever we must in these last days!

Acts 4:27-33

For truly in this city there were gathered together against Your set-apart Servant יהושע, whom You anointed, both Herodes and Pontius Pilate, with the gentiles and the people of Yisra'ĕl to do whatever Your hand and Your purpose decided before to be done."And now, יהוה, look on their threats, and give to Your servants all boldness to speak Your word, by stretching out Your hand for healing, and signs, and wonders to take place through the Name of Your set-apart Servant יהושע."And when they had prayed, the place where they came together was shaken. And they were all filled with the Set-apart Spirit, and they spoke the word of Elohim with boldness. And the group of those who believed were of one heart and one being. And no one claimed that any of his possessions was his own, but they had all in common. And with great power the emissaries gave witness to the resurrection of the Master יהושע, and great favour was upon them all.

Day By Day

It is time, the hour is drawing ever so close. Let me warn those of you who are still connected via social tracking. I urge you now, delete all of your social profiles. Disconnect from the internet as much as possible!! For some of you, I know you can **NOT** due to your calling, jobs, or your absolute final mission for **Yahuah** . The majority of you **CAN** and **SHOULD DISCONNECT RIGHT NOW!!!** I believe this is a firm warning from the Ruach HaKodesh today. Understand that you will not be able to delete your entire digital footprint but at least your social and then pray for protection, pray the blood of **Yahusha** over you and your family for **YaH** to keep your digital footprint hidden from the evil ones! Trust **THE MOST HIGH, HE** promises to supply what we need in every area of our lives **DAY BY DAY** ! Humbly, come before **HIM** and ask and then wait. Waiting is the hardest part. Pray for patience and do not allow hasatan or his minions to deceive you by telling you lies. Expect and be on your guard always!

And He who was sitting on the throne said, "See, I make all *matters* new." And He said to me, "Write, for these words are true and trustworthy."

And He said to me, "It is done! I am the ' **Aleph' and the 'Taw** ', the Beginning and the End. To the one who thirsts I shall give of the fountain of the water of life without payment.

"The one who overcomes shall inherit all this, and I shall be his Elohim and he shall be My son. Revelation 21: 5-7

The Natsarim Vow in the Last Days--My Story

For the past 6 months, **ABBA** has had me living the Natsarim Vow. I did not know of the Natsarim or Nazarite Vow, although I have read Numbers 6 many times before it just never caught my attention. I have not perfectly participated but, my longing desire to be holy and live righteously has fueled my interest in living this way. Having not cut my hair and it growing into dreadlocks, which I did to mark my 40th birthday three years ago. Next, **ABBA** led me to cover my head as an act of respect and submission unto **HIM** out of love. Next, I stopped wearing jeans, pants, and began to dress modestly. This included wearing linen more and long skirts and dresses. I did drink wine on Pesach and a few Shabbats but have not wanted any in a while. I praise YaH for this because at one point in my life I drank a bottle of wine a night easily!! (before my conversion) The Ruach has whispered to me repeatedly about diet, to stop eating food sacrificed to idols, to eat veggies and fruits. To eat like the disciples. I have been completely convicted to fast as I mentioned earlier. I am rededicating myself to YaH daily. I know a lot of what I mentioned above is not in the Natsarim Vows. I believe **ABBA** , speaks to each of us differently because we are all being sanctified day after day and we are not in the same place. Bottom line is that the Natsarim Vow is a personal decision and requires only four things to do as stated in Numbers 6.

What is the *" Nazarite Vow"?*

It is a period of time for one to dedicate oneself to **YAHUAH** . It is available to all!! It is a vow of aspiration of desire and is strictly voluntary. The goal is to be totally set apart and draw close to **YaH** through strict obedience. **YAHUAH** is to be our pleasure, we are to love **YAHUAH** , go to **HIS** altar. To be fully committed to walk in the **" WAY".** We are **NOT** our own. We were bought with a high price! Taking this vow is a privilege as we consecrate ourselves to **YaH** . To **LIVE** to **HIM** and pursue **HIM** with a pure heart.

Four Fold Consecration

- overcome worldly pleasures
- overcome rebellion
- overcome death
- overcome natural affection
- **Food** - One is to abstain from all grapes, wine, alcohol.
- **Appearance** - One is **NOT** to cut their hair.
- **Attitude** - One is to have a desire to be holy.
- **Associations** - One is **NOT** to come near to a dead body.

In these days of tribulation we must choose to be and remain **Set Apart/ Qodesh** . As a *Son or Daughter of Zadok* , **YOU** have been chosen to be a Natsarim in these last days! This is a very serious calling. To whom much is given, much is required! We must stand out in hopes that the lost, broken, and hurting will bear witness and be drawn to us so we can share the testimony of **YAHUSHA** . Living the Natsarim Vow will draw us ever closer to **ABBA** and into **HIS** secret place. This is key for survival. The enemy is working overtime to irritate and destroy us by any and all means. We are to be awake and watching, keeping our focus at all times on **YAHUSHA** . Being led by the Ruach HaKodesh in all spirit and truth. Living this requires great discipline and self control. For we are to store treasures in heaven and not on this earth.

I am rededicating myself now. I crave righteousness and holiness. My prayer is for **YaH** to create in me a clean heart and renew a right spirit. To be obedient and eat only fruits and vegetables. The enemy has been successful in deceiving Believers by in the way we eat, what we eat, and when we eat by telling us that food does not matter and we do not have to be obedient to Torah. This is the lie that has been sown into western Christianity for the last 200 years or more. Living a life of obedience to Torah, Fear of Yahuah, and discipline to not act on temptations placed before us shows **ABBA** our heart.

Raw Life

The authentic practice of our faith is the means of furthering the Kingdom of Yahuah on earth. Living a raw life as a Son or Daughter of Zadok and a Natsarim requires us to fulfill the Natsarim Vow (if you feel led too). Daily we face an opportunity to demonstrate our **LOVE** , **OBEDIENCE** , and **RESPECT** for YaH and **HIS** commands. We must exude passion for the Covenant of Yahuah Elohim, so purpose in your heart today **NOT** to defile yourself anymore. If we are obedient to YaH's Covenant, **HE** will move in our situations. The benefits of our Covenant relationship far out way anything that the world could give us as we will receive greater intimacy with **ABBA** and will be blessed with many spiritual blessings. In this last hour many of us know that we have gone through a purification process being purified by **HIS   WORD** .

Choosing obedience results in an inner peace resulting from the fulfillment of the will of Yahuah which radiates inward and outward. It is better to suffer death than transgress the **LAW** of Elohim. We must be engulfed in the knowledge of Torah so much that it consumes our whole being so that we can **NOT** be persuaded. This is important for Natsarim in these last days. Our roots must run deep in the **WORD** , and by exuding our great **LOVE** for YaH and the **FEAR** of YaH this will keep us from rebellion and disobedience in the hour of testing that is to come.

" Blessed is **HE** who meditates on wisdom and reasons with intelligence, who studies her ways in his heart and ponders her secrets." **Ecclesiasticus 14: 20,21**

At this point in this manual of instruction for the last days and tribulations to come, I have found myself in a struggle both spiritually and physically. The enemy has tempted me to abandon the things that YaH has told me to do; such as how I dress, what I eat, and how I live my daily. It started as a logical temptation, that I had to wear jeans to "work" in because I could not wear a long dress as it would get in the way and people may question my "why". Next, it was the busyness of life itself that presented temptations as "acceptable" for a time. A few days ago, I searched my heart and asked myself, " Why would I disregard what my Father has asked me to do, just to present myself acceptable to the world?" I am sharing this because these very temptations will creep in at this hour to distract us from the "greater things". We must be **ALERT** to everything!!! This must be the urgency in our spirit. Just as the **WORD** warns us;

Be alert and of sober mind. Your enemy the devil prowls around like a roaring lion looking for someone to devour. 1 Peter 5:8

In my weakness, I repented and thanked YaH for teaching me how easy it was to stumble when my eyes are **NOT** fixed on Yahusha. We, the Ekklesia of Natsarim, the Sons and Daughters of Zadok are living in treacherous times. For our enemy knows his time is short and is throwing every stone and shooting every arrow at us that he can to cause to stumble. Never before in time has there been such a fervency to be steady and alert!!

So put away all malice and all deceit and hypocrisy and envy and all slander. Like newborn infants, long for the pure spiritual milk, that by it you may grow up into salvation— if indeed you have tasted that Yahuah is good. As you come to him, a living stone rejected by men but in the sight of Adonai chosen and precious, you yourselves like living stones are being built up as a spiritual house, to be a holy priesthood, to offer spiritual sacrifices acceptable to Adonai through Yahusha HaMashiach. For it stands in Scripture:

"Behold, I am laying in Zion a stone, a cornerstone chosen and precious,and whoever believes in him will not be put to shame." So the honor is for you who believe, but for those who do not believe, "The stone that the builders rejected has become the

cornerstone," and "A stone of stumbling, and a rock of offense." They stumble because they **disobey the word** , as they were destined to do. But you are a chosen race, a royal priesthood, a holy nation, a people for his own possession, that you may proclaim the excellencies of him who called you out of darkness into his marvelous light. Once you were not a people , but now you are YaH's people; once you had not received mercy, but now you have received mercy.

Beloved, I urge you as sojourners and exiles **to abstain from the passions of the flesh,** which wage war against your soul. Keep your conduct among the Gentiles honorable, so that when they speak against you as evildoers, they may see your good deeds and glorify Yahuah Elohim on the day of visitation. **1 Peter 2: 1-12**

Let us learn as Daniel learned to live Godly lives in a pagan society. This book is for that very purpose. We know that the struggle is very real but our passion and desire for YaH must be greater than all things in this world!!

Grievances of Passionate Eating becoming the OVERCOMER!

HE who overcomes, I shall make him a supporting post in the Dwelling Place of My **ELOHIM** , and he shall by no means go out. And I shall write on him the Name of My **ELOHIM** and the name of the city of My **ELOHIM** , the renewed Yerushalayim, which comes down out of heaven from My **ELOHIM** , and My renewed Name. Revelation 3:12

(I am including the following after much prayer and seeking guidance from the Ruach HaKodesh, that it will be of useful wisdom for the coming time of tribulation. As I have stated previously, that fasting is a weapon against hasatan and demons and his principalities. I have edited and modified the paragraph below that was taken from the book- The Essene Science of Fasting to give **ALL GLORY, ALL PRAISES, AND ALL HONOR TO YAHUAH!!)**

YAHUSHA SPEAKING:

And He said to them, "Are you also without understanding? Do you not perceive that whatever enters a man from outside is unable to defile him, because it does not enter his heart but his stomach, and is eliminated, thus purging all the foods?" And **HE** said, "What comes out of a man, that defiles a man. For from within, out of the heart of men, proceed evil reasonings, adulteries, whorings, murders, thefts, greedy desires, wickedness, deceit, indecency, an evil eye, blasphemy, pride, foolishness. All these wicked *matters* come from within and defile a man." **Mark 7: 18-23**

Renew yourselves and fast. For I tell you truly, that hasatan and his plagues may only be cast out by fasting and by prayer. Go by yourself and fast alone, and show your fasting to no man. **YAHUAH** our **ELOHIM** shall see it and great shall be your reward. And fast till all evils depart from you. For I tell you truly, except you fast,(as **YAHUSHA** fasted and was tested by hasatan himself)

Then יהושע was led up by the Spirit into the wilderness to be tried by the devil. **Matthew 4:1**

Fast and pray fervently, seeking the power of the **LIVING ELOHIM** for your healing. While you fast, pray and draw close to the **Father** ; for he that seeks shall find. So let us always eat from the table of **ADONAI** : the fruits of the trees, the grain and grass of the field, the milk of beasts, and the honey of bees. For everything beyond these and that is mixed by man; these are of hasatan doings, and lead by the way of sins and of dis-eases unto death. But the foods which you eat from the abundant table of **YAHUAH** give strength and youth to your body, and you can never see dis-ease. For the table of **YAHUAH** fed Methuselah of old, and I tell you truly, if you live even as he lived, then will **YAHUAH** the living **ELOHIM** give you also long life upon the earth as was his.

For I tell you truly, the **ELOHIM** of the **LIVING** is richer than all the riches of the earth, and his abundant table is richer than the richest table of feasting of all the rich upon the earth. Eat, therefore, all your life at the table of **YAHUAH** , and you will never see want.

But **HE** answering, said, "It has been written, 'Man shall not live by bread alone, but by every word that comes from the mouth of יהוה.' Matthew 4:4

Take heed, therefore, and defile not your body which is the **TEMPLE OF THE RUACH HAKODESH** with all kinds of abominations. Be content with two or three sorts of food, which you will find always upon the table of **YAH** . And desire not to devour all things which you see around you. For I tell you truly, if you mix together all sorts of food in your body, then the peace of your body will cease, and **ENDLESS WAR WILL RAGE IN YOU!** (I found this fascinating because it is so true and in my life it has been the very cause of my backsliding with food, pharmaceuticals, and drink.)

Or do you not know that your body is the Dwelling Place of the Set-apart Spirit who is in you, which you have from Elohim, and you are not your own? 1 Corinthians 6:19

And when you eat, never eat unto fullness. Flee the temptations of hasatan, and listen to the voice of the Ruach HaKodesh within. For hasatan and his power is to tempt you always, to eat more and more. But live by the spirit, and resist the desires of the body/flesh. And your fasting is always pleasing in the eyes of **YAHUAH** . So give heed to how much you have eaten, only eat until you are full.

Let the weight of your daily food be not less than a mina, but mark that it goes not beyond two. Then, will the angels of **YAHUAH** whom are there ministering to us serve you always, and you will never fall into the bondage of hasatan and of his dis-eases . For I tell you truly, he who eats at the demands of the flesh will soon find themselves in bondage. Eat only when the sun is highest in the heavens, and again when it is set. And you will never see dis-ease brought on by temptation of food or drink, for such finds favor in the eyes of **YAHUAH.**

From the coming of the month of Iyyar, eat barley; from the month of Sivan, eat wheat, the most perfect among all seed-bearing herbs. And let your daily bread be made of wheat, that YaH may take care of your body. From Tammuz, eat the sour grape. In the month of Elul, gather the grapes that the juice may serve you as drink. In the month of Cheshvan, gather the sweet grape, sweetened and dried by the sunshine , that it may increase your bodies. You should eat figs rich in juice in the months of Av and Shebat. Eat them with the meat of almonds in all the months when the trees bear no fruits. And the herbs which come after rain, these eat in the month of Tevet, that your blood may be cleansed. And in the same month begin to eat also the milk of your animals, because for this did **YAHUAH** give the herbs of the fields to all the animals which render milk, that they might with their milk feed man. I tell you, happy are they that eat only at the table of YAHUAH, and eschew all the abominations of hasatan. Eat not unclean foods as in the **TORAH** . For your YaH knows well what is needful for you and your body, and where and when. And **HE** gives to all peoples of all kingdoms for food that is best for each. Eat not as the heathen do, who stuff themselves in haste.

And put a knife to your throat If you are a man given to appetite. Do not desire his delicacies, For that food is deceptive. Do not labour to be rich. Cease from your own understanding! Do you set your eyes on that which is not? For riches certainly make themselves wings; They fly away like an eagle to the heavens. Do not eat the bread of *one having* an evil eye, Nor desire his delicacies; For as he reckons in his life, so is he. "Eat and drink!" he says to you, But his heart is not with you. **Proverbs 23: 2-7**

Therefore, since Messiah suffered in the flesh, arm yourselves also with the same mind, because he who has suffered in the flesh has ceased from sin, so that he no longer lives the rest of his time in the flesh for the lusts of men, but according to the desire of Elohim. For we *have spent* enough of our past lifetime in doing the desire of the gentiles, having walked in indecencies, lusts, drunkenness, orgies, wild parties, and abominable idolatries, in which they are surprised that you do not run with them in the same flood of loose behaviour, blaspheming, who shall give an account to Him who is ready to judge the living and the dead. For this reason the Good News was also brought to those who are dead, so that, whereas they are judged according to men in the flesh, they might live according to Elohim in the spirit. But the end of all has drawn near. Therefore be sober-minded, and be attentive in the prayers. And above all have fervent love for one another, because love covers a great number of sins. **1 Peter 4: 1-8**

For the table of YAHUAH is as an altar, and he who eats at the table of YaH, is in a temple. For I tell you truly, the body is turned into a temple, and there inwards into an altar, for those who obey the commandments of YaH.

And Elohim, who raised up the Master, shall also raise us up through His power. Do you not know that your bodies are members of Messiah? Shall I then take the members of Messiah and make them members of a whore? Let it not be! Or do you not know that he who is joined to a whore is one body? For He says, "The two shall become one flesh." And he who is joined to the Master is one spirit. Flee whoring. Every sin that a man does is outside the body, but he who commits whoring sins against his own body. Or do you not know that your body is the Dwelling Place of the Set-apart Spirit who is in you, which you have from Elohim, and you are not your own? For you were bought with a price, therefore esteem Elohim in your body and in your spirit, which are of Elohim.
1 Corinthians 6: 14-20

THE INTERCESSORS BURDEN

WARfare is our UPGRADE....

CommonUnion/Communion is our weapon and one we must learn to exercise as if our lives depended on it!! Communion is a supernatural blood transfusion. The benefits through faith (emunah) in **Yahusha our MaShiach** .

- the ability to conceive physically and spiritually.
- it releases the elixir of life to become more like YaH.
- It emits a portion of divine energy.
- brings the fullness of Yahuah manifest in our lives.

- brings healing both spiritually and physically.
- causes one bear much fruit.
- to abide in **HIM** and **HE** in **YOU!**
- Increasingly gain the mind of **YaH.**

יהושע therefore said to them, "Truly, truly, I say to you, unless you eat the flesh of the Son of Adam and drink His blood, you possess no life in yourselves.

He who eats My flesh and drinks My blood possesses everlasting life, and I shall raise him up in the last day. **John 6:53-54**

We must take communion more than ever, it is just as important as prayer and Torah, for it is our lifeline. It is through these three things that will enable us to survive all that is coming soon.

The cup of blessing which we bless, is it not a sharing in the blood of Messiah? The bread that we break, is it not a sharing in the body of Messiah?

Because there is one bread, we, who are many, are one body, for we all partake of the one bread. **1 Corinthians 10: 16-17**

In the days to come it will be those who exude faith (emunah), meekness, love (ahavah), and a holy boldness to go forth as seasoned Natsarim to bring in the last harvest. The Sons and Daughters of Zadok stand under the blood stained banner of **Yahusha** willing to be partakers of **HIS** conflicts and wage a determined **WAR** against the powers of darkness. hasatan has a dark army waiting to be activated. These soldiers of darkness are everyone and no one. Some are people possessed by demons and as of right now can still receive **Yahusha** and be saved.The enemy has cleverly deceived them with promises of great power and prestige. In order to receive their "prize" they must tirelessly recruit for the coming **WAR** . If they keep choosing not too then they will be absolved into darkness and forever a servant of hasatan.

The time of trouble has been increasing more and more over the last 100 years. The final manuscript of creation's redemption is at hand. Men's hearts are failing them for **FEAR** of the things that are rapidly approaching. We know and expect hasatan to throw at us everything he can. There will be a false return of Yahusha. **BEWARE!!** Just as the **WORD** says that even some of the elect will be deceived!! With technology at his fingertips he will manipulate everything we are waiting for. hasatan is always seeking out the weak minded to manipulate first, offering them a "way out" and spreading lies to keep them behind the veil. In my opinion, one of the ways he will try to deceive many is through fear of what is coming. Through manipulation of the mind and thoughts he will twist reality; seeking to compartmentalize the end of days events to signaling them out one by one. This paired with the influx of false teachers and prophets utilizing social media as his megaphone to the masses for complete control mind, body and soul in his web of well planned deception offering a safety net of lies leading the sheep to the slaughter one by one. he will form his one world government of "safety and salvation.". Instead,what I think is the possibility of all end days events occurring simultaneously at one time, making us much further along and much closer to the return of our Messiah!

See how good and how pleasant it is for brothers to dwell together in unity –
Like the precious oil on the head, Running down on the beard, The beard of Aharon, Running down on the collar of his robes –Like the dew of Ḥermon, That comes down on the mountains of Tsiyon. For there יהוה commanded the blessing, Life forever! Psalm 133

Remember all this is about preparation for the persecution. To stay armored up and teach others as well, knowing that the battle belongs to Yahuah. The **TORAH** is our spiritual weapon against the spirit of deception in these end days. For those that have not studied as a good Berean will not have access to this weapon. It is imperative we read, study, remember, and teach others now!! Yahuah has given us HIS precious stones the five books of **TORAH.**

Now all these things happened unto them as types, and they are written for our admonition, upon whom the **ends of the ages will come.** 1 Corinthians 10:11

Paul seems to be convinced that they were penned for the benefit of the last generation! You see beloved, the reason why Paul could come to his conclusion was because he understood the prophetic nature of the **TORAH** . He knew that the prophecies of the past were prophetic blueprints for the future. What's most significant though is the fact that he believed their greatest significance was for the last generation, which I believe we are that generation! During the writing of this manual one event has continued to be a constant over and over again bearing witness to those in the end days. That is the event of Yahuah taking Israel out of Egypt, the Exodus. We know that there will come a **Second Exodus.** (If you have not studied the **Second Exodus** I would encourage you to seek YaH and study the events of the first Exodus and the truth will be made clear.) Take a look at the specific stories Paul said were so significant to the last generation. **I Corinthians 10:1-2** is a clear reference to the splitting of the Red Sea. **I Corinthians 10: 3-4** is a reference to Yahuah's provision of bread and water to Israel once they had left Egypt. **I Corinthians 10: 5-10** is a reference to events that occurred during their wilderness journeys as recorded in the book of Numbers. Paul stated that these events are the ones that were written for the benefit of the last generation. So what's the connection between these events and the last generation?

The exodus from Egypt and the journey to the **Promised Land** were simply prophetic shadows of a **Greater, Second Exodus** and journey which is to occur in the last days. As stated earlier in the book the plagues of the Exodus will once again play out in the end days. Which points to why **TORAH** is so intertwined with Revelation.

We will make a final exodus out of the **"world systems"** and journey through the **"wilderness"** as we are told, **"come out of her my people!"**

We all will encounter the wilderness journey. It is Yahuah's way of sorting out the true **Natsarim** from those who are "luke warm". We have all had to go through the refiner's fire being sanctified and cleansed to mature and have a passionate desire for holiness and righteousness. Upon coming out of the wilderness which can also illude to (tribulation) we will then be brought into the **Promised Land as the Bride.**

"Guard to do every command which I command you today, that you might live, and shall increase, and go in, and shall possess the land of which יהוה swore to your fathers. "And you shall remember that יהוה your Elohim led you all the way these forty years in the wilderness, to humble you, prove you, to know what is in your heart, whether you guard His commands or not. "And He humbled you, and let you suffer hunger, and fed you with manna which you did not know nor did your fathers know, to make you know that man does not live by bread alone, but by every *Word* that comes from the mouth of יהוה "Your garments did not wear out on you, nor did your foot swell these forty years. "Thus you shall know in your heart that as a man disciplines his son, so יהוה your Elohim disciplines you, therefore you shall guard the commands of יהוה your Elohim, to walk in His ways and to fear Him. "For יהוה your Elohim is bringing you into a good land, a land of streams of water, of fountains and springs, that flow out of valleys and hills, a land of wheat and barley, of vines and fig trees and pomegranates, a land of olive oil and honey, a land in which you eat bread without scarcity, in which you do not lack at all, a land whose stones are iron and out of whose hills you dig copper. "And you shall eat and be satisfied, and shall bless יהוה your Elohim for the good land which He has given you. "Be on guard, lest you forget יהוה your Elohim by not guarding His commands, and His right-rulings, and His laws which I command you today, lest you eat and shall be satisfied, and build lovely houses and shall dwell in them, and your herds and your flocks increase, and your silver and your gold are increased, and all that you have is increased, that your heart then becomes lifted up, and you forget יהוה your Elohim who brought you out of the land of Mitsrayim, from the house of bondage, who led you through that great and awesome wilderness – fiery serpents and scorpions and thirst – where there was no water, who brought water for you out of the flinty rock, who fed you in the wilderness with manna, which your fathers did not know, in order to humble you and to try you, to do you good in the end, Deuteronomy 8: 1-16

Moses was speaking to those who made it through the trials of the wilderness. Our wilderness experiences have been training and equipping us for the coming tribulation. Some of us have had to face giants and situations that were mightier than us. We will have to war with things none have had to face since the time of the first exodus.

The training and equipping that we now need to take part in is that of warring with the unseen world in intense battles and stand confidently in our authority as conquerors!! This will help us conquer tribulation and usher in the Millennial Reign! That's why the **TORAH** gave us a picture of Israel going up against super-sized (*Numbers 13:33 & Deuteronomy 3:1-11*) giants and cities fortified to the heavens as she went to possess the land. It was all to teach us about the final battles which will be waged by us mere humans against hasatan and his demonic spirits, all of whom are mightier than we.

KEY _ to victory is that our weapons are made mighty through Yahusha to the pulling down of hasatan's kingdom.

To prepare you need to read the **TORAH** and ask the Ruach HaKodesh to guide you line by line for the perpetual revelation of understanding for tribulation. I could write it all out here for you line by line but, that would not benefit you at all. You must learn the **TORAH** as I must and bind it to your arm. Write it upon your heart as many of us already have. This will be ongoing training until the very end, Natsarim!

Now is the time the ingathering of the nations and the dispersed of Israel into a remnant of Judah!!

And it shall be that all who are left from all the gentiles which came up against Yerushalayim, shall go up from year to year to bow themselves to the Sovereign, יהוה of hosts, and to observe the **Festival of Booths** . And it shall be, that if anyone of the clans of the earth does not come up to Yerushalayim to bow himself to the Sovereign, יהוה of hosts, on them there is to be no rain. And if the clan of Mitsrayim does not come up and enter in, then there is no *rain* . On them is the plague with which יהוה plagues the gentiles who do not come up to observe the **Festival of Booths** . This is the punishment of Mitsrayim and the punishment of all the gentiles that do not come up to observe the **Festival of Booths** . Zechariah 14: 16-19

Blessed are those doing His commands, so that the authority shall be theirs unto the tree of life, and to enter through the gates into the city. Revelation 22:14

Paul's example is for us today; Natsarim breaking bread together. Listening to the reading of Scripture, having the **FIRE** of the Ruach HaKodesh blaze within each of our spirits. Emunah/Faith that moves mountains and boldness that stands tall in the face of adversity and persecution. In Acts 20:7-12 Paul is preaching and he preached late into the night and a man became overcome with sleep and fell three floors to the ground below. Paul ran down and picked him up and said, "don't worry there is still life in him." Then he went back upstairs with the man and Paul broke bread and ate and kept talking till daybreak.

These are the keys we must use in these end days from the above **WORD.**

KEY - have faith, bold faith, expectant faith

KEY- Communion, Common Union of Natsarim, itself is a miracle weapon.

These qualities are prominent in Acts 19: 11, and 12. We are to believe and pray for Yahuah to anoint our hands, so that aprons and handkerchiefs or anything we touch will carry the healing anointing to give to the sick so they are cured and so evil spirits come out of them!

KEY - Knowing **YOUR AUTHORITY**

We must pray against the spirit of unbelief. For without faith it is impossible to please YaH. How can we do anything if we do not really have faith? The hour is soon upon us where the called out ones are to form small house churches as in the days of the early Apostles. We must pray for the anointing to fall on our hands, mouth, and feet as **FIRE** from the Ruach!! It is the Ruach who will give and guide us in all wisdom and truth, giving us discernment of all things, matters, peoples, and places. Pray fervently for the **FIRE** of the Ruach to fall! **WALK confidently IN YOUR AUTHORITY and POWER given us by YAHUSHA HAMASCHIACH.** We are to Praise and Worship loudly and everywhere.

We know we must choose Yahuah over man! Obedience to Yahuah comes before obedience to man. Acts 5:30 and the Ruach HaKodesh is given to those who obey Yahuah!! Acts 5:32

KEY- Be joyful and glad of sufferings and humiliation for the sake of the name of Yahusha.

KEY- We must recognize the gifts and abilities in others as to assign those who are of good reputation, filled with the Spirit, and with wisdom.

KEY - Those who are intercessors they must devote themselves to prayer and service of the WORD.

KEY - Choose the side of humility. Be humble in all things and in all ways.

KEY - Choose the side of gentleness. Seek harmony and peace.

Another example for us is Philip in Samaria- Acts 8: 4-8. He worked miracles and unclean spirits came shrieking out of many who were possessed and several paralytics and cripples were cured from Philips preaching and praying. Also, in the end days let us remember Stephan our Beloved Brother, and his example. We know persecution is coming to America. It has already started in other parts of the world and is quickly increasing day by day. We must resist the temptations of our body (flesh), and mind during the time our lives are being persecuted!! No matter what kind of persecution it is. Remember Stephan and pray, cry out as he did in our final earthly moments, " Yahusha receive my spirit and do not hold this sin against them." If we do this we will leave another example for those who are witnesses in the hour of our departure.

Watch and pray so that you will not enter into temptation. For the spirit is willing, but the body is weak." **Mark 14:38**

Greater level of consecration is demanded NOT required.   Not Optional.

THE CALL is available to everyone- who will answer. Will you?

In the surrender, power is released, direction is given and peace is maintained. This is because one has given themselves over to Yahuah, for HIS purposes. In this moment the greatest level of freedom in this life is attained because we know that we NO longer belong to ourselves.

Simplicity of surrender---loose the spirit of rebellion and obey YaH!

What have you been holding on to?

What have you overlooked and Yeah is saying HE wants it?

Joel 2: 20- Anointing of the End Days= Prophecy the possible in the impossible.

Raise the DEAD, heal the sick, cast of demons, prophesy, faith that will throw mountains into the water **PRAISE YAHUAH!! PRAISE YAHUSHA HAMASHIACH!**

The blessing of being nameless and faceless, be who YaH made YOU! HE will give you a new name and a white stone.

The LAND is mine. It is mine to give to HIM. It is flowing with milk and honey. ABBA I pray for revelation on how to overcome the giants in the land. This is a generational blessing and mission. Show me my part in this Father. Follow the path the Ruach HaKodesh leads me on and press in to ABBA, HE will provide fresh manna day by day.

The world is weariness to the righteous but the next is theirs! The righteous depart from this habitation without FEAR, they have a store of works preserved in treasuries in heaven. We have entered into a "new time", one where the Natsarim must be absolute in all things, they must live the truth, speak the truth, and continue to seek the truth.

We know we are the Nation of Natsarim but do we know the fullness of our mission on a larger scale? What is our purpose in these end of days?

You can reference the WORD for this vision in Acts 2: 42-47 and Acts 4:32-35

- They are faithful to the brotherhood. (Common Unity)
- They will break bread together and pray together daily.

- They will share in the faith and walk the "narrow road" together.
- They will work many signs and miracles in the last days.
- Upon each is a great **FEAR of YAHUAH.**
- Brothers and Sisters (Natsarim) will sell all their possessions and goods and distribute the proceeds among all Natsarim according to what each needs.
- They will be filled with awe.
- They will be covered in the anointing and possess the FIRE of the Ruach HaKodesh in a new and powerful way to usher in the last harvest of souls.
- Each day they will all with one heart and one mind worship and praise Adonai!
- They will be abandoned to Yahusha and have their minds on HIM and things above.
- They will meet together in houses and safe haven to break bread and share food joyfully.
- They will be hated, persecuted, tortured, and murdered for their love and faithfulness to Yahusha HaMashiach.
- They keep the commandments, practice self-control and discipline their flesh.
- They will operate in a powerful boldness when sharing the gospel.
- They know their authority and use it. They will be demon slayers and prayer warriors.
- They love their enemies and love others.
- They know the WORD and stand strong in tribulation.

Our obedience evokes bitterness in this world. We know our very survival is in YaH's power. We consider all Believers to be on the path of redemption through repentance and immersion in the name of Yahusha and obedient to the Covenant of Yahusha through the Set Apart Spirit of Elohim. We who consider ourselves Natsarim of the last days take 1 Peter 1:16 seriously; " *Be holy as I am holy.* " Our desire is to walk in holiness, never compromising any aspect of Yahuah's WORD or our walk. We will also take every opportunity to teach people between clean and unclean. As Natsarim we are opposed to all system regimes. We offer ourselves daily as a living sacrifice to Yahuah and we have died to everything else. Death to personal agendas, death to pride of life, death to fleshly pursuits, death to our version of life. Once we were slaves and in bondage just like ancient Israel,in Babylon/Mitrayim. Now we have been saved, set free, tried and tested.

In these last days as Natsarim we must be committed to consecration and live as the example, be the light, exude love and walk in truth. It is a great privilege to consecrate oneself to Yahuah. To pursue HIM out of a pure heart and a need to live in the principle of a Natsarim.

The world has famously set *"responsibility traps"* .You may be asking yourself what is that all I know is that I work, pay my bills, love my family and YAH and that is what I was taught to do. Oh, friend you and I have been deceived as now everything that was once in the dark has now come into the light. Since the very beginning a plan was put into place and successfully executed while we were sleeping. Society set traps...they told you that you are a victim. We have been/were programmed since birth and trained in the " *way of the world* " being indoctrinated from Kindergarten to High School onto College and then adulthood then you have kids and the cycle begins again all the while growing in power while we were sleeping. You were told that you can not think for yourself, that you can not make decisions for yourself or even your loved ones, that you are unable to manage your own money, that you do not know your own body or what it needs, somethings are just too hard for you and the stress is just too much (insert need for drugs to keep you asleep). You have been told that you can't actually buy things with cash (i.e. cars, homes etc.) and that you had to go to college to get a "real job" and going into debt was for you just part of "building your credit score" unknowingly keeping you a slave with the guarantee to them that you would always be under their control. They conveniently made society "the helpless victim". This program has worked like a charm until NOW!! People have been waking up. They began with simple questions like, "why can't I just pay cash for that?" which then led to the questioning of everything. Like the famous movie, The Matrix, Neo woke up. The Most High, has been bringing what was hidden into the light over the past few years with this year being the **BIG REVEAL!   HE wants HIS people FREE** so HE began little by little revealing truths and destroying the falsehoods, lies, and deception crippling hasatans plans for the end of days. The Most High knew all along while watching him, manipulate the masses and bury the real truths. Masquerading as an Angel of Light. And Yahuah our Elohim, sat in silence allowing hasatan to spin his web of deceit, maybe even allowing him to think he had the upper hand for the moment. In reverent patience and wisdom the Almighty watched HIS clock, then the hour struck and with one little snap of HIS finger the deceit, darkness, and lies were shattered and eyes began to see and ears began to hear. My Beloveds, it is time for **WAR** . The countdown has begun. The shaking is increasing. The time is **NOW to RISE UP.** Have courage to fight the battles ahead knowing that our treasures are not here but, in the world to come as we are sojourners. ABBA is pouring forth a fire of boldness and faith to bring the last harvest in. Yes, judgement is coming and even here now. ABBA's judgement is to wake people up, yes even the evil people HE wants all people to have the opportunity to repent/teshuvah and come to Yahusha.

Psalm 83
O Elohim, do not remain silent! Do not be speechless, And do not be still, O Ĕl!
For look, Your enemies make an uproar, And those hating You have lifted up their heads.
They craftily plot against Your people, And conspire against Your treasured ones.
They have said, "Come, And let us wipe them out as a nation, And let the name of Yisra'ĕl be remembered no more."
For they have conspired together with one heart; They have made a covenant against You –

The tents of Eḏom and the Yishma'ĕlites, Mo'aḇ and the Hagarites,

Geḇal, and Ammon, and Amalĕq, Philistia with the inhabitants of Tsor,

Ashshur also has joined with them, they have helped the children of Lot. Selah.

Do to them as to Miḏyan, As to Sisera, As to Yaḇin at the wadi Qishon ,
Who perished at Ĕndor, Who became as dung for the ground.

Make their nobles like Orĕḇ and like Ze'ĕḇ, And all their princes like Zeḇaḥ and Tsalmunna,

Who has said, "Let us take possession of the pastures of Elohim For ourselves."

O my Elohim, make them as whirling dust, As stubble before the wind!

As a fire consumes a forest, And as a flame sets mountains on fire,

So pursue them with Your whirlwind, And frighten them with Your storm.

Fill their faces with shame, And let them seek Your Name, O יהוה.

Let them be ashamed and alarmed forever; And let them become abashed and perish,

And let them know that You, Whose Name is יהוה, You alone are the Most High over all the earth.

On July 22, 2019, I was given a **WORD of WARNING.** It was **JOB 24.** All I can say is stop reading this and open your Bible and read it. It is a stern warning, I believe for the judgement that is coming, if it has not already come while you are reading this.

Ancient Path Life- Return to what we formally knew. YAH instilled within each of us a desire to honor HIS creation, to live simply.

What is your plan B when all else fails?   To the unprepared?

Noahide Laws--5G---AI--- Transition-- Transhumanism- Fallen Angels

The time of sleeping is over either you wake up or you stay asleep and subject yourself to becoming a slave of what is coming. Everything we need to know is found in the **WORD of Yahuah** . There is nothing new under the sun, what has been is what will be and what will be is what has been (paraphrase).

How to Stay a Light in These End of Days:

The Seed is The Word of Yahuah. **Yahusha is the WORD** . (Luke 8:11)

In order for you to change and transform into who Yahuah has called you to be, you must plant the seed in your heart and in your mind.

Apply the WORD to your life daily. Meditate on it day and night. **(Joshua 1:8).**

This is what it means to have a renewal of your mind **(Romans 12:2).**

When you plant the seed (The **WORD** of Yahuah) in the dead areas of your life, you will begin to bring forth good fruits **(Galatians 5:22-23)**

This is the glorified state that YaH wants us all to reach in an effort to be and remain "lights" in this dark world. Make every effort to examine yourself daily. The Most High has stressed this to me over the past 12 months. When we take time to evaluate ourselves daily; we will ensure that we do **NOT** step off the **NARROW ROAD!** Think about the following questions and ask for ABBA's help. HE knows our struggles in this world. Where are your dead areas? What bad fruits do you need to uproot and begin planting godly seeds in?□

We need Yahusha/Yeshua/Jesus it is **HIS POWER** that helps us overcome! If we do **NOT** understand this very simple act of surrender and release our WILL to HIM then we will fail and fall miserably. **HIS POWER SET US FREE** and where we are weak ; **HE is STRONG!**

Over the past year we have been thrust rapidly into the end of days. Time has quickened, there are wars and rumors of wars, famine, dis-eases and pestilences unheard of, animals dying all over the world, division among the nations (**nations=people**). People full of demons and enraged, social persecution against Natsarim **(Endtime Believers)** , Brother turning against brother, those openly practicing witchcraft and the occult in our face, the rise of maniacs, earthquakes and volcanoes and so much more. There is a food crisis and financial crisis coming very soon as Yahuah brings judgement to the countries and cities who have turned against **HIM** . I have been assigned the task of writing about the coming events.

Understand that the enemy is throwing everything at us; we now witness demons in the flesh masquerading as humans. We should be aware that the enemy will use our loved ones and friends against us in these last days. People can come under demonic influence and attack. Things like this will become more and more frequent in the days ahead.

The wicked and worldly will say to us *"Adapt or Die."*

Frequency/ Signal adaptors

PRAYER FOR THE SAFE HAVENS -FOUND IN EZEKIEL 34:25-31:

From Sister Elizabeth Marie of LatterRain333 YouTube Channel

I will make a covenant of peace with them, and cause wild beasts to cease from the land; and they will dwell safely in the wilderness and sleep in the woods.

I will make them and the places all around My hill a blessing; and I will cause showers to come down in their season; there shall be showers of blessing.

Then the trees of the field shall yield their fruit, and the earth shall yield her increase. They shall be safe in their land; and they shall know that I am YAHUAH their ELOHIM, when I have broken the bands of their yoke and delivered them from the hand of those who enslaved them.

And they shall no longer be a prey for the nations, nor shall beasts of the land devour them; but they shall dwell safely, and no one shall make them afraid.

I will raise up for them a garden of renown, and they shall no longer be consumed with hunger in the land, nor bear the shame of the Gentiles anymore.

Thus they shall know that I, the YAHUAH their ELOHIM, am with them, and they, the house of Israel, are My people, says ADONAI.

You are My flock, the flock of My pasture; you are men, and I am your ELOHIM, YAHUAH says ADONAI. Then they cry out to יהוה in their distress, And He brings them out of their troubles. He caused the storm to be still, So that its waves were silent. And they rejoice because they are hushed; And He leads them to the haven of their delight.

Psalms 107:28-30

For in the time of trouble He shall hide me in His pavilion; In the secret place of His

tabernacle *He shall hide me ;He shall set me high upon a rock. Psalms 27:5*

The mountains will bring peace to the people,

And the little hills, by righteousness. Psalms 72:3

Incline Your ear to me, Deliver me speedily; Be a rock of refuge to me, A house of defence to save me. For You are my rock and my stronghold; For Your Name's sake lead me and guide me. Psalms 31:2-3

The spirit of reason will become an enemy to people in the near future.

Quantum D Wave = open portals for demons and dimensions. Agenda of hasatan and his evil spirits, principalities, and dark spirits. This is technology given from the Fallen Angels and Nephilim. This along with Cern and the rise of the Beast System and the NWO and the stage is set. Breeding of A.I. merged with human DNA beings are probably already in our population just like the reptilian race and demonic presence has been proven. PRAISE YAH HE WILL DESTROY THEM ALL ON HIS DAY OF RECKONING!

"Flee from the midst of Baḇel, and let each one save his life! Do not be cut off in her crookedness, for this is the time of the vengeance of יהוה, the recompense He is repaying her. "Come out of her midst, My people! And let everyone deliver his being from the burning displeasure of יהוה. " **Jeremiah 51: 6, 45**

The counterfeit is in every place that Yahuah has created.Understand that hasatan mimics...it ALL!

Jerusalem vs. Rome/Babylon
Yahuah vs. hasatan/Ba'al
The Shema vs. The Cross/The Trinity
Yahusha vs. Jesus/Tammuz
The Sabbath vs. Sunday
The Passover Lamb vs. Easter/The Ishtar Pig
The Holy Days vs. Holidays
The Law vs. Lawlessness
The Spirit of Truth vs. The Spirit of Error
The Spirit of Yahuah vs. the Spirit of the False Messiah/Incarnation
The Nazarene vs. Christianity

Hebrews 5:14
"But solid food is for the mature whose senses have been trained by practice to discern both good and evil."

"Therefore write down what you have seen, what is, and what will happen after these things." Revelation 1:19 This is my assignment for these End Days and Tribulation even unto the end of all things; for in the Shamayim there is a library where all things have been recorded. I am humbled and blessed for such an assignment.

Hear, O Yisra'ěl: יהוה our Elohim, יהוה is one! "And you shall love יהוה your Elohim with all your heart, and with all your being, and with all your might. "And these Words which I am commanding you today shall be in your heart, and you shall impress them upon your children, and shall speak of them when you sit in your house, and when you walk by the way, and when you lie down, and when you rise up, and shall bind them as a sign on your hand, and they shall be as frontlets between your eyes. "And you shall write them on the doorposts of your house and on your gates. "And it shall be, when יהוה your Elohim brings you into the land of which He swore to your fathers, to Aḇraham, to Yitsḥaq, and to Ya'aqoḇ, to give you great and good cities which you did not build, and houses filled with all kinds of goods, which you did not fill, and wells dug which you did not dig, vineyards and olive trees which you did not plant, and you shall eat and be satisfied – be on guard, lest you forget יהוה who brought you out of the land of Mitsrayim, from the house of bondage. "Fear יהוה your Elohim and serve Him, and swear by His Name. **Deuteronomy 6: 4-13**

"Therefore take courage, men, for I believe Elohim that it shall be according to **the way** it was spoken to me." **Acts 27:25**

" *The Melody of My Word is the Tapestry of My Creation!" saith Yahuah*

The Shofar is our alarm clock and it is sounding now... **WAKE UP!**

 A WORD from YAHUAH ELOHIM delivered to Amaliyah bat Yahuah- - Abba Yahuah says; I love those who come naked and barefoot before me because I get to dress them. But understand this, that in the last days; hard times will come—for people will be lovers of self, lovers of money, boastful, arrogant, blasphemers, disobedient to parents, ungrateful, unholy,hardhearted, unforgiving, backbiting, without self-control, brutal, hating what is good, treacherous, reckless, conceited, lovers of pleasure rather than lovers of God, holding to an outward form of godliness but denying its power. Avoid these people! For, among these are those who slip into households and deceive weak women weighed down with sins, led away by various desires, always learning yet never able to come to the knowledge of truth. **2 Timothy 6: 1-7**

"Know ye, therefore, my children, that in the last times Your sons will forsake singleness And will cleave unto insatiable desire; And leaving guilelessness, will draw near to malice; And forsaking the commandments of the Lord, They will cleave unto Beliar. And leaving husbandry, They will follow after their own wicked devices, And they shall be dispersed among the Gentiles, And shall serve their enemies." **Testament of Issachar, 6:1-2.**

"And honour shall be turned into shame, And strength humiliated into contempt, And probity destroyed, And beauty shall become ugliness...And envy shall rise in those who had not thought aught of themselves, And passion shall seize him that is peaceful, And

many shall be stirred up in anger to injure many; And they shall rouse up armies in order to shed blood, And in the end they shall perish together with them." **2 Baruch 27** .
Ministry of Darkness---Black Awakening--- **BE READY EVEN NOW!**
The essence of a life not of this world is the **obliteration of SELF!**

Times of stress, tribulations have been recycled over and over since the time of the book of Acts...all have believed they were living in the last days. Paul is saying that within this extended period of time there will come repetitive cycles of distress, times of stress, perilous times, when all the conditions which he describes with these chilling words will obtain.

Shabbat is faithful resistance to the chaotic world!
This world and universe are constantly moving toward greater and greater disorder this is the result of it dying. It must come full circle just as our lives come full circle. From the moment we are born into this world we begin to die. Just as Yahuah created this world and universe it began to die when sin entered into.

" *The same is true of life itself. The normative state of living things is death. We humans are only alive because we are constantly making ourselves live. The body is dying due to lack of oxygen, but we are constantly breathing in oxygen to keep it going. The body is disintegrating, but we are replenishing lost cells every time we eat. The body is being tugged toward Earth by gravity, but we force ourselves to stand and sit upright. We are, in effect, continually pumping life into an inanimate collection of atoms that we call our body. Life is not simply a state of being; it is a state that we are choosing to perpetuate. And that which is true on a physical level is always mirrored on a spiritual level." Rabbi Shaul Rosenblatt*

Abba wants a mature grown up family--blue and red tassels are a warriors robe
YaH's WORD- WILL- WAYS
The very essence for all sin is the doubting or denial of the aforementioned.
The Tree of Life produces the fruits of holiness, cleanliness, purity, perfection, and truth.
DE-CEP-TION
Peace today equals compromise--look around the world is in an erotic chaos! There are zero morals among the masses, zero boundaries, and everything is all about "me". it is becoming hasatan's DisneyLand! The mass deception began a few years ago and like clock work is right on schedule with the **"END DAYS"** clock! As a Believer and Follower of Yahusha HaMashiach , maybe you were confidently alert to the deception and watched it creep into churches and worship services under the guise of, "let's be cool to win souls". I must warn you we have just crossed over to a whole new level of mass deception, with Preachers, Teachers, and the like professing the name of Jesus aka Yahusha HaMasciach and talking the talk and perceiving to the untrained eye to walk the walk. To a "lukewarmer" this is sooo awesome that your favorite hip hop, rock, actor, etc. etc. you love professes J.C. aka Yahusha so come on y'all let go to there church!! **MASS DECEPTION!!!** We have reached a whole new level of deception in the world...the enemy knows how little time he has and so he has started to roll out his end days deception agenda; "pretend to embrace Yahusha and become wolves among the sheep".

How does he do this? hasatan owns the music/ movie industry and so he calls to action his servants.   The influencers of our pop culture sold their souls and their brand new assignment is to go "sell salvation"! Praise Yahusha! **BE ALERT BELOVEDS! BE ALERT!!**

Micro to Macro from cells to cycles we are only set to 120 The truth within the 120! Humans live to 120 years old...there is a deeper connection and meaning here. I have yet to have all revealed to me, I included it here for you to pray and seek ABBA for the meaning as I feel it has to do with the days we are living in. Count each day and mark with its own uniqueness. We receive gifts everyday. It is up to us to decide if we will accept them or not!

CURRENCY OF TRIBULATION

LOVE & FORGIVENESS are particles and the currency of tribulation and of heaven.

WARNING- Earthquakes and Tsunamis

Amid the solar storm.

Gravitational pull of the planet will be felt tomorrow!

WARNING YaH's Vengeance is coming!

People's hearts have grown cold

Animals acting out of their norm.

Anger rising, Wars and rumors of wars.

Hatred of Believers- Lawlessness

Wildfires in various places are out of control...

Transhumanism and the U.S. and Israeli military. Splicing DNA and adding infrared eyes of the reptile and super hearing from a dolphin will make a new kind of soldier and this is a mild transformation add in when the Fallen Angels open the Portals and "higher consciousness" for demons to enter and control the transhuman! The droids will undoubtedly round up the Believers like cattle into FEMA camps....run to the wilderness Beloveds.Abba reminded me of this song, as HE said everyone knows what is about to happen and the times we are headed into.

SIGNS, SIGNS, EVERYWHERE THERE ARE SIGNS- As the song goes:

Signs Signs

Everywhere there's signs

Screwing up the scenery

Breaking my mind

Do this, don't do that

Can't you read the sign

And the sign says "Anybody caught trespassing will be shot on sight"

So I jumped the fence and I yelled at the house, Hey! What gives you the right

To put up a fence And keep me out Or to keep Mother Nature in

If God was here He'd tell it to your face Man You're some kind of sinner

Oh Say now mister Can't you read

You got to have a shirt and tie to get a seat

You can't watch No You can't eat You ain't supposed to be here

And the sign says "You got to have a membership card to get inside" Huh

And the sign says "Everybody welcome Come in Kneel down and pray"

But then they passed around a plate at the end of it all
And I didn't have a penny to pay
So I got me a pen and paper And I made up my own little sign
I said Thank you Lord for thinking about me. I'm alive and doing fine.

Super Black Moons

Dis-eases and Plagues strange and unusual--flesh eating bacteria, bubonic plague. Pestilences have been released. The water will be poisoned and there will be a shortage so I encourage you now to stock up! Stay away from GMO--these are genetically modified foods. Not only that, these "fake foods" have been injected with micro sized nanobots. The nanos will alter your DNA and will transform you from a human to a transhuman. If that happens you **CAN NOT BE** accepted into **YAHUAH's KINGDOM!!** **That is why you must heed this warning and pray the BLOOD of YAHUSHA over your body, mind, soul, spirit, mind, thoughts, emotions and DNA.**

Holes in the sun directed at earth will cause plasm storms and with Planet X. I believe that just before this Planet hits ours that the rapture will take place. Many have had prophetic dreams and visions of a plasma sky and then at the blink of an eye they were raptured up and bodies changed. Continue to pray about this. I do believe this is a possibility, and yes some will hate us, some will mock us, some will curse us. Count it all joy in suffering as Yahusha did. Great persecution is coming to America and we must ready ourselves mind, body and soul. So much is happening everyday it is almost impossible to keep up. I am going to give a short report today and in the coming days I will go into more detail about these things.

Some other events that have already happened!

The honey bee population is almost extinct. There are mosquitos carrying disease that when bitten affects the brain.

The government accidently released weaponized ticks that can and did spread lymes disease. These were intended to be released with those we are at war with but instead they let them loose here. Ooops!! This is just another tactic of the enemy.

Beware the Noahide Laws --do your homework- I recommend watching all the videos from Israeli News Live as they have been researching this matter a long time to let us know the information. These laws have already been signed and approved by our President!

5G -- is **ALREADY HERE!** 5G/6G will kill humanity and animals and other wildlife. Already many birds, butterflies and other important wildlife to our ecosystem have been found falling out of the sky and dying in between two 5G towers.

55 or so birds fell to the ground with their eyes bleeding in Australia last week.

Demons are taking the shape of humans and revealing themselves. There is proof. This means that the natural world is meshing with the supernatural world.

The State of Israel is gaining power and the end goal is for the U.S. to submit to them. Beware the false *"alien invasion"* is fast approaching as the media, world science and technology prepare to roll it out.

A.I. technology is much farther along than the public has been told or even thought. They have made robo bees not to pollinate the world but to be used as surveillance and weapons as they are armed and dangerous.

The **LGBTQ Agenda** is working towards anti semetic laws which will involve the Noahide Laws.

Earthquakes continue all around the world at an alarming rate. Volcanic activity has increased.

I did not talk about the fallen angels who are working with the governments of Israel and the U.S. and doing human DNA testing. Nor did I share about the Black Awakening and the Demonic Super Soldiers for that information I can refer you to Russ Dizdar's Shatter the Darkness website where you can read all about it. You really must!

My goal is not to alarm you or scare you. It is to present only the truth, and you must search the matter out for yourself. Beloved, we are heading into tribulation quickly and if you were still sleeping concerning these matters then I hope I made you aware of what is happening or made you curious to investigate yourself. If you don't want to believe it that is entirely up to you. The truth always sets one **FREE!**

PRAY, INTERCEDE, FAST. ...that is what is needed right now. I love you and I am praying for you! If you have any questions please drop it below in the comments. Have a beautiful SHABBAT SHALOM!! We know the **RETURN OF OUR KING IS SOON!! HALLELUYAH! Baruch haba b'shem Adonai!** (Blessed is He who comes in the name of Elohim.)

But as it has been written, "Eye has not seen, and ear has not heard, nor have entered into the heart of man what Elohim has prepared for those who love Him." *1 Corinthians 2:9*

Prophetic Declaration of Identity

You/I are a son [or daughter] of Yahuah Elohim, begotten by the Ruach HaKodesh, a child of the Promise. You have been given the Birthright with all of the blessings of heaven and earth at your disposal, to be used in accordance with the divine plan that the Spirit is outworking in the earth daily. As part of the Body of Christ, positioned under the Head, you have been given all authority in both heaven and earth. It is your/my calling to have dominion over the creation itself and to exercise that authority as Yahusha HaMashiach did when He ministered in the earth. You have authority over time and distance, governments, principalities and powers, nature, disease, and death itself. You/I are the righteousness of Yahuah in Yahusha, called to show forth the glory of Adonai to every creature, that all may know both the character and the works of Yahuah through YOU/ME. So come forth this day and subdue all things under your feet. Bring order out of chaos, deliverance from bondage, light out of darkness, health out of sickness, and life out of death. Praise Yahuah! Barak Yahuah in Yahusha! HalleluYaH!

Natsarim's Prayer
Father, may YOUR NAME be held holy. enable us to have sound minds in these last days. Help us to live wisely. To abide in the shelter of YOUR arms. Keep us focused on

things above and not below. Let us never lean on our own understanding!! Show us those things that give us fuzzy thinking instead of clear mindedness. May we be able to focus on Your precious Word to define our thinking and decision-making. Make clear to us the areas where we are lacking in self-control and discipline; help us to resist the enemy in these areas so that he will flee from us! Help us to know how to pray what is on Your heart! We desire powerful, Spirit-filled lives of prayer that will bring You glory in these last days! Teach us to pray, ABBA! In Yahusha's Name Amein!

You see Beloved, I never sought for perfection, just broken and contrite hearts. For then I will deliver, I will answer. Depending on self is a futile activity for man is limited, but when one aligns himself with Me, all is possible, even attainable, for I Am the Great I Am. Now My name will be great in all the earth. My display, the display of My power unleashed, now at hand. Victory shall emit from My camp and utter ruin and devastation to the camp of the enemy. I have now had enough. My children serve Me with nothing, while those I gave more have sold their souls for a trinket of fools gold.

Now Beloveds, remember, when I bring you into the land that I have promised, keep yourselves separated from the heathen and do not do as they do, lest I smite you with a curse. I have, for My purposes, separated you from the world. You are to be in it, not of it. My Spirit will dwell in you, and where I Am there is only truth and holiness. The circumcision was painful, but necessary to prepare for My coming to dwell in you.

Be still and know that I Am. I shall exalt My name in all the earth. Man think himself to be clever, but fools I say.

Does one suppose that I do not see man's plans and schemes?

I shall shatter them every one.

Behold, the tabernacle of Yahuah is with men.

I shall dwell among My people. I will be their Elohim, they will be My people.

For My name sake shalll perform this, beloved

My people have played the harlot, but My covenant was and is to rescue them and cause them to return to their land. My covenant still stands. Will My people repent and align themselves? That is the question for every man. Know now that I have begun My approach. I will visit everyone, open up and let Me sup with you. Let us commune together.

I will release My power from on high to My readied vessels. This is the time that I have spoken of. Behold, behold your Elohim. For I Am will answer from on high. Rejoice Zion for your king has come. Rejoice Zion, your victory is won. Let the high praise of Yahuah be in your mouth. Let the hallelujahs begin, says Yahuah.

Exodus 34: 5-10, Deuteronomy 4, Psalm 51:17, Psalm 46:10, Deuteronomy 6-11, John 15:19, Revelation 21:1-7, Ezekiel 36: 19-24, Revelation 3:20, Zechariah 9

Psalm 10--- **The Righteous do NOT fear the Reapers**

Walk in Integrity

A psalm of David.

Adonai, who may dwell in Your tent? Who may live on Your holy mountain? The one who walks with integrity, who does what is right, and speaks truth in his heart, who does not slander with his tongue, does not wrong his neighbor, and does not disgrace his friend,
Psalm 15:1-3 TLV
Under the Shadow of HIS WINGS..
We will dwell.

One *matter* I asked of יהוה – this I seek: To dwell in the House of יהוה All the days of my life, To see the pleasantness of יהוה, And to inquire in His Hĕ̱kal. For in the day of evil He hides me in His booth; In the covering of His Tent He hides me; On a rock He raises me up.   And now my head is lifted up above my enemies all around me; And I offer in His Tent with shouts of joy; I sing, yea, I sing praises to יהוה. **Psalm 27: 4-6**
"And He made My mouth like a sharp sword, in the shadow of His hand He hid Me, and made Me a polished shaft. In His quiver He hid Me." **Isaiah 49:2**
"And I have put My Words in your mouth, and with the shadow of My hand I have covered you, to plant the heavens and lay the foundations of the earth, and to say to Tsiyon, 'You are My people.' " **Isaiah 51:16**

ABBA YAHUAH, Teach me to abide in YOU.
Shifting and Sifting---The Wheat from the Chaff
CHAFF, n.

1. The husk, or dry calyx of corn, and grasses. In common language, the word is applied to the husks when separated from the corn by thrashing, riddling or winnowing. The word is sometimes used rather improperly to denote straw cut small for the food of cattle.

2. Refuse; worthless matter; especially that which is light, and apt to be driven by the wind. In scripture, false doctrines, fruitless designs, hypocrites and ungodly men are compared to chaff. Ps. 1:4 ; Jer. 23:28 ; Is. 33:11 ; Mat. 3:12 .
"As the darnel, then, is gathered and burned in the fire, so it shall be at the end of this age. "The Son of A̱dam shall send out His messengers, and they shall gather out of His reign all the stumbling-blocks, and those doing lawlessness, and shall throw them into the furnace of fire – there shall be wailing and gnashing of teeth. "Then the righteous shall shine forth as the sun in the reign of their Father. He who has ears to hear, let him hear! **Matthew 13: 40-43**

What is a shadow?

: partial darkness or obscurity within a part of space from which rays from a source of light are cut off by an interposed opaque body
: a reflected image
: shelter from danger or observation
: an imperfect and faint representation
: an imitation of something ;copy: the dark figure cast upon a surface by a body intercepting the rays from a source of light : PHANTOM
5780 5781 5782 5783 5784 5786 5787 5788 5789 5790 5791 5792 5793
2020 2021 2022 2023 2024 2025 2026 2027 2028 2029 2030 2031 2032
Enoch was born 7th in the 1st week while **JUDGEMENT & RIGHTEOUSNESS** still endured
2nd week GREAT WICKEDNESS & DECEIT sprung up; in it shall be the first END. In it a man shall be saved (Noah) after unrighteousness shall grow up and law shall be made for the sinners. (Possibly Enoch's Death)
3rd week at its close a man shall be elected as the plant of RIGHTEOUS JUDGEMENT-- (Abraham??) or (Flood)
4th week visions of the holy & righteous shall be seen, and a law for ALL generations & enclosure (Tabernacles??) shall be made for them--(Moses and the Law??)
5th week at its close the HOUSE of GLORY & DOMINION shall be built forever!! (King David- Solomon??)
6th week all who live in it shall be BLINDED & the hearts of all them shall godlessly forsake WISDOM. And in it a man shall ascend. At its close the house of DOMINION shall be burnt with FIRE and the whole race of the CHOSEN root shall be dispersed. (Yahusha?Resurrection and Dispersion)
7th week shall an APOSTATE GENERATION arise. many shall be its deeds & all its deeds shall be apostate. And at its close shall be elected; the elect righteous of the eternal plant of righteousness, to receive SEVENFOLD INSTRUCTION concerning all HIS CREATION(Early Church)
8th week is of RIGHTEOUSNESS & a SWORD (the WORD??) shall be given to it that RIGHTEOUS JUDGEMENT shall be executed on the oppressors.Sinners shall be delivered into the hands of the righteous. At its close they shall acquire houses through their righteousness.
9th week the RIGHTEOUS JUDGEMENT shall be revealed to the whole wor ld (YAHUSHA's RETURN??) all the works of the godless shall vanish from all the earth & the world shall be WRITTEN down for destruction
10th week in the 7th part there shall be great **ETERNAL JUDGEMENT,** HE will execute vengeance among the angels (Fallen Angels) and the 1st heaven shall pass away and the NEW HEAVEN shall appear & all the powers of the heavens shall give SEVENFOLD LIGHT. After that shall be many weeks without number for ever all shall be in GOODNESS & RIGHTEOUSNESS & SIN shall no more be mentioned for ever!!! (Final Judgement)

Spiritual DNA of the Remnant
KNOW- STRONG- DO
See Daniel 11:32 YaH's Word says in the end days that a nation will rise (Nation of Natsarim) 1 Peter 2:9 Deut. 32:31

Matthew 24--

Abide in the place of the anointing

The Remnant (Natsarim) will begin to minister for 3 1/2 years ushering in the last harvest --possibly the first 3 years of Tribulation

During the last 3 1/2 years of Tribulation Natsarim will flee to safe havens or places of refuge...see below

Gen 1: 1-31 Gen 6: 1-22 Exo 23: 20 Psa 23: 6 Psa 31:19 Matt 25: 34 John 14:2 1 Cor 2:9 Heb 11:7 & 16 Rev 12:6

Pray for food, food and water that is "safe" to consume.

Food shortages will begin and continue...

Few people seem to care about or understand the dangers of consuming genetically modified foods. Who is even paying attention or listening to the increasingly long list of food recalls? Our government does not require the food we import to pass the same safety laws as food grown domestically in America.

But take great heed to do the commands and the law, which Moses the servant of the Yahuah commanded you to do; to love the Yahuah our Elohim, to walk in all his ways, to keep his commands, and to cleave to him, and serve him with all your mind, and with all your soul. *Joshua 22:5 Septuagint*

The Reckoning

I am including these powerful prayers for the Natsarim aka. The Remnant; because I felt led by the Ruach to do so, these will be extremely helpful in the days ahead and I am so grateful to Mary Lou Lake for writing and making them available for FREE.

Prayers for Release

Developed by: Mary Lou Lake- Author of " *What Witches Don't Want Christians to Know*"
MORNING PRAYER :

Father,I declare that You are the One True GOD YAHUAH,   the Most High, the God of Abraham, Isaac and Jacob. I ask You to forgive   my sins and   cleanse me of all unrighteousness, create in me a clean heart and renew a right spirit within me. I plead the blood of YAHUSHA/ YAHSHUA over my eyes and ears and over the eyes and   ears of my family, so we can see and hear the truth, and I ask You to shield us from all forms of mind control that can enter the eye gates   and ear gates. I declare that we have access to the   whole   armor   of YAHUAH, according to Ephesians 6; our loins are girt about with truth, and our feet are shod with the preparation of the gospel of peace. We have the breastplate of righteousness/ set apartness, the shield of faith/

emunah, the helmet of our salvation and the Sword/Dagger of the Spirit, which is the Word of YAHUAH. As we commit our works unto You, our thoughts will be established according to Proverbs 16:3. Father, I ask You to apply the blood of YAHUSHA/ YAHSHUA to any doors that I have open to the enemy that I am unaware of, and I ask You to reveal these doors to me so they can be closed forever. I take the authority that Yahusha gave me over all the power of the enemy according to Luke 10:19. I stand upon YOUR WORD in Matthew 16:19 that I have been given the keys to the Kingdom and what I bind on Earth will be bound in Shamayim/Heaven, and what I loose on Earth will be loosed in Shamayim/Heaven. I take authority over the kingdom of darkness in every plain of existence that has access to me, and I bind the power of the enemy to affect me or my family, and I loose the power of the Kingdom of Yahuah to form impenetrable shields in every dimension-- above, below and all around, in the Name of Yahusha/ Yahshua. I stand upon the promise in Your Word that says that NO weapon formed against me shall prosper, according to Isaiah 54:17. I stand upon the 91st Psalm that no evil shall befall me, neither shall any plague come nigh my dwelling. The 91st Psalm also promises that Your holy angels have been given charge over me and my family to keep us in all our ways. Father, I ask You to send extra angels for reinforcement during times of spiritual warfare, In Yahusha's' Name. Father, I ask You to forgive the sins of all of my ancestors (and the ancestors of my children and grandchildren), and I plead the blood of Yahusha/Yahshua over my DNA and the DNA of all of my descendants, which cleanses our bloodlines of all iniquity. I bind the power of any generational or familiar spirits to attach or influence us, and I loose the power of the Kingdom of Yahuah within us and around us as we keep Your commandments. I declare that our family is free to walk in the blessings of Deuteronomy 28. I ask You to forgive the sins of all individuals being used by the enemy to combat our family (and ministry). I ask You to forgive the sins of all of their ancestors, and I plead the blood of Yahusha/Yahshua over their bloodlines all the way to the DNA level, breaking the power of iniquity. I ask You to break all of their occult power to the highest levels, making it impossible for them to be used by the kingdom of darkness to harm anyone. I ask You to save their souls, deliver and heal them. I plead the blood of Yahusha/Yahshua over every action and every word spoken against me and my family, nullifying the demonic power. I command any evil spirits sent on assignment against me and my family to return to the place they were sent from. I bind these spirits from harming those that sent them, but I pray that their defeat in their mission would serve as a testimony of Your greatness and the victory that Yahusha/Yahshua won for believers, in Yahusha's Name. Father, I ask You to remove my DNA and the DNA of my family from any hair, blood or any other contact object in the hands of the enemy and break all conduits to our physical bodies, in Yahusha's Name. Father, I ask You to forgive the sins that have allowed technology to be used as a weapon against Your Creation. I ask You to place shields between me and my family and all broadcasts of the enemy through the airways, TVs, computers, phone lines, electric lines and satellites. I Stand upon the promises in Your Word that You are our shield. I ask You to purify our air, water and food, in Yahusha's Name. Father, I ask You to forgive the sins done on the roadways, railroad tracks, and waterways. I ask You to forgive the sins of any individuals or groups that have adopted the roadways, and I ask You to break any occult connections that would give power to the kingdom of darkness. Father, I ask You to provide divine protection during any modes of transportation. I ask You to surround our vehicles with. Your holy angels to insure safe travel, in Yahusha's Name. Father, lead me in paths of righteousness today and attune my ears to Your voice that I may follow You.I ask You to fill me with a hunger for Your Word, that I may know You more. I give You all of my praise, my worship, honor, and the glory, In the Name of Your Beloved Son Yahusha. Amein

Definition of **transhumanism:**

"Transhumanism is an international intellectual and cultural movement supporting the use of science and technology to improve human mental and physical characteristics and capacities. The movement regards aspects of the human condition, such as disability, suffering, disease, aging, and involuntary death as unnecessary and undesirable."
But there are a growing number of scientists all over the world that are absolutely convinced that dramatic advances in nanotechnology and biotechnology will enable humanity to far surpass any limitations that we are experiencing now. To many of these scientists, transhumanism has become the overriding philosophy of their lives. It is almost a religion to many of them.In fact it is believed by many transhumanists that we are on the verge of seeing an entire new "species" created. The transhumanist version of the future includes many different "lines" of humanity. In fact, many transhumanists are very open about the fact that humanity as we know it will eventually go out of existence as far more superior forms take over.

Guess what? If you are not a fan of human upgrades and speak out against it rest assure that you will be labeled and outsider, or worse you will be targeted as a "anti semetic".

"Being human is so yesterday" New York Times columnist Ashlee Vance described the moment that transhumanists are most looking forward to. It is known as "the Singularity", and in her article Vance described the Singularity as "a time, possibly just a couple decades from now, when a superior intelligence will dominate and life will take on an altered form that we can't predict or comprehend in our current, limited state."

Many transhumanists believe that once the Singularity occurs those who embrace transhumanism will have dramatically enhanced intelligence and will be able to live for hundreds of years, and those that do not embrace transhumanism will slowly die off as they cling to their antiquated philosophies.

Forced Manipulation--Workings of Entities of Darkness

Look up 1 Samuel 19:20= this verse is a prophetic activator for 5780 because the words/letters add up to 5780

20/20 vision means to see clearly at a distance. The great divide.

2 Timothy 3:7---This verse has always haunted me--it causes me to examine my motives of study especially the **WORD of YaH** .

Collapse of the financial system begins with only one domino---then another and another and another. One at a time things collapse like bursts of dynamite; suddenly burst after burst until all is blown up!

Fast for the sake of the Kingdom--

The Ekklesia of Natsarim will gather in the near future and sing the Song of Moseh! It will be written on our hearts and a light in our thoughts as we gather and sing this to Yahuah! (Revelation 15: 3-4)

The Song of Moses (Tree of Life Version)

"Give ear, O heavens, and I will speak! Let the earth hear the words of my mouth.

May my teaching trickle like rain, my speech distill like dew— like gentle rain on new grass, like showers on tender plants.

For I will proclaim *Adonai* 's Name, ascribe greatness to our God!

The Rock—blameless is His work. Indeed, all His ways are just. God of faithfulness without iniquity, righteous and upright is He.

Did it corrupt Him? No! The blemish is His children's— a generation crooked and twisted.

Is this how you pay back *Adonai* , O foolish, unwise people? Isn't He your Father who ransomed you? He made you and established you.

"Remember the days of antiquity, understand the years across generations. Ask your father and he will tell you, your elders and they will say to you.

When Elyon gave nations their heritage, when He separated the sons of man, He set boundaries for the people by the number of *Bnei-Yisrael* .

But *Adonai*'s portion is His people— Jacob is the share of His inheritance.

He found him in the wilderness land, in the void of a howling waste. He surrounded him, cared for him, guarded him as the pupil of His eye.

As an eagle stirs up its nest, hovers over its young, He spreads His wings, catches him, lifts him up on His pinions.

Adonai alone guided him— there was no foreign god with him.

He made him mount the heights of the land. so he ate the produce of the field. He suckled him with honey from a rock, with oil from a flinty boulder.

Butter of cattle and milk of a flock, with fat of lambs, rams of the Bashan and he-goats, with fat of the kidneys of wheat, and blood of grapes you drank.

But Jeshurun grew fat and kicked— you got fat, you grew thick, you gorged! He forsook God who made him. He mocked the Rock of his salvation.

They made him jealous with strangers, with abominations they angered Him.

They sacrificed to demons, a non-god, gods they had not known— to new ones who came in lately, ones your fathers had not dreaded.

The Rock who birthed you, you ignored. You forgot God who brought you forth.

" *Adonai* saw, and He spurned His sons and His daughters out of vexation.

He said, "I will hide My face from them, I want to see their hereafter. For they are an upside down generation, children with no faithfulness in them.

They made Me jealous with a non-god. They vexed Me with airy idols. So I will make them jealous with non-people. With a foolish nation I will vex them.

For fire has ignited in My nostrils— it will burn to *Sheol* beneath, devour the earth and her produce, and scorch the foundations of mountains.

I will heap calamities upon them. With My arrows I will finish them.

Wasted by famine, ravaged by plague and pestilence so bitter, fangs of beasts I'll let loose on them, with venom of creepers in the dust.

Outside the sword deals death, and inside terror— to both young men and young women, infants, with men of gray hair.

I would have said, 'I will hack them to pieces, make the memory of them cease from mankind,'

except I dread the taunt of the enemy, lest their foes might misconstrue— lest they say, 'Our hand is held high, and *Adonai* has not done all this.'

For they are a nation lacking counsel, among them there is no understanding.

"If they were wise, they would discern this, they would understand their hereafter.

How can one chase a thousand and two put ten thousand to flight, unless their Rock had sold them and *Adonai* had handed them over?

Surely their rock is not like our Rock, as even our enemies judge.

For their vine is from the vine of Sodom and from the terraces of Gomorrah. Its grapes are grapes of poison— bitter clusters on it.

Venom of serpents is their wine— poison of vipers so cruel.

Is it not stored up with Me, sealed up in My treasuries?

Vengeance is Mine, and payback, for the time when their foot staggers. Surely their day of disaster is near— what is prepared rushes on them.

For *Adonai* will judge His people— for His servants, He will relent when He sees that strength is gone and no one is left, slave or free.

He will say, 'Where are their gods, the "rock" they took refuge in?

Who ate the fat of their sacrifices and drank the wine of their libation? Let them rise up and help you and be a shelter over you!

See now that I, I am He! There are no other gods beside Me. I bring death and give life, I have wounded but I will heal, and none can rescue from My hand.'

"Yes, I lift My hand up to heaven and say, 'As I Myself live forever,

when I sharpen My lightning sword and My hand seizes it in judgment, I will return vengeance on My foes, and those who hate Me I will pay back.

I will make My arrows drunk from blood, and My sword will devour flesh— the blood of the slain and the captive, the head of the leaders of the enemy.'

Make His people rejoice, O nations, for He will avenge the blood of His servants. He will return vengeance on His foes, and atone for the land of His people."

Then Moses came and spoke all the words of this song in the ears of the people—he and Joshua son of Nun.

When Moses finished speaking all these words to all Israel,

he said to them, "Put in your hearts all the words that I call as witness against you today—that you may command your children to keep and do all the words of this *Torah* .

For it is not an empty thing for you, because it is your life! By this word you will prolong your days on the land, which you are crossing over the Jordan to possess."

On that very day, *Adonai* spoke to Moses saying,

"Go up this mountain of the Avarim, Mount Nebo, which is in the land of Moab facing Jericho, and see the land of Canaan, which I am giving to *Bnei-Yisrael* as a possession. On the mountain that you are ascending, there be gathered to your people—as Aaron your brother died on Mount Hor and was gathered to his people—

because you both broke faith with Me among *Bnei-Yisrael* at the waters of Meribath-kadesh in the wilderness of Zin, because you did not treat Me as holy in the midst of *Bnei-Yisrael* .

For you will see the land from afar, but you will not enter there, into the land that I am giving to *Bnei-Yisrael* ."

FOCUS

F aithful/Follow

O ffering/Opposition/Operation or Operating/Obedience/Orders

C ompassion/Clarity/Confidence

U nified

S ervant/Savior

Yahusha HaNazeret VaMelech HaYehudim--Yahusha of Nazareth, the King of the Jews

Blessed be the Name of Yahusha HaMashiah!

Baruch Attah Adonai, Yavenu, Elohenu, Avenu, Melchenu, Melek ha Olam!

The main question of 4Q246 (*Aramaic Apocalypse*)- - Col. 1

1. [   ] rested upon him, he fell before the throne
2. [… k]ing, rage is coming to the world, and your years
3. […]. . . your vision, all of it is about to come unto the world.
4. [… mi]ghty [signs], distress is coming upon the land
5. […] great slaughter in the provinces
6. […] king of Assyria [and E]gypt
7. […] he will rule over the land
8. […] will do and all will serve
9. [… gr]eat will be called and he will be designated by his name.

Col II

1. He will be called the Son of Elohim, and they will call him the Son of the Most High like a shooting star.
2. that you saw, so will be their kingdom, they will rule several years over
3. the earth and crush everything, a people will crush another people and nation (will crush) nation.
4. Until the people of God arises and makes everyone rest from warfare.
5. Their kingdom will be an eternal kingdom, and their paths will be righteous. They will judge
6. the earth with truth, and all (nations) will make peace. The warfare will cease from the land,
7. and all (nations) will worship him. The great Elohim will be their help,
8. He Himself will fight for them, putting peoples into their power, all of them
9. He will cast them away before him, His dominion will be an everlasting dominion and all the abysses.

Appointed Times

Sabbatical Years - Jubilee Years

Exodus 23:10-11: Instructions for land rest
Leviticus 25:9-:Jubilee: Blow the trumpet on
Atonement
Leviticus 25: 10-17: A jubilee rest

Deuteronomy 15:1: Release of debt every 7 years for the brethren
Deuteronomy 31: 10-11: Read Deuteronomy on the 7th year Sabbatical
2 Chronicles 36:21: Yahuah can enforce obedience
Ezekiel 20:12: All Sabbaths are a sign
Ezekiel 46:17: Sabbatical years observed in the Kingdom
SABBATICAL YEARS: 2022- 2023
Notes;

1900s- 1960s **The Hook- Rise of The Satanic Super Soldiers**
Hasatan's Implantation of Joy

Time of the Nazi Reign aka Naphalim/ Nephilim Agenda: like with Moses the children in the wilderness evil within darkness and then and it came time for Joshua to lead Israel into promised Land and Abba gave orders to kill call of the Giants in the land AKA Nephilim.. and they did not they let some live and they lived with them and peace stop what am I saying that the Nazis are Nephilim. The Americans we're supposed to imprison or kill the remaining Nazis, the scientists, the generals, the Colonel's etc instead they partnered with them, brought them to America and put them under the cover of darkness AKA deep state to work with fallen angels. To develop technology AI weaponize medicine, pharmakeia and other dark and evil things that would thrust us forward as a world leader and the most powerful. They have developed human genomes altered DNA status through forced vaccinations in hospitals, prisons and government and schools. The remnant that is rising is an enemy of the state and their job if you put us down which is impossible because if yahuah is for us who can be against us. and that is why they poison the food poison the water poison the air what's the American Church Gray fat and lazy.

Harvesting Generation--Wealth Transfer
Expanded Psalm 23

Adonai is my [good, good] Shepherd; I shall not want [any good thing]. He makes me to lie down [resting] in green pastures [full of money]: He leads me beside the still waters [of His Word, which run deep]. He restores my soul [my mind, will, emotions, imagination and thought life to be in conformity with His desires and plans for my life]: He leads me in the paths of righteousness [my right standing in and with Him] for His name's sake [His name is glorified when the world can see His blessings in and on me].

Yea, though I walk through the valley of the shadow of death [it's a valley of shadows and not a valley of death], I will fear no evil [for I have not been given a spirit of fear, but of power, of love and of a sound mind]: for YOU are with me [and will never leave or forsake me]; Your rod [the Word] and Your staff [the Ruach HaKodesh] they comfort me [as I walk in the reverential fear of Adonai and comfort of the Ruach Hakodesh].

You prepare a table [a banqueting table full of all good things] before me in the presence of my enemies [so my enemies can see that you are a good, good Elohim]: You anoint my head with oil [with the power of the Ruach Hakodesh and
Anointing of Yahusha]; my cup runs over [it overflows with blessings so that I may be a blessing to others].

Surely [without a doubt] goodness and mercy [and I receive both in abundance] will follow [and overtake] me all the days of my life [which shall be long upon the earth]: and I will dwell in the house of Adonai [in my mansions in Glory] for ever [and ever, unto the ages of the ages yet to come]. In Yahusha's Name. Amein.

[Scripture references: John 10:11, 14:23-24; Hab. 2:14; Acts 3:19; Rom. 5:17-18, 12:2; 2 Tim. 1:7; Matt. 28:20; Heb. 13:5; Acts 9:31; Song 2:4; Psa. 92:10; Luke 12:32; Deut. 28:1-2; Psa. 91:16; John 14:2-3; Rev. 22:1-5]

Lost in Translation

Reflecting on the ancient lives of Abraham, Isaac, and Jacob all the way back to Adam and Eve will empower us to return to the origin-al plan of Yahuah Elohim for mankind. What do I mean? As I was studying the WORD on a Shabbat day in November, I heard the Ruach say; " learn the ancient language for it will be a cover of protection in the future." DING!! Light bulb moment...YaH was revealing to me that as all things move forward in the prophetic we are in a sense; moving backward too. Since HE knows the END from the BEGINNING. We pray and ask "for the ancient path." The Natsarim seek it out and YaH gives insight to revelations.

Yahuah is releasing to HIS CHOSEN their land. **eretz = land (not earth).**

Jubilee's xxiii 26-32 (Sacred Texts Version)

26. And in those days the children will begin to study the laws,
And to seek the commandments,
And to return to the path of righteousness.
27. And the days will begin to grow many and increase amongst those children of men,
Till their days draw nigh to one thousand years,
And to a greater number of years than (before) was the number of the days.
28. And there will be no old man
Nor one who is not satisfied with his days,
For all will be (as) children and youths.
29. And all their days they will complete and live in peace and in joy,
And there will be no hasatan nor any evil destroyer;
For all their days will be days of blessing and healing,
30. And at that time the Yahuah will heal His servants,
And they will rise up and see great peace,
And drive out their adversaries.
And the righteous will see and be thankful,
And rejoice with joy for ever and ever,
And will see all their judgments and all their curses on their enemies.
31. And their bones will rest in the earth,

And their spirits will have much joy,
And they will know that it is Yahuah Elohim who executeth judgment,
And showeth mercy to hundreds and thousands and to all that love Him.
32. And do thou, Moses, write down these words; for thus are they written, and they record (them) on the heavenly tables for a testimony for the generations for ever.

MANNA PORTION

The manna had the following characteristics:
Small: Speaks of the humility of Christ.
Round : Speaks of the perfection of His life.
White : Speaks of the purity of His character.
Hoar frost-like : Speaks of the ability to impart life and energy.
Coriander seed-like: Speaks of the aromatic flavour given off when crushed, as in the Cross.
Herb like : Speaks of health to all who partake of it.
Fresh oil : Speaks of the anointing of the Holy Spirit.
Like honey: Speaks of the sweetness of the Word of God.
Like bdellium (white pearl) : Speaks of the pearl of great price, and the gates of the Eternal City.

The spirit is king; the soul is a servant to the spirit; and the body is a slave to the soul.

Have this attitude in yourselves, which also was in Messiah Yeshua, Philippians 2:5
Otiot= Sacred Signs
There are a number of elements to each of the 22 characters:
– the name of the character;
– what the name of the character means;
– the visual of the character;
– the function of the character;

Anti Semitism is hasatan's survival plan. Unknowing victims are eating from the table of demons, feasting on hate, wickedness, pride, jealousy, anger, rage, ...
Preparation for Tribulation is not just physical but also spiritual. I have been speaking of this often throughout this book, it is imperative that you listen now!!!
 I understand that it is a challenge in discarding much of the lies of Christianity because most have become dogmatically fused in one's mind. I believe thus far until Yahuah reveals to me differently, that The Mark of the Beast" is a literal mark and a spiritual mark

that is what one has ingrained in One's Own Mind. Literal because those that belong to hasatan will wear it to buy and sell. It is hasatans branding mankind.

 ABBA, told me a year ago that HE was going to turn the pyramids upside down. I have spent the last year praying and seeking what the pyramid represented. Now, I have understanding. If you believe your **"church"** , **"denomination"** or **"religion"** is **"called out"** but is under the registry of the agency of the powers-that-be **(the government securities)** , and have a **"pyramid hierarchical structure";** your church is not really **"called out"** .It is not a **"congregation"** or **"assembly"** of Yahushua, rather a pyramid hierarchical structure, which controls or enslaved the people below, or what the Revelations call "Nicolaitans Rev 2:6 , 16 ". That is why it is called **"church"** , a departure from the "Old Testament congregation or assembly".

Nicolaitans = "destruction of people"
1) a sect mentioned in Rev_2:6,Rev_2:15
There are congregations of Yahushua inside these churches. Some are perhaps innocent, and some just wanted to hang in there because of the fellowship or something else. Meaning the whole world is not aware, it is ruled by one power, it is already in a **"New World Order"** , in other words, the whole world is deceived. If you come to this realization, then you would know what it means to **"come out of her"** when you, yourself, are already out of **"her"** . For then, you shall begin to see things in a new light, and shall see things of her, that you would not see when you are still with her. But the powers-that-be, the agents of the hasatan, have changed the translation of the word **"ekklesia"** from **"congregation"** or **"assembly"** to the word **"church"** , so that it would be easy for them to gain control and divide the **"congregation"** .
I know that throughout this book I repeat things often. It is only because as each page, topic and word given is being given by the Ruach Hakodesh in the order I have been led to place them. Brothers and Sisters, this manual will be a necessary tool for tribulation! We have little time left to work and prepare. ABBA, is still waking people up thus adding to the number of the remnant. YaH is patient and HE forces NO ONE to come to HIM exercising their YaH given free will.
Believer's will be classified as **lethal and a harmful dis-ease to the NWO!**
*Yahusha said to him, "I am the Way (**follow His example**) , and the Truth (**He lived by the Torah, preached and taught it**) , and the Life (**believe that He is the root of David, Rev 5:5 , 22:16 , traced to Adam son of Elohim, He is 100% human, 1Jn 5:6-10 , see: The Spirit of Prophecy He is not YHWH who became a man, that is a doctrine of incarnation, emanation, virgin birth, original sin and trinity inserted in the Gospels**) . No one comes to the Father except through Me (by following His example, for He is a man, 100% human, we have no excuse, however, the decrees of the Torah have been covered by grace because of His blood for all who believe and obey; but if we nail the*

130

Torah to the cross of Jesus Christ, so will grace be removed to cover us, let us not be fooled). (John 14:6 The Scriptures 1998+)

Pray to be found worthy of the test. This will be the test of all tests in that last hour. Yahusha in the garden of Gethsemane weeping and crying out to The Father; and like HIM we must pray and cry out--parallels the WORD; where we are weak; HE is strong!

Underground Railroad is Activated

On or before certain events listed below occur....

*When you see the abomination that makes desolation----will activate all over the world YaH's Underground railroad to protect HIS elect.

"So when you see the 'abomination that lays waste, spoken of by Dani'ĕl the prophet, set up in the set-apart place" – he who reads, let him understand –"then let those who are in Yehudah flee to the mountains." **Matthew 24:15,16**

Believer's went underground during the persecutions in Rome. They literally lived in the vast network of catacombs beneath the city of Rome. Visitors to Rome today can visit the places where they lived, including large cavernous rooms where they met for worship and prayer, and hundreds of tombs carved into the sides of the tunnels for those who died during this time.

Tribes of "underground" believers during the Tribulation Period will no doubt form their own alliances for survival, including sharing of resources, bartering, and standing guard for one another. They may well have the use of the Internet, satellite communication, and other high tech methods in their struggle. According to Revelation 12, which records the cosmic drama of Israel and the Dragon, Antichrist will be thwarted in his attempt to capture the fleeing remnant of Israel and will be enraged at "the rest of her offspring" who are described as true believers in Yahusha (Revelation 12:14-17). We the Natsarim aka underground followers of Yahusha; during The Tribulation period will receive special divine guidance and help to flee, because it will be protected by Yahuah. Many have already been instructed to build these places of refuge, as I have. The Nation of Natsarim will come together as I have shared earlier as in the book of Acts but even greater in love and fellowship.

Some of the Natsarim will become martyr's. That is just a fact. Yahuah will give us boldness as nothing we have ever experienced before to stand and be found worthy in the end. The Greek word "martyr" actually means "witness" or "one who gives a testimony.

"And in the latter days it shall be that the mountain of the House of יהוה is established on the top of the mountains, and shall be exalted above the hills. And peoples shall flow to it.

And many nations shall come and say, "Come, and let us go up to the mountain of יהוה, to the House of the Elohim of Ya'aqoḇ, and let Him teach us His ways, and let us walk in His paths. For out of Tsiyon comes forth the Torah, and the word of יהוה from Yerushalayim." **Micah 4:1-2**

Era of Evil--Demons of Death

And He said to them, "When I sent you without a purse and bag and sandals, did you lack any?" And they said, "None at all." And He said to them, "But now, let him who has a purse take it, likewise also a bag. And let him who has no sword sell his garment and buy one. "For I say to you that what has been written has yet to be accomplished in Me, 'And He was reckoned with lawless ones.' For that which refers to Me has an end to.",and they said, "Master, look, here are two swords." But He said to them, "That is enough!" **Luke 22: 35-38**

And take heed to yourselves, lest your hearts be weighed down by gluttony, and drunkenness, and worries of this life, and that day come on you suddenly. "For it shall come as a snare on all those dwelling on the face of all the earth. "Watch then at all times, and pray that you be counted worthy to escape all this about to take place, and to stand before the Son of Aḏam." **Luke 21:34-36**

And coming to the place, He said to them, "Pray that you do not enter into trial." **Luke 22:40**

And there shall be signs in the sun, and moon, and stars, and on the earth anxiety of nations, in bewilderment at the roaring of the sea, and agitation, men fainting from fear and the expectation of what is coming on the earth, for the powers of the heavens shall be shaken. "And then they shall see the Son of Aḏam coming in a cloud with power and much esteem. "And when these *matters* begin to take place, look up and lift up your heads, because your redemption draws near." **Luke 21:25-28**

And they shall fall by the edge of the sword, and be led away captive into all nations. And Yerushalayim shall be trampled underfoot by the gentile until the times of the gentiles are filled. **Luke 21:24**

And He said, "See that you are not led astray, for many shall come in My Name, saying, 'I am,' and, 'The time is near.' Then do not go after them. "But when you hear of fighting and unrests, do not be alarmed, for these have to take place first, but the end is not immediately." Then He said to them, "Nation shall rise against nation, and reign against reign. "And there shall be great earthquakes in various places, and scarcities of food and deadly diseases. And there shall be horrors, and great signs from heaven. "But before all this, they shall lay their hands on you and persecute you, delivering you up to the congregations and prisons, and be brought before sovereigns and rulers for My Name's sake. "And it shall turn out to you for a witness. "Therefore, resolve in your hearts not to premeditate on what to answer. "For I shall give you a mouth and wisdom which all your adversaries shall not be able to refute or resist. "And you shall also be betrayed by parents and brothers and relatives and friends. And some of you shall be put to death. "And you shall be hated by all because of My Name. "But not a hair of your head shall be lost at all. "Possess your lives by your endurance! **Luke 21:8-19**

"While you have the light, believe in the light, so that you become sons of light." These *words* יהושע spoke, and went off and were hidden from them. **John 12:36**

"These *words* I have spoken to you, so that you do not stumble. "They shall put you out of the congregations, but an hour is coming when everyone who kills you shall think he is rendering service to Elohim. "And this they shall do to you because they did not know the Father, nor Me. "But I have said these *words* to you, so that when the hour comes you remember that I told them to you. And these *words* I did not say to you at the beginning, for I was with you. **John 16: 1-4**

And who is the one doing evil to you, if you become imitators of the good? But even if you suffer for righteousness' sake, you are blessed. "And do not fear their threats, neither be troubled." But set apart יהוה Elohim in your hearts, and always be ready to give an answer to everyone asking you a reason concerning the expectation that is in you, with meekness and fear, having a good conscience, so that when they speak against you as doers of evil, those who falsely accuse your good behaviour in Messiah, shall be ashamed. For it is better, if it is the desire of Elohim, to suffer for doing good than for doing evil. **1 Peter 3: 13-17**

In the same way, husbands live understandingly together, giving respect to the wife, as to the weaker vessel, and as being heirs together of the favour of life, so that your prayers are not hindered. To sum up, let all of you be like-minded, sympathetic, loving as brothers, tenderhearted, humble-minded, not returning evil for evil or reviling for reviling, but on the contrary blessing, knowing that you were called to this, in order to inherit a blessing. For "He who wishes to love life and see good days, let him keep his tongue from evil, and his lips from speaking deceit, let him turn away from evil and do good, let him seek peace and pursue it. **1 Peter 3: 7-11**

Integrity of the heart on every matter. Whatever you believe is a small matter of sin, is the exact opposite in heaven and hell.

Meditate on the following---have you repented for every single thing??

But as for the cowardly, and untrustworthy, and abominable, and murderers, and those who whore, and drug sorcerers, and idolaters, and all the false, their part is in the lake which burns with fire and sulphur, which is the second death." Revelation 21:8
**Look to JOB=Tribulation and Hour of Testing and Temptation
JOB 22: 21-30**

Reconcile now with Him and have *shalom* — in this way prosperity will come to you.

Accept instruction from His mouth and store up His words in your heart. If you return to

Shaddai, you will be restored; if you remove iniquity far from your tent and throw your gold in the dust, and the gold of Ophir to the rocks in the wadis, then *Shaddai* will be your gold and your precious silver. Surely then *Shaddai* will be your delight and you will lift up your face to God. You will pray to Him and He will hear you, and you will fulfill your vows. What you decide will be done, and light will shine on your ways. When people are brought low, and you say, 'Lift them up!' then He will save the downcast. He will deliver even one who is not innocent, who will be delivered by the cleanness of your hands."

Are you ready?

VISION = SEE= WATCH= SPEAK AND SEE! SEE WHAT YOU SPEAK!

20= KAPH --Pictograph= OPEN PALM

To Bend, to Allow, to Open

To Tame or Sundue

The WORK of YAHUSHA

The Filling of the Ruach

The Year of the Appointed Time- Visions

chazah: see, behold

Original Word: חָזָה

Part of Speech: Verb

Transliteration: chazah

Phonetic Spelling: (khaw-zaw')

Definition: se e, behold

Appointed time, place, and season. Valley of Vision Isaiah 22

Yesha'yahu (Isaiah) 61:1-3

THE RUACH ADONAI YAHUAH is upon me; because YAHUAH has anointed me to preach the Besorah unto the meek; he has sent me to bind up the brokenhearted, to proclaim liberty to the captives, and the opening of the prison to them that are bound; 2 To proclaim the acceptable year of YAHUAH, and the day of vengeance of our ELOHIYM; to comfort all that mourn; 3 To appoint unto them that mourn in Tsiyon, to give unto them beauty for ashes, the oil of joy for mourning, the garment of praise for the ruach of heaviness; that they might be called oaks of righteousness, the planting of YAHUAH, that he might be glorified.

YAHUAH is GLORIFIED in HIS CREATION
- The Atom: the atom consists of three parts, protons, neutrons, and electrons.
- Matter: Solid, liquid, and gas.
- Space: Length, width, and depth.
- Time: Is threefold, past, present, and future.
- People: All people come from one of three extractions, Mongoloid, Negroid, and Caucasian.

- The flesh: has three layers of skin; the epidermis, the dermis, and the subcutaneous tissue.
- Family: The family consists of a man, woman, and children.
- The sun emits three types of rays alpha, beta, and gamma. These rays are classified as light, heat and actinic rays. The sun emits light rays that can be seen but not felt, heat rays which can be felt yet not seen and actinic rays which can not be seen or felt.
- The actinic rays (those which can't be seen or felt) picture Yahuah our Father.
- The light rays which can be seen but not felt picture Yahusha; the Word of YaH showing up in human form.
- The chemical rays that can be felt yet not seen picture Yahuah the Ruach HaKodesh.
- There are three basic elements in the soil which cause plants to grow; nitrogen, phosphorus and potash.
- Colors: There are three primary color pigments from which all other colors are derived, red, yellow and blue.
- Blood: solids consist of three main cells, platelets, red cells, and white cells.
- Human capability is thought, word and deed.

Even the most basic forms of life reflect our triune Maker, basic cell structure; true wall, plasma membrane, and nuclear membrane. All are inextricably intertwined and interdependent.

The apostle Paul likened the believer to Yahuah's **Temple ,** (1 Cor.3:16 & 6:19) which was divided into three parts; the Holy of Holies, the Holy place, and the outer court, thus once again providing a striking resemblance to man's spirit, soul, and body. The priority and order are obvious, spirit, soul, and body…not body, soul, and spirit.

Courtesy: perfectingofthesaints.org

Our flesh manifests its nature through rebellion and a self-centered life. The flesh is enmity with the spirit. Our flesh is the by-product of a fallen state (i.e. sin) When one is born into the physical realm wearing our established fleshly nature, we are in a fallen state therefore full of sin (darkness) . It is crucial to spiritual growth that the believer is able to **discern** that which stems from the spirit or soul from that which emanates from his flesh.

Fellowship with Yahuah Elohim intensifies the magnetic pull of the spirit and stifles the influence of the body. Conversely, fellowship with the world coupled with neglect of YaH and His Word strengthens the flesh, grieving and quenching the indwelling Ruach HaKodesh.

When the soul is yielded to the YaH's influence (the Ruach HaKodesh) working through the believer's spirit, he is said to be **"walking in the Ruach/Spirit".**

FALLEN ANGEL SPIRITS/ NEPHILIM/ AI

The human race has already been infiltrated. Some people (Deep State/ Wicked people) who did not have the indwelling of the Ruach HaKodesh, have had their minds and bodies taken over by these dark spirits (Nephilim), These people are no longer active within their body, they have given themselves over to these Nephilim. The same is true for the reptilians--there are people possessed by "unclean spirits" whose eyes/ears/noses shift from human to reptile. They are completely taken over. Many times it is a "free will" offering how they become possessed. Next, I want to mention AI- as I have stated previously in this book, AI will become merged with human flesh. I believe it already has! It will be sold to the public under the description of "upgrade your life-be better than your best human self by merging with AI to give you superhuman qualities!" They will also claim it to be for the better of mankind/humankind and claim it will save lives, cure the incurable dis-eases. Change your reality to what you desire.

Everything will point to self satisfaction, self-gratification, selfish pride, self-serving, I, me and what YOU WANT YOU CAN HAVE. STAY ALERT NATSARIM! PAY ATTENTION! ABBA, is giving us greater levels of discernment than ever! ALL you need to do when confronted with one of the above is pray and rebuke it in Yahusha's Name!

Second Book of Hermas- YAHUAH's COMMANDS
Command 1- Believe in ONE ALAHYIM
Command 2- Avoid Detraction- Do Alms- Deeds with Simplicity
Command 3- Seek Truth- Avoid Lying
Command 4- Put Away One's Wife
Command 5- Be Patient and Long Suffering
Command 6- Every man has Two Angels--Angel of Righteousness/ Angel of Iniquity
Command 7- FEAR YAHUAH/ NOT hasatan
Command 8- Flee from Evil/ DO GOOD
Command 9- Ask of YAHUAH daily and without doubting
Command 10- DO NOT grieve the RUACH
Command 11- Spirits and Prophets are to be tried by their works and of two or threefold spirit.
Command 12- The Commands of YAH are NOT impossible/ hasatan is NOT to be feared by them that believe

KEY FOR SURVIVAL IN THE END OF DAYS
Purify your heart from doubting and put on emunah and trust in YAHUAH and thou shall receive all you shall ask.
Desire RIGHTEOUSNESS armed with the FEAR OF YAH!
THE HOUSE OF YASHRAEL, THE NATSARIM WE OBEY YAH WITH A PURE HEART; WE LOVE YAHUAH AND YAHUSHA; WE AND OUR CHILDREN AND GRANDCHILDREN WALK IN YAH'S COMMANDS!
ЧА ﮑ-ﮑﮯﻮ- Mish'pahah

The ancient walled city of the Bible had the most in common with the modern city. It was most often a center of apostasy, a base for imperialism, a treasure trove for plundering tyrants, a monument to human pride, vainglory and rebellion against God... The city provides no ideal for culture since it is opposed to biblical culture. Like Babel, the prototype, it has been erected in defiance of God's design for a decentralized agrarian civilization." Howard King- "A Christian-Agrarian Critique of Technological Society"

Time, Place, Proximity, Mutual Concerns, and Mutual Kindness

By time, I mean years. The more the better. Generations are best.

By place, I mean a home where a family lives, on a section of land that the family has, over time (maybe even generations) cared for and grown to love. Proximity is the state or quality of being near. A new kind of community has emerged in recent years with the advent of the internet. Such a community can be good. But it can never be the best form of community because there is little proximity. Virtual proximity just isn't the same as physical proximity and never will be. Mutual concerns arise out of a mutual worldview. Worldview boils down to fundamental ideas about what is right and wrong, good and bad. Worldview is at the root of religious belief. Generally speaking, rural folks share similar belief systems. They may not all agree on religious doctrines but they think alike on many core issues. One example of this becomes clear during a national election when the rural areas of the nation typically vote the same (i.e., the "red states"). Mutual kindness is when people in the community interact by speaking, visiting, working, caring, sharing, and giving to each other in some way, to some degree, preferably on a daily basis. This kind of best community was once the norm in most rural areas of America. It was also found in small rural towns and villages. But as agrarian culture has given way to modern, industrialized culture, the social fabric of rural communities has become more and more threadbare.

YAHUAH TzEVAOT
ADONAI YAHUSHAHaMaShiach
RUACH ha'QODOSH

SEVEN FOLD DOCTRINE

RUACH EMUNAH - The Ruach of Faith
RUACH CHOKMAH - The Ruach of Wisdom
RUACH NETSACH - The Ruach of Longsuffering
RUACH CHECED - The Ruach of Mercy
RUACH MISHPAT - The Ruach of Judgment
RUACH SHALOM - The Ruach of Peace
RUACH RAHTSON - The Ruach of Benevolence

SEVEN RUACHOTH OF YAH

RUACH YAHUAH - The Ruach of YAHUAH
RUACH CHOKMAH - The Ruach of Wisdom
RUACH BIYNAH - The Ruach of Understanding
RUACH ETSAH - The Ruach of Counsel
RUACH GEVURAH - The Ruach of Strength
RUACH DA'ATH - The Ruach of Knowledge
RUACH YIR'AH - The Ruach of the Fear of YAHUAH

Chanok (Enoch) 62:2-4
YAHUAH TSEVA'OTH sat upon the throne of his glory. 3 And the RUACH TSEDAQAH was poured out over him. The word of his mouth shall destroy all the sinners and all the wicked, who shall perish at his presence.
Yesha`yahu (Isaiah) 11:2-5
And the RUACH YAHUAH shall rest upon him, the RUACH CHOKMAH and BIYNAH, the RUACH ETSAH and GEVURAH, the RUACH DA'ATH and of the YIR'AH of YAHUAH; 3 And shall make him of quick understanding in the fear of YAHUAH: and he shall not judge after the sight of his eyes, neither reprove after the hearing of his ears: 4 But with righteousness shall he judge the poor, and reprove with equity for the meek of the earth: and he shall smite the earth with the rod of his mouth, and with the breath of his lips shall he slay the wicked. 5 And righteousness shall be the belt of his loins, and faithfulness the belt of his reins.

Compare these SEVEN RUACHOTH with the seven days of Creation.

Chanok (Enoch)	Yesha`yahu (Isaiah)	Verses
RUACH RAHTSON	RUACH YAHUAH	Bere'shiyth 1:2-3
RUACH CHOKMAH	RUACH CHOKMAH	Bere'shiyth 1:3-5 (1 st day)
RUACH NETSACH	RUACH BIYNAH	Bere'shiyth 1:6-8 (2 nd day)
RUACH SHALOM	RUACH ETSAH	Bere'shiyth 1:9-13 (3 rd day)

RUACH MISHPAT	RUACH GEVURAH	Bere'shiyth 1:14-19 (4 th day)
RUACH CHECED	RUACH DA'ATH	Bere'shiyth 1:20-23 (5 th day)
RUACH EMUNAH	RUACH YIR'AH	Bere'shiyth 1:24-31 (6 th day)

Chizayon (Revelation) 1:19-20
Write the things אֶת eth which you have seen, and the things which are, and the things which shall be hereafter; 20 The mystery of the seven stars which you saw in my right hand, and the seven golden menoroth. The seven stars are the angels of the seven called out assemblies: and the seven menoroth which you saw are the seven called out assemblies.

The Ancient Agrarian Principles of Agriculture

Agrarian: *a·grar·i·an - adjective 1. pro-farmer: promoting the interests of farmers, especially by seeking a more equitable basis of land ownership an agrarian political party 2. of rural life: dominated by or relating to farming or rural life 3. of land: relating to land, especially its ownership and cultivation noun (plural a·grar·i·ans) land reformer: somebody, often a member of an agrarian political movement, who believes in the fair distribution of land, especially the redistribution of large amounts of land owned by the rich < agr- "field, land"] -a·grar·i·an·ism, noun*

1 – **Earth Ownership Principle:** The earth is the Yahuah's and all that it contains.
2 – **First Farmer Principle:** YAH is the First Farmer, the author and initiator of agriculture.

3 – **First Farmer Relationship Principle:** Those who practice agriculture need to have a good relationship with the First Farmer.

4 – **High Calling Principle:** Those who practice agriculture have a high calling from YAH, which is full of dignity and purpose.

5 – **Sacred Work Principle:** Those who practice agriculture should strive to honor and glorify YAH through their work.

6 – **Dominion Principle:** Farmers are commanded by YAH to have dominion over the creation.

7 – **Bounty Principle:** Farmers are commanded by YAH to be fruitful and produce bounty from the land and animals that God has entrusted to them.

8 – **Stewardship Principle:** Farmers are commanded by YAH to steward the land, natural resources, farm animals and crops that He has placed in their care.

9 – **Diversity Principle:** Yahuah delights in the diversity of his creation and farmers should strive to encourage and maintain the diversity that He created.

10 – **Neighborly Love Principle:** Those who practice agriculture should treat their neighbors as they would wish to be treated themselves.

The application of these principles will not be easy. That said, the apostle Paul's words ring true for us when he commands us to not be conformed to this world, but to be transformed by the renewing of our minds, that we may prove what is the good, acceptable and perfect will of Yahuah.

WORDS RELATED TO AGRARIAN

rural, agricultural , natural , peasant , rustic , <u>uncultivated</u> , undomesticated HUS'BANDRY , n. The business of a farmer, comprehending agriculture or tillage of the ground, the raising , managing and fattening of cattle and other domestic animals, the management of the dairy and whatever the land produces.

1. Frugality; domestic economy; good management; thrift. But in this sense we generally prefix good; as good husbandry.
2. Care of domestic affairs.

Ancient Way of Life Common Union of the CommUnity of Natsarim
Common Life
Mornings Belong to YAH-RISE UP to WARship...
Sound off -Lift your arms, shout for joy, give HIM GLORY & PRAISE HIM then call FIRE down from the shamayim.
The Two Paths or The Two Trees
It says of the Common Union and of the end of days; keep the unity of the spirit in the bond of shalom, be renewed in the spirit of our mind. We renew our minds by eating the WORD daily; it is our nourishment. Do NOT grieve the Ruach Hakodesh in any way. We are sealed by the Ruach HaKodesh intoCommon Life
Common Prayer- Common Praise- Common Scripture Studies.The essence of the community of spirit is truth, light and love.
Weekly Rhythm

Monthly Rhythm
Annual Rhythm
Time- Treasure---Talent
What am I doing with the time given me?
What do I place value on or in?
What is my YAH given talent?
Am I using it to HIS GLORY?
Know your identity and talents before coming into the Tribe.
Founders are usually visionaries who need gifted managers to carry out the vision.
The Situation Room-
Place and time set aside to discuss prophecy/end of days/scripture studies/job assignments/gift assignments/ order and structure YaH requires/ Personal issues or emotions/deliverance ministry/ threats from NWO
The Upper Room-
Place for intimacy with YAH, one on one prayer and communing with The Most High.
The LIVING Room-
Place to gather for worship and WARship Psalms, Prayer, Spiritual Warfare, Scripture Reading & Studies
OBEDIENT IN HIS CREATION
The melody of YAH's heart can be heard amidst all of HIS created things. Innocence and unperverted it once was. It will again be pure after it is brought through the fire of purification. All unholiness must be seared off. The rebirth welcomed after the pain. I pray, 'YAH strengthen me today to walk into the fire, so I may emerge clean and pure before you Master."

Rod and staff comfort me- ---like herding--staying faithfully in YAH's borders YAH's discipline is protection of HIS people.

fam·ine *noun* \'fa-mən\ : extreme and protracted shortage of food, resulting in widespread hunger and a substantial increase in the death rate

geno·cide *noun* \'je-nə-ˌsīd\ : the deliberate and systematic destruction of a racial, political, or cultural group
War time--YaH is positioning HIS people to organise them into camps during the wars.

TEHILLIM FOR THE END DAYS
WARSHIP & PRAYS
PSALMS FOR THE END of Days

4-

1 Answer me when I call, O Elohim of my righteousness! You gave relief to me when I was in distress; Show favour to me, and hear my prayer.

2 Till when, O you sons of men, Would you turn my esteem to shame, Would you love emptiness, seek falsehood? Selah.

3 But know that יהוה has separated a kind one for Himself; יהוה hears when I call to Him.

4 Tremble, and do not sin. Speak within your heart on your bed, and be still. Selah.

5 Offer slaughterings of righteousness, And trust in יהוה.

6 Many are saying, "Who would show us good?" יהוה, lift up the light of Your face upon us.

7 You have put more gladness in my heart, Than in the season that their grain and wine increased.

8 I lie down in peace altogether, and sleep; For You alone, O יהוה, make me dwell in safety.

5

1 Give ear to my words, O יהוה, Consider my meditation.

2 Attend to the voice of my cry, My Sovereign and my Elohim, For unto You I pray.

3 O יהוה, in the morning You hear my voice; I present myself to You in the morning, And I look up.

4 For You are not an Ěl taking delight in wrong, Nor does evil dwell with You.

5 The boasters do not stand before Your eyes; You hate all workers of wickedness.

6 You destroy those speaking falsehood; יהוה loathes a man of blood and deceit.

7 But I, I enter Your house In the greatness of Your kindness; I bow myself toward Your set-apart Hěk̲al in Your fear.

8 O יהוה, lead me in Your righteousness because of those watching me; Make Your way straight before my face.

9 For there is no stability in their mouth; Their inward part is destruction; Their throat is an open grave; They flatter with their tongue.

10 Declare them guilty, O Elohim! Let them fall by their own counsels; Thrust them away for their many transgressions, Because they have rebelled against You.

11 But let all who take refuge in You rejoice; Let them ever shout for joy, because You shelter them; And let those who love Your Name exult in You.

12 For You bless the righteous, O יהוה; You surround him with favour as with a shield.

6

1 O יהוה, do not rebuke me in Your displeasure, Nor discipline me in Your wrath.

2 Show favour to me, O יהוה, for I am fading away; O יהוה, heal me, for my bones have been troubled.

3 And my being has been greatly troubled; And You, O יהוה – till when?

4 Return, O יהוה, rescue my life! Oh, save me for Your kindness' sake!

5 For in death there is no remembrance of You; Who gives You thanks in the grave?

6 I have grown weary with my groaning; Every night I flood my bed; I drench my couch with my tears.

7 My eye has grown dim because of grief; It grows old because of all my adversaries.

8 Depart from me, all you workers of wickedness; For יהוה has heard the voice of my weeping.

9 יהוה has heard my pleading; יהוה receives my prayer.

10 Let all my enemies be ashamed and greatly troubled; They turn back suddenly, ashamed.

8

1 O יהוה, our Master, how excellent is Your Name in all the earth, You who set Your splendour above the heavens!

2 Out of the mouth of babes and infants You have founded strength, Because of Your adversaries, To put an end to enemy and avenger.

3 For I see Your heavens, the work of Your fingers, The moon and the stars, which You have established.

4 What is man that You remember him? And the son of man that You visit him?

5 Yet You have made him a little less than Elohim, And have crowned him with esteem and splendour.

6 You made him rule over the works of Your hands; You have put all under his feet,

7 All sheep and oxen, And also the beasts of the field,

8 The birds of the heavens, And the fish of the sea, Passing through the paths of the seas.

9 O יהוה, our Master, How excellent is Your Name in all the earth!

9

1 I praise You, O יהוה, with all my heart; I declare all Your wonders.

2 I rejoice and exult in You; I sing praise to Your Name, O Most High.

3 When my enemies turn back, They stumble and perish before You.

4 For You executed my right and my cause, You sat on the throne judging in righteousness.

5 You have rebuked the gentiles, You have destroyed the wrong, You have wiped out their name forever and ever.

6 The enemy is no more – ruins everlasting! And You have uprooted the cities; Even their remembrance has perished.

7 But יהוה abides forever, He is preparing His throne for judgment.

8 And He judges the world in righteousness, He judges the peoples in straightness.

9 And יהוה is a refuge for the crushed one, A refuge in times of distress.

10 And those who know Your Name trust in You, For You have not forsaken those who seek You, O יהוה.

11 Sing praises to יהוה, who dwells in Tsiyon! Declare His deeds among the peoples.

12 For He remembers the seekers of bloodshed, He does not forget the cry of the afflicted.

13 Show favour to me, O יהוה! See my affliction by those who hate me, You who lift me up from the gates of death,

14 So that I declare all Your praise In the gates of the daughter of Tsiyon. I rejoice in Your deliverance.

15 The gentiles have sunk down in the pit which they made; In the net which they hid, their own foot is caught.

16 יהוה has made Himself known, He has done right-ruling; The wrong is snared in the work of his own hands. Meditation. Selah.

17 The wrong return to the grave, All the gentiles that forget Elohim.

18 For the needy is not always forgotten; Neither the expectancy of the poor lost forever.

19 Arise, O יהוה, Do not let man prevail; Let the gentiles be judged before Your face.

20 Put them in fear, O יהוה, Let the gentiles know they are *but* men. Selah.

11

1 In יהוה I have taken refuge; Why do you say to me, "Flee to your mountain like a bird"?

2 For look! The wrong bend a bow, They set their arrow on the string, To shoot in darkness at the upright in heart.

3 When the foundations are destroyed, What shall the righteous do?

4 יהוה is in His set-apart Hĕḵal, The throne of יהוה is in the heavens. His eyes see, His eyelids examine the sons of men.

5 יהוה tries the righteous, But His being shall hate the wrong And the one who loves violence.

6 Upon the wrong He rains snares, Fire and sulphur and a scorching wind Are the portion of their cup.

7 For יהוה is righteous, He has loved righteousness; The upright shall see His face.

12

1 Save, יהוה, for the kind one is no more! For the trustworthy have ceased from among the sons of men.

2 They speak falsehood with each other; They speak *with* flattering lips, a double heart.

3 יהוה does cut off all flattering lips, A tongue that speaks swelling words,

4 Who have said, "With our tongue we do mightily; Our lips are our own; Who is master over us?"

5 "Because of the oppression of the poor, because of the sighing of the needy, I now arise," says יהוה, "I set in safety – he pants for it."

6 The Words of יהוה are clean Words, Silver tried in a furnace of earth, Refined seven times a .

7 You guard them, O יהוה, You preserve them from this generation forever.

8 The wrong walk around on every side, When worthlessness is exalted among the sons of men.

13

1 How long would You forget me, O יהוה? Forever? How long would You hide Your face from me?

2 How long would I take counsel in my being, Grief in my heart day by day? How long would my enemy be exalted over me?

3 Look! Answer me, O יהוה my Elohim; Enlighten my eyes, Lest I sleep in death;

4 Lest my enemy say, "I have prevailed against him," *Lest* my adversaries rejoice when I am moved.

5 But I have trusted in Your kindness; My heart rejoices in Your deliverance.

6 I sing to יהוה, Because He has been good to me.

14

1 The fool has said in his heart, "There is no יהוה." They have done corruptly, They have done an abominable deed, There is no one who does good.

2 יהוה looked down from the heavens on the sons of mankind, To see if there is a wise one, seeking יהוה.

3 They have all turned aside, They have together become filthy; No one is doing good, not even one.

4 Have all the workers of wickedness no knowledge, Who eat up my people as they eat bread, And do not call on יהוה?

5 There they are in great fear, For יהוה is with the generation of the righteous.

6 You would put to shame the counsel of the poor, But יהוה is his refuge.

7 O that the deliverance of Yisra'ĕl Would be given out of Tsiyon! When יהוה turns back the captivity of His people, Let Ya'aqoḇ rejoice, let Yisra'ĕl be glad.

18

1 I love You, O יהוה, My strength.

2 יהוה is my rock and my stronghold and my deliverer; My Ěl is my rock, I take refuge in Him; My shield and the horn of my deliverance, my high tower.

3 I call upon יהוה, the One to be praised, And I am saved from my enemies.

4 The cords of death surrounded me, And the floods of Beliya'al made me afraid.

5 The cords of the grave were all around me; The snares of death were before me.

6 In my distress I called upon יהוה, And to my Elohim I cried; He heard my voice from His Hěḵal, And my cry went before Him, into His ears.

7 And the earth shook and trembled; Even the foundations of the mountains were troubled And they shook, because He was wroth.

8 Smoke went up from His nostrils, And consuming fire from His mouth; Coals were kindled by it.

9 And He bowed the heavens and came down, And thick darkness was under His feet.

10 And He rode upon a keruḇ, and flew; He flew upon the wings of the wind.

11 He made darkness His covering; Around Him His booth, Darkness of waters, thick clouds of the skies.

12 From the brightness before Him, His thick clouds passed, hail and coals of fire.

13 And יהוה thundered in the heavens, And the Most High sent forth His voice, Hail and coals of fire.

14 And He sent out His arrows and scattered them, And much lightning, and confused them.

15 And the channels of waters were seen, And the foundations of the world were uncovered At Your rebuke, O יהוה, At the blast of the breath of Your nostrils.

16 He sent from above, He took me; He drew me out of many waters.

17 He delivered me from my strong enemy, And from those hating me, For they were stronger than I.

18 They confronted me in the day of my calamity, But יהוה was my support.

19 And He brought me out into a large place; He delivered me for He delighted in me.

20 יהוה rewarded me according to my righteousness; According to the cleanness of my hands He repaid me.

21 For I have guarded the ways of יהוה, And have not acted wrongly against my Elohim.

22 For all His right-rulings are before me, And I did not turn from His laws.

23 And I am perfect before Him, And I guard myself from my crookedness.

24 And יהוה repays me according to my righteousness, According to the cleanness of my hands before His eyes.

25 With the kind You show Yourself kind; With the perfect one You show Yourself perfect;

26 With the clean You show Yourself clean; And with the crooked You show Yourself twisted.

27 For You save the afflicted people, But bring down those whose eyes are haughty.

28 For You Yourself light my lamp; יהוה my Elohim makes my darkness light.

29 For with You I run against a band, And with my Elohim I leap over a wall.

30 The Ĕl – His way is perfect; The Word of יהוה is proven a ; He is a shield to all who take refuge in Him.

31 For who is Eloah, besides יהוה? And who is a rock, except our Elohim?

32 It is Ĕl who girds me with strength, And makes my way perfect,

33 Making my feet like the feet of deer, And sets me on my high places,

34 Teaching my hands for battle, So that my arms shall bend a bow of bronze.

35 And You give me the shield of Your deliverance; And Your right hand supports me, And Your lowliness makes me great.

36 You enlarge my step under me; And my feet shall not slip.

37 I pursue my enemies and overtake them; And do not turn back till they are destroyed.

3 8 I crush them, and they are unable to rise; They fall under my feet.

39 And You gird me with strength for battle; Cause my adversaries to bow under me.

40 And You have made my enemies turn their backs, As for those hating me, I cut them off.

41 They cry – but no one is there to save, To יהוה – but He answers them not.

42 And I beat them as dust before the wind; I empty them out like dirt in the streets.

43 You deliver me from the strivings of the people, You set me at the head of the nations; A people I have not known serve me.

44 As soon as they hear of me they obey me; The foreigners submit to me.

45 The foreigners fade away, And come frightened from their strongholds.

46 יהוה lives! And blessed is my Rock! And exalted is the Elohim of my deliverance,

47 The Ĕl who avenges me, And He humbles the peoples under me;

48 My deliverer from my enemies. You lift me up above those who rise against me; You deliver me from a man of violence.

49 Therefore I give thanks to You, O יהוה, among nations, And I sing praise to Your Name,

50 Making great the deliverance of His sovereign, And showing kindness to His anointed,

To Dawiḏ and his seed, forever.

19

1 The heavens are proclaiming the esteem of Ĕl; And the expanse is declaring the work of His hand.

2 Day to day pours forth speech, And night to night reveals knowledge.

3 There is no speech, and there are no words, Their voice is not heard.

4 Their line has gone out through all the earth, And their words to the end of the world. In them He set up a tent for the sun,

5 And it is like a bridegroom coming out of his room, It rejoices like a strong man to run the path.

6 Its rising is from one end of the heavens, And its circuit to the other end; And naught is hidden from its heat.

7 The Torah of יהוה is perfect, bringing back the being; The witness of יהוה is trustworthy, making wise the simple;

8 The orders of יהוה are straight, rejoicing the heart; The command of יהוה is clear, enlightening the eyes;

9 The fear of יהוה is clean, standing forever; The right-rulings of יהוה are true, They are righteous altogether,

10 More desirable than gold, Than much fine gold; And sweeter than honey and the honeycomb.

11 Also, Your servant is warned by them, In guarding them there is great reward.

12 Who discerns mistakes? Declare me innocent from those that are secret,

13 Also keep Your servant back from presumptuous ones, Do not let them rule over me. Then shall I be perfect, and innocent of great transgression.

14 Let the words of my mouth and the meditation of my heart Be pleasing before You, O יהוה, my rock and my redeemer.

20

1 יהוה does answer you in the day of distress! The Name of the Elohim of Ya'aqoḇ does set you on high!

2 He does send you help from the set-apart place, And does uphold you from Tsiyon!

3 He does remember all your offerings, And does accept your burnt offering! Selah.

4 He does give you according to your heart, And fills all your plans!

5 We sing of Your deliverance, And in the Name of our Elohim we set up a banner! יהוה does fill all your requests!

6 Now I know that יהוה shall save His Anointed; He answers him from His set-apart heavens With the saving might of His right hand.

7 Some *trust* in chariots, and some in horses, But we remember the Name of יהוה our Elohim.

8 They, they have bowed down and fallen; But we have risen and are established.

9 Save, יהוה! Let the Sovereign answer us in the day we call.

21

1 The sovereign rejoices in Your strength, O יהוה; And how greatly he exults in Your deliverance!

2 You have given him the desire of his heart, And You have not withheld the request of his lips. Selah.

3 For You put before him the blessings of goodness; You set a crown of fine gold on his head.

4 He asked life from You, and You gave it to him – Length of days forever and ever.

5 Through Your deliverance his esteem is great; You have laid excellency and splendour on him.

6 For You have made him most blessed forever; You have made him glad with the joy of Your presence.

7 For the sovereign is trusting in יהוה, And through the kindness of the Most High he is not moved.

8 Your hand reaches all Your enemies; Your right hand reaches those who hate You.

9 You make them as a furnace of fire in the time of Your presence; יהוה does swallow them up in His wrath, And fire does consume them.

10 You destroy their fruit from the earth, And their seed from among the sons of men.

11 For they held out evil against You; They devised a plot; they do not prevail.

12 For You make them turn their back, When You aim with Your bowstring toward their faces.

13 Be exalted, O יהוה, in Your strength! We sing and we praise Your might.

22

1 My Ěl, My Ěl, why have You forsaken Me – Far from saving Me, *far from* the words of My groaning?

2 O My Elohim, I call by day, but You do not answer; And by night, but I find no rest.

3 Yet You are set-apart, Enthroned on the praises of Yisra'ěl.

4 Our fathers trusted in You; They trusted, and You delivered them.

5 They cried to You, and were delivered; They trusted in You, and were not ashamed.

6 But I am a worm, and no man; A reproach of men, and despised by the people.

7 All those who see Me mock Me; They shoot out the lip, they shake the head, *saying* ,

8 "He trusted in יהוה, let Him rescue Him; Let Him deliver Him, seeing He has delighted in Him!"

9 For You are the One who took Me out of the womb; Causing Me to trust *while* on My mother's breasts.

10 I was cast upon You from birth. From My mother's belly You have been My Ěl.

11 Do not be far from Me, For distress is near; For there is none to help.

12 Many bulls have surrounded Me; Strong ones of Bashan have encircled Me.

13 They have opened their mouths against Me, As a raging and roaring lion.

14 I have been poured out like water, And all My bones have been spread apart; My heart has become like wax; It has melted in the midst of My inward parts.

15 My strength is dried like a potsherd, And My tongue is cleaving to My jaws; And to the dust of death You are appointing Me.

16 For dogs have surrounded Me; A crowd of evil ones have encircled Me, Piercing My hands and My feet;

17 I count all My bones. They look, they stare at Me.

18 They divide My garments among them, And for My raiment they cast lots.

19 But You, O יהוה, do not be far off; O My Strength, hasten to help Me!

20 Deliver My life from the sword, My only *life* from the power of the dog.

21 Save Me from the mouth of the lion, And from the horns of the wild beasts! You have answered Me.

22 I make known Your Name to My brothers; In the midst of the assembly I praise You.

23 You who fear יהוה, praise Him! All you seed of Ya'aqoḇ, esteem Him, And fear Him, all you seed of Yisra'ĕl!

24 For He has not despised Nor hated the affliction of the afflicted; Nor has He hidden His face from Him; But when He cried to Him, He heard.

25 From You is My praise in the great assembly; I pay My vows before those who fear Him.

26 The meek ones do eat and are satisfied; Let those who seek Him praise יהוה. Let your heart live forever!

27 Let all the ends of the earth Remember and turn to יהוה, And all clans of the nations Bow themselves before You.

28 For the reign belongs to יהוה, And He is ruling over the nations.

29 All the fat ones of the earth Shall eat and bow themselves; All who go down to the dust bow before Him, Even he who did not keep alive his own life.

30 A seed shall serve Him. It is declared of יהוה to the *coming* generation.

31 They shall come and declare His righteousness To a people *yet* to be born a , For He shall do it!

31

1 In You, O יהוה, I have taken refuge; Let me never be ashamed; Deliver me in Your righteousness.

2 Incline Your ear to me, Deliver me speedily; Be a rock of refuge to me, A house of defence to save me.

3 For You are my rock and my stronghold; For Your Name's sake lead me and guide me.

4 Bring me out of the net which they have hidden for me, For You are my stronghold.

5 Into Your hand I commit my spirit; You have redeemed me, O יהוה Ĕl of truth.

6 I have hated those who observe lying vanities; But I trust in יהוה.

7 I exult and rejoice in Your kindness, For You have seen my affliction; You have known the distresses of my life,

8 And You have not shut me up into the hand of the enemy. You have set my feet in a large place.

9 Show me favour, O יהוה, for I am in distress; My eye, my being and my body have become old with grief!

10 For my life is consumed in sorrow, And my years in sighing; My strength fails because of my crookedness, And my bones have become old.

11 I am a reproach among all my adversaries, But most of all among my neighbours, And a dread to my friends; Those who see me outside flee from me.

12 I have been forgotten like someone dead from the heart; I have been like a missing vessel.

13 For I hear the evil report of many; Fear is from all around; When they take counsel together against me, They plot to take away my life.

14 But I, I have put my trust in You, O יהוה; I have said, "You are my Elohim."

15 My times are in Your hand; Deliver me from the hand of my enemies, And from those who pursue me.

1 6 Make Your face shine upon Your servant; Save me in Your kindness.

17 Do not let me be ashamed, O יהוה, For I have called upon You; Let the wrong be ashamed; Let them be silenced in the grave.

18 Let lips of falsehood be stilled, Which speak recklessly against the righteous, With pride and scorn.

19 How great is Your goodness, Which You have laid up for those fearing You, Which You have prepared for those taking refuge in You In the sight of the sons of men!

20 In the secrecy of Your presence You shall hide them from the plots of man; You shelter them in a booth from the strife of tongues.

21 Blessed be יהוה, For He has made marvellous His kindness to me in a strong city!

22 And I, I have said in my haste, "I am cut off from before Your eyes," Yet You heard the voice of my prayers When I cried out to You.

23 Love יהוה, all you His kind ones! For יהוה guards the trustworthy ones, And exceedingly repays the doer of pride.

24 Be strong, and let Him strengthen your heart, All you who are waiting for יהוה.

36

1 Transgression speaks to the wrong within his heart; Fear of Elohim is not before his eyes.

2 For he flatters himself in his own eyes, To find his crookedness to be hated.

3 The words of his mouth are wickedness and deceit; He has ceased to be wise, to do good.

4 He plots wickedness on his bed; He sets himself in a way that is not good; He does not despise evil.

5 O יהוה, Your kindness is in the heavens, And Your trustworthiness reaches to the clouds.

6 Your righteousness is like the mighty mountains; Your right-rulings are a great deep; O יהוה, You save man and beast.

7 How precious is Your kindness, O Elohim! And the sons of men take refuge in the shadow of Your wings.

8 They are filled from the fatness of Your house, And You give them drink from the river of Your pleasures.

9 For with You is the fountain of life; In Your light we see light.

10 Draw out Your kindness to those who know You, And Your righteousness to the upright in heart.

11 Let not the foot of pride come against me, And the hand of the wrong drive me away.

12 There the workers of wickedness have fallen; They have been overthrown And have been unable to rise.

39

1 I have said,"Let me guard my ways Against sinning with my tongue; Let me guard my mouth with a muzzle, While the wrongdoer is before me."

2 I became dumb, keeping still; I was silent, from good; And my pain was stirred.

3 My heart was hot within me; While I was meditating, the fire burned. Then I spoke with my tongue:

4 "יהוה, let me know my end, And the measure of my days, what it is, Let me know how short-lived I am.

5 "See, You have made my days as handbreadths, And my lifetime is as non-existence before You; Only, all men standing, are all breath. Selah.

6 "As but a shadow each one walks; They busy themselves, only in vain; He heaps up *wealth* , But knows not who gathers them.

7 "And now, יהוה, what do I wait for? My expectancy is in You.

8 "Deliver me from all my transgressions; Do not make me the reproach of the foolish.

9 "I was dumb, I did not open my mouth, Because it was You who did it.

10 "Turn aside Your stroke from me; I am overcome by the blow of Your hand.

11 "When You chastise man for crookedness with reproofs, You consume what he loves, like a moth; All men are but a breath. Selah.

12 "Hear my prayer, O יהוה, And give ear to my cry; Do not be silent at my tears; For I am a stranger with You, A sojourner, as all my fathers were.

13 "Look away from me, That I might brighten up, Before I go away and am no more."

40

1 I waited, waited for יהוה; And He inclined to me, and heard my cry.

2 And He drew me Out of the pit of destruction, Out of the muddy clay, And He set my feet upon a rock, He is establishing my steps.

3 Then He put a new song in my mouth; Praise to our Elohim; Many do see it and fear, And trust in יהוה.

4 Blessed is that man who has made יהוה his trust, And has not turned to the proud, And those turning aside to falsehood.

5 O יהוה my Elohim, many are the wonders Which You have done, and Your purposes toward us; There is no one to compare with You; I declare and speak: They are too many to be numbered.

6 Slaughtering a and meal offering You did not desire; You have opened my ears; Burnt offering and sin offering You did not ask for.

7 Then I said, "See, I have come; In the scroll of the Book it is prescribed for me.

8 I have delighted to do Your pleasure, O my Elohim, And Your Torah is within my heart a ".

9 I have proclaimed the good news of righteousness, In the great assembly; See, I do not restrain my lips, O יהוה, You know.

10 I did not conceal Your righteousness within my heart; I have declared Your trustworthiness and Your deliverance; I did not hide Your kindness and Your truth From the great assembly.

11 Do not withhold Your compassion from me, O יהוה; Let Your kindness and Your truth always watch over me.

12 For evils without number have surrounded me; My crookednesses have overtaken me, And I have been unable to see; They became more than the hairs of my head; And my heart has failed me.

13 Be pleased, O יהוה, to deliver me; O יהוה, hasten to help me!

14 Let those who seek to destroy my life Be ashamed and abashed altogether; Let those who are desiring my evil Be driven back and put to shame.

15 Let those who say to me, "Aha, aha!" Be appalled at their own shame.

16 Let all those who seek You Rejoice and be glad in You; Let those who love Your deliverance always say, "יהוה be exalted!"

17 But I am poor and needy; Let יהוה think upon me. You are my help and my deliverer; O my Elohim, do not delay!

41

1 Blessed is he who considers the poor; יהוה does deliver him in a day of evil.

2 יהוה does guard him and keep him alive; He is blessed on the earth, And You do not hand him over To the desire of his enemies.

3 יהוה sustains him on his sickbed; In his weakness on his bed You bring a change.

4 As for me, I said, "O יהוה, show me favour; Heal me, for I have sinned against You."

5 My enemies speak evil of me, "When he dies his name shall perish."

6 And when one comes to visit, he speaks falsely; His heart gathers wickedness to itself; He goes out, he speaks of it.

7 All who hate me whisper together against me; They plot evil to me, *saying* ,

8 "A matter of Beliya'al is poured out on him, That when he lies down, he would not rise again."

9 Even my own friend in whom I trusted, who ate my bread, Has lifted up his heel against me.

10 But You, יהוה, show me favour and raise me up, And let me repay them.

11 By this I know that You did delight in me, Because my enemy does not shout for joy over me.

12 And I, You uphold me in my integrity, And set me before Your face forever.

13 Blessed be יהוה Elohim of Yisra'ĕl From everlasting to everlasting! Amĕn and Amĕn.

42

1 As a deer longs for the water streams, So my being longs for You, O Elohim.

2 My being thirsts for Elohim, for the living Ĕl. When shall I enter in to appear before Elohim?

3 My tears have been my food day and night, While they say to me all day, "Where is your Elohim?"

4 These I remember, and pour out my being within me. For I used to pass along with the throng; I went with them to the House of Elohim, With the voice of joy and praise, A multitude keeping a festival!

5 Why are you depressed, O my being? And *why* are you restless within me? Wait for Elohim: for I shall yet thank Him, *For* the deliverance of His face!

6 O my Elohim, my being is depressed within me; Therefore I remember You from the land of the Yarděn, And from the heights of Ḥermon, From Mount Mits'ar.

7 Deep calls to deep at the sound of Your waterfalls; All Your waves and breakers passed over me.

8 By day יהוה commands His kindness, And by night His song is with me; A prayer to the Ěl of my life.

9 I say to Ěl my Rock, "Why have You forgotten me? Why do I go mourning because of the oppression of the enemy?"

10 My enemies have reproached me, Like a crushing of my bones, While they say to me all day long, "Where is your Elohim?"

11 Why are you depressed, O my being? And why are you restless w ithin me? Wait for Elohim: for I shall yet thank Him, the deliverance of my face, And my Elohim.

44

1 O Elohim, we have heard with our ears, Our fathers have related to us, The work You did in their days, In the days of old.

2 You drove out the nations with Your hand, But them You planted. You afflicted peoples, and sent them out.

3 For not by their own sword did they possess the land, Neither did their own arm save them; But it was Your right hand and Your arm, And the light of Your face, Because You delighted in them.

4 You Yourself are my Sovereign, O Elohim; Command deliverances for Ya'aqoḇ.

5 Through You we push our enemies; Through Your Name we tread down those who rise up against us.

6 For I do not trust in my bow, And my sword does not save me.

7 For You have saved us from our enemies, And have put to shame those who hated us.

8 In Elohim we shall boast all day long, And praise Your Name forever. Selah.

9 Yet You have rejected us and put us to shame, And You do not go with our armies.

10 You make us turn back from the adversary, And those who hate us have plundered us.

11 You do give us as sheep to be eaten, And You have scattered us among the gentiles.

12 You sell Your people for no value, And have set no high price on them.

13 You make us a reproach to our neighbours, A scorn and a mockery to those round about us.

14 You make us a proverb among the nations, A shaking of the head among the peoples.

15 My reproach is always before me, And the shame of my face has covered me,

16 Because of the voice of the slanderer and blasphemer, Because of the enemy and avenger.

17 All this has come upon us; But we have not forgotten You, Neither have we been false to Your covenant.

18 Our heart has not turned back, Neither has our step swerved from Your way,

19 Yet You have crushed us in the place of jackals, And covered us with the shadow of death.

20 If we have forgotten the Name of our Elohim, Or stretched out our hands to a foreign mighty one,

21 Would Elohim not search this out? For He knows the secrets of the heart.

22 But for Your sake we are killed all day long; Reckoned as sheep for the slaughter.

23 Awake! Why do You sleep, O יהוה? Arise! Do not reject us forever.

24 Why do You hide Your face, Ignoring our affliction and our oppression?

25 For our being is bowed down to the dust; Our body cleaves to the earth.

26 Arise, be our help, And redeem us for Your kindness' sake.

45

1 My heart is overflowing with a goodly word; I address my works to the Sovereign; My tongue is the pen of a speedy writer.

2 You are more handsome than the sons of men; Favour has been poured upon Your lips; Therefore Elohim has blessed You forever.

3 Gird Your sword upon *Your* thigh, O Mighty One, Your excellency and Your splendour.

4 And ride prosperously in Your splendour, On the matter of truth and humility, righteousness; And let Your right hand lead You to awesome *matters* .

5 Your arrows are sharp In the heart of the Sovereign's enemies – Peoples fall under You.

6 Your throne, O Elohim, is forever and ever; The sceptre of Your reign Is a sceptre of straightness.

7 You have loved righteousness and hated wrongness a ; Therefore Elohim, Your Elohim, has anointed You With the oil of gladness more than Your companions.

8 All Your garments are myrrh and aloes, cassia; Out of the palaces of ivory, Stringed instruments have made You glad.

9 Daughters of sovereigns are among Your precious ones; At Your right hand stands the sovereigness in gold from Ophir.

10 Listen, O daughter, and see, And incline your ear, And forget your own people and your father's house;

11 And let the Sovereign delight in your loveliness; Because He is your Master – bow yourself to Him.

1 2 And the daughter of Tsor with a gift, The rich among the people seek your favour.

13 The daughter of the Sovereign Is all esteemed within *the palace* ; Her dress is embroidered with gold.

14 She is brought to the Sovereign in embroidered work; Maidens, her companions following her, Are brought to You.

15 They are brought with gladness and rejoicing; They enter the Sovereign's palace.

16 Instead of Your fathers are Your sons, Whom You appoint princes in all the earth.

17 I cause Your Name to be remembered in all generations; Therefore the people praise You forever and ever.

46

1 Elohim is our refuge and strength, A help in distress, soon found.

2 Therefore we do not fear, Though the earth reels And mountains topple into the heart of the seas.

3 Let its waters rage, foam; Let mountains shake with its swelling. Selah.

4 A river whose streams Make glad the city of Elohim, The set-apart dwelling of the Most High.

5 Elohim is in her midst, she does not topple; Elohim does help her when morning turns.

6 The gentiles shall rage, Reigns shall topple; He shall give forth His voice, The earth melts.

7 יהוה of hosts is with us; The Elohim of Ya'aqoḇ is our refuge. Selah.

8 Come, see the works of יהוה, The ruins He has wrought on the earth,

9 Causing *all* fighting to cease, Unto the end of the earth. He breaks the bow and shatters the spear; He burns the chariot with fire.

10 Be still, and know that I am Elohim; I am exalted among nations, I am exalted in the earth!

11 יהוה of hosts is with us; The Elohim of Ya'aqoḇ is our refuge. Selah.

47

1 Oh, clap your hands, all you peoples! Shout to Elohim with a voice of singing!

2 For יהוה Most High is awesome; A great Sovereign over all the earth.

3 He subdues peoples under us, And nations under our feet.

4 He chooses our inheritance for us, The excellence of Ya'aqoḇ whom He loves. Selah.

5 Elohim shall go up with a shout, יהוה with the sound of a ram's horn.

6 Sing praises to Elohim, sing praises! Sing praises to our Sovereign, sing praises!

7 For Elohim is Sovereign of all the earth; Sing praises with understanding.

8 Elohim shall reign over the nations; Elohim shall sit on His set-apart throne.

9 Nobles of peoples shall be gathered together, The people of the Elohim of Aḇraham.

For the shields of the earth belong to Elohim; He shall be greatly exalted.

48

1 Great is יהוה, and greatly to be praised In the city of our Elohim, His set-apart mountain.

2 Pretty on high, The joy of all the earth, Is Mount Tsiyon on the sides of the north, The city of the great Sovereign.

3 Elohim is in her citadels; He is known as her refuge.

4 For look, the sovereigns met, They passed by together.

5 They saw, so they marvelled; They were alarmed, they hastened away.

6 Trembling took hold of them there, Pain, as of a woman in labour,

7 With an east wind You break the ships of Tarshish.

8 As we have heard, so we have seen In the city of יהוה of hosts, In the city of our Elohim, Elohim establishes her forever. Selah.

9 We have thought, O Elohim, of Your kindness, In the midst of Your Hĕḵal.

10 According to Your Name, O Elohim, So is Your praise to the ends of the earth; Your right hand is filled with righteousness.

11 Let Mount Tsiyon rejoice, Let the daughters of Yehuḏah exult, Because of Your right-rulings.

12 Walk about Tsiyon, And go all around her. Count her towers;

13 Set your heart upon her rampart; Go through her citadels; So that you report it to the coming generation.

14 For this Elohim is our Elohim, Forever and ever; He Himself leads us, Even to death.

49

1 Hear this, all you peoples; Give ear, all you inhabitants of the world,

2 Both sons of mankind and sons of man, Rich and poor together.

3 My mouth speaks wisdom, And the meditation of my heart brings understanding.

4 I incline my ear to a parable; I expound my riddle on the lyre.

5 Why should I fear in the days of evil, When the crookedness of my supplanters surrounds me?

6 Those who are trusting in their riches And who are boasting in their great wealth?

7 A brother does not redeem anyone at all, Neither give to Elohim a ransom for him;

8 For the redemption of their lives is costly, And it shall cease forever;

9 That he should still live forever, *And* not see the Pit.

10 For he sees wise men die, The foolish and the ignorant both perish, And shall leave their wealth to others.

11 Their graves are their houses, forever; Their dwelling places, to all generations; They call *their* lands after their own names.

12 But man does not remain in esteem, He is like the beasts that perish.

13 This way of theirs is folly to them, Yet their followers are pleased with their words. Selah.

14 Like sheep they shall be laid in the grave; Death shall shepherd them; And the upright rule over them in the morning; And their form is consumed in the grave, Far from their dwelling.

15 But Elohim does redeem my being From the power of the grave, For He does receive me. Selah.

16 Do not be afraid when a man becomes rich, When the wealth of his house increases;

17 For when he dies he takes none of it; His wealth does not go down after him.

18 Though while he lived he blessed himself, And though they praise you when you do well for yourself,

19 He has to go to the generation of his fathers; They never see the light.

20 Man, who is rich, Yet does not understand, Shall be like the beasts, They shall perish.

51

1 Show me favour, O Elohim, According to Your kindness; According to the greatness of Your compassion, Blot out my transgressions.

2 Wash me completely from my guilt, And cleanse me from my sin.

3 For I know my transgressions, And my sin is ever before me.

4 Against You, You alone, have I sinned, And done evil in Your eyes; That You might be proven right in Your words; Be clear when You judge.

5 See, I was brought forth in crookedness, And in sin my mother conceived me.

6 See, You have desired truth in the inward parts, And in the hidden part You make me know wisdom.

7 Cleanse me with hyssop, and I am clean; Wash me, and I am whiter than snow.

8 Let me hear joy and gladness, Let the bones You have crushed rejoice.

9 Hide Your face from my sins, And blot out all my crookednesses.

10 Create in me a clean heart, O Elohim, And renew a steadfast spirit within me.

11 Do not cast me away from Your presence, And do not take Your Set-apart Spirit from me.

12 Restore to me the joy of Your deliverance, And uphold me, Noble Spirit!

13 Let me teach transgressors Your ways, So that sinners turn back to You.

14 Deliver me from blood-guilt, O Elohim, Elohim of my deliverance, Let my tongue sing aloud of Your righteousness.

15 O יהוה, open my lips, And that my mouth declare Your praise.

16 For You do not desire slaughtering, or I would give it; You do not delight in burnt offering.

17 The slaughterings of Elohim are a broken spirit, A heart broken and crushed, O Elohim, These You do not despise.

18 Do good in Your good pleasure to Tsiyon; Build the walls of Yerushalayim.

19 Then You would delight in slaughterings of righteousness, In burnt offering and complete burnt offering; Then young bulls would be offered on Your altar.

52

1 Why do you boast in evil, O mighty man? The kindness of Ěl is all day long!

2 Your tongue devises destruction, Like a sharp razor, working deceit.

3 You loved evil more than good, Lying more than speaking righteousness. Selah.

4 You loved all devouring words, O tongue of deceit.

5 Let Ěl also break you down forever, Take you and pluck you out of your tent. And He shall uproot you From the land of the living. Selah.

6 And let the righteous see and fear, And laugh at him, *saying* ,

7 "See the man who did not make Elohim his strength, But trusted in his many riches, Being strong in his destruction."

8 But I am like a green olive tree In the House of Elohim, I have trusted in the kindness of Elohim Forever and ever.

9 I thank You forever, Because You have done it; And in the presence of Your kind ones I wait on Your Name, for it is good.

53

1 The fool has said in his heart, "There is no Elohim." They have done corruptly, And they have done abominable unrighteousness; No one does good.

2 Elohim looked down from the heavens on the children of men, To see if there is a wise one, seeking Elohim.

3 They have all turned aside; They have together become filthy; No one is doing good, not even one.

4 Have the workers of wickedness no knowledge, Who eat up my people as they eat bread, And do not call on Elohim?

5 There they are in great fear, Where no fear was, For Elohim shall scatter the bones Of him who encamps against you. You shall put them to shame, For Elohim has rejected them.

6 O that the deliverance of Yisra'ĕl Would be given out of Tsiyon! When Elohim turns back the captivity of His people, Let Ya'aqob rejoice, let Yisra'ĕl be glad.

54

1 O Elohim, save me by Your Name, And rightly rule me by Your might.

2 Hear my prayer, O Elohim; Give ear to the words of my mouth.

3 For strangers have risen up against me, And cruel men have sought after my life; They have not set Elohim before them. Selah.

4 See, Elohim is my helper; יהוה is with those who sustain my life.

5 He repays evil to my enemies. Cut them off in Your truth.

6 Voluntarily I slaughter to You; I praise Your Name, O יהוה, for it is good.

7 For He has delivered me out of all distress; And my eye has looked upon my enemies.

55

1 Give ear to my prayer, O Elohim, And do not hide Yourself from my plea.

2 Give heed to me, and answer me; I wander and moan in my complaint,

3 Because of the noise of the enemy, Because of the outcry of the wrong; For they bring down wickedness upon me, And in wrath they hate me.

4 My heart is pained within me, And the frights of death have fallen upon me.

5 Fear and trembling have come upon me, And shuddering covers me.

6 And I said, "Who would give me wings like a dove! I would fly away and be at rest.

7 "See, I would wander far off, I would lodge in the wilderness. Selah.

8 "I would hasten my escape From the raging wind and storm."

9 Confuse, O יהוה, divide their tongues, For I saw violence and strife in the city.

10 Day and night they go around it on its walls; Wickedness and trouble are also in the midst of it.

11 Covetings are in its midst; Oppression and deceit do not vanish from its streets.

12 It is not an enemy who reproaches me – That I could bear; Nor one who hates me who is making himself great against me – Then I could hide from him.

13 But it was you, a man my equal, My companion and my friend.

14 We took sweet counsel together, We walked to the House of Elohim in the throng.

15 Let death come upon them; Let them go down into the grave alive, For evil is in their dwellings, in their midst.

16 I, I call upon Elohim, And יהוה saves me.

17 Evening and morning and at noon I complain and moan, And He hears my voice.

18 He has redeemed my life in peace From the battle against me, For there were many against me.

19 Ěl, even He who sits *enthroned* from of old, Does hear and afflict them – Selah – Those with whom there are no changes, Those who do not fear Elohim.

20 He has put forth his hands against those Who were at peace with him; He has broken his covenant.

21 His mouth was smoother than curds, Yet in his heart is fighting; His words were softer than oil, But they are drawn swords.

22 Cast your burden on יהוה, And let Him sustain you; He never allows the righteous to be shaken.

23 For You, O Elohim, do bring them down To the pit of destruction; Men of blood and deceit do not reach half their days; But I, I trust in You.

56

1 Show me favour, O Elohim, For man would swallow me up; Fighting all day long, he oppresses me.

2 My enemies would swallow me up all day long, For many are fighting against me, O Most High.

3 In the day I am afraid, I trust in You.

4 In Elohim, whose Word I praise, In Elohim I have trusted; I do not fear; What could flesh do to me?

5 All day long they twist my words; All their thoughts are against me for evil.

6 They stir up strife, they hide, They watch my steps, As they lie in wait for my life.

7 Because of wickedness, cast them out. Put down the peoples in displeasure, O Elohim!

8 You have counted my wanderings; You put my tears into Your bottle; Are they not in Your book?

9 My enemies turn back in the day I call; This I know, because Elohim is for me.

10 In Elohim, whose Word I praise, In יהוה, whose Word I praise,

11 In Elohim I have trusted; I do not fear; What could man do to me?

12 On me, O Elohim, are Your vows; I render praises to You,

13 For You have delivered my life from death, My feet from stumbling, That I might walk before Elohim, In the light of the living!

57

1 Show me favour, O Elohim, show me favour! For in You my being is taking refuge; And in the shadow of Your wings I take refuge, Until destruction passes by.

2 I cry out to the Most High Elohim, To Ěl who is perfecting *all matters* for me.

3 He sends from the heavens and saves me; He reproaches the one who would swallow me up. Selah. Elohim sends forth His kindness and His truth.

4 My being is in the midst of lions; I lie *among* those who breathe fire, Whose teeth are spears and arrows, And their tongue is a sharp sword.

5 Be exalted, O Elohim, above the heavens; Let Your esteem be above all the earth.

6 They have prepared a net for my footsteps; My being was bowed down; They have dug a pit before me; They fell into the midst of it! Selah.

7 My heart is firm, O Elohim, My heart is firm; I sing and praise.

8 Awake, my esteem! Awake, harp and lyre! I awake the dawn.

9 I praise You among the peoples, O יהוה; I sing to You among the nations.

10 For Your kindness is great up to the heavens, And Your truth unto the clouds.

11 Be exalted above the heavens, O Elohim; Let Your esteem be above all the earth.

58

1 Would you indeed speak righteousness, in silence? Do you judge straightly, you sons of men?

2 No, in heart you work unrighteousness; On earth you weigh out the violence of your hands.

3 The wrong have been estranged from the womb; These who speak lies go astray from birth.

4 Their poison is like the poison of a snake; Like a deaf cobra that stops its ear,

5 So as not to hear the voice of whisperers, Or a skilled caster of spells.

6 O Elohim, break their teeth in their mouth! Break out the fangs of the young lions, O יהוה!

7 Let them melt, let them vanish as water; Let Him aim His arrows that they be cut down;

8 Like a snail which melts away as it moves, Like a woman's stillbirth, Let them not see the sun!

9 Before your pots feel the thorns, Whether green or ablaze, He sweeps them away.

10 The righteous rejoices when he has seen the vengeance, He washes his feet in the blood of the wrong,

11 And man says, "Truly, the righteous are rewarded; Truly, there is an Elohim judging in the earth."

59

1 Deliver me from my enemies, O my Elohim; Set me on high from those who rise up against me.

2 Deliver me from the workers of wickedness, And save me from men of blood.

3 For look, they have lain in wait for my life; Mighty men assemble against me, For no transgression or sin of mine, O יהוה,

4 For no guilt *of mine* ! They run and prepare themselves. Awake to help me, and see!

5 And You, יהוה Elohim of hosts, Elohim of Yisra'ěl, Awake to punish all the gentiles; Show no favour to any wicked traitors. Selah.

6 They return at evening, They howl like a dog, And go around the city.

7 See, they belch out with their mouth, Swords are in their lips, For who is listening?

8 But You, יהוה, laughs at them, You mock all the gentiles.

9 O my Strength, I wait for You; For Elohim is my strong tower, My Elohim of kindness.

10 Elohim does go before me, He lets me look upon my enemies.

11 Do not slay them, lest my people forget; Scatter them by Your power, And bring them down, O יהוה our shield.

12 The sin of their mouth is the words of their lips, And they are captured in their pride, And for the cursing and lying they utter.

13 Bring *them* to an end in wrath, Bring *them* to an end, That they be no more; And let them know That Elohim is ruling in Ya'aqoḇ To the ends of the earth. Selah.

14 And at evening they return, They howl like a dog, And go around the city.

15 They wander up and down for food, And whine if they are not satisfied.

16 And I, I sing of Your power; And in the morning I sing aloud of Your kindness; For You have been my strong tower And a refuge in the day of my distress.

17 O my Strength, to You I sing praises; For Elohim is my strong tower, My Elohim of kindness.

60

1 O Elohim, You have rejected us; You have broken us; You have been displeased; Turn back to us!

2 You have made the earth tremble; You have broken it; Heal its breaches, for it is shaken.

3 You have let Your people see hardship; You have made us drink the wine of trembling.

4 You have given a banner to those who fear You, That it might be lifted up Because of the truth. Selah.

5 That those You love might be rescued, Save with Your right hand and answer me.

6 Elohim has spoken in His set-apartness, "I exult, I portion out Shekem And measure out the Valley of Sukkoth.

7 "Gil'ad is Mine and Menashsheh is Mine, And Ephrayim is the defence of My head,

Yehudah is My lawgiver.

8 "Mo'ab is My wash-pot, Over Edom I cast My shoe, Shout loud, O Philistia, because of Me."

9 Who would bring me to the strong city? Who shall lead me to Edom?

10 Have not You, O Elohim, rejected us? And You do not go out, O Elohim, With our armies!

11 Give us help from distress, For the help of man is naught.

12 In Elohim we do mightily, And He treads down our adversaries!

61

1 Hear my cry, O Elohim, Listen to my prayer.

2 From the end of the earth I call unto You, When my heart is faint; Lead me to the rock that is higher than I.

3 For You have been my refuge, A strong tower in the face of the enemy.

4 Let me dwell in Your Tent forever, Let me take refuge in the shelter of Your wings. Selah.

5 For You, O Elohim, have heard my vows; You have given me the inheritance Of those who fear Your Name.

6 You add days to the days of the sovereign, His years as many generations.

7 Let him dwell forever before Elohim. Prepare kindness and truth to preserve him!

8 So I sing praise to Your Name forever, When I pay my vows day by day.

62

1 My being finds rest in Elohim alone; From Him is my deliverance.

2 He alone is my rock and my deliverance, my strong tower; I am not greatly shaken.

3 How long would you assail a man? You crush him, all of you, Like a leaning wall, a tottering fence.

4 They plotted to topple him from his high position; They delight in lies; They bless with their mouth, But in their heart they curse. Selah.

5 My being, find rest in Elohim alone, Because my expectation is from Him.

6 He alone is my rock and my deliverance, my strong tower; I am not shaken.

7 My deliverance and my esteem *depend* on Elohim; The rock of my strength, my refuge is in Elohim.

8 Trust in Him at all times, you people; Pour out your heart before Him; Elohim is a refuge for us. Selah.

9 Sons of Aḏam are but a breath, Sons of men are a lie; If weighed in the scales, They are altogether lighter than breath.

10 Do not trust in oppression. And do not become vain in robbery; If riches increase, Do not set your heart on them.

11 Elohim has spoken once, Twice I have heard this: That strength belongs to Elohim.

12 And kindness is Yours, O יהוה; For You reward each one according to his work.

64

1 Hear my voice, O Elohim, in my meditation; Guar d my life from the threats of the enemy.

2 Hide me from the secret plans of the evil-doers, From the tumult of the workers of wickedness,

3 Who sharpen their tongue like a sword, And aim their arrows, a bitter word,

4 To shoot in ambush at someone blameless, They shoot at him suddenly and do not fear.

5 They arm themselves with an evil word; They talk of hiding snares; They have said, "Who sees them?"

6 They search out unrighteousnesses, "We have perfected a well searched out plan." For the inward part of man, and heart, are deep.

7 But Elohim does shoot at them with an arrow; Their wounds shall be sudden.

8 And they cause one to stumble, Their own tongue is against them; All who see them flee away.

9 And all men fear, And declare the work of Elohim. And they shall wisely consider What He has done.

10 The righteous rejoice in יהוה, And shall take refuge in Him, And all the upright in heart praise *Him* .

65

1 To You, stillness, praise, in Tsiyon, O Elohim; And to You a vow is paid.

2 To You who hears all prayer, all flesh comes.

3 Crooked matters were mightier than I; As for our transgressions, You do cover them.

4 Blessed is the one You choose, And bring near to dwell in Your courts. We are satisfied with the goodness of Your house, Your set-apart Hĕḵal.

5 By awesome deeds in righteousness You answer us, O Elohim of our deliverance, The Trust of all the ends of the earth, And the distant seas;

6 Who established the mountains by His strength, Being girded with might;

7 Who stills the roaring of the seas, The roaring of their waves, And the uproar of the peoples.

8 And they who dwell in the farthest parts, Are afraid of Your signs; You make the outgoings of the morning and evening rejoice.

9 You have visited the earth and watered it, You greatly enrich it; The river of Elohim is filled with water; You provide their grain, For so You have prepared it.

10 Its ridges have been filled, Its furrows have been deepened, You make it soft with showers, You bless its growth.

11 You have crowned the year with Your goodness, And Your paths drip with fatness.

12 The pastures of the wilderness drip, And the hills are girded with rejoicing.

13 The meadows are dressed in flocks, And valleys are covered with grain; They shout for joy and sing.

66

1 Shout with joy to Elohim, All the earth!

2 Sing out the splendour of His Name; Make His praise esteemed.

3 Say to Elohim, "How awesome are Your works! Through the greatness of Your power Your enemies pretend obedience to You.

4 "All the earth bow to You, They sing praises to You, They praise Your Name." Selah.

5 Come and see the works of Elohim, Awesome acts toward the sons of men.

6 He has turned the sea into dry land, They went through the river on foot. There we rejoiced in Him,

7 Who rules by His power forever; His eyes keeping watch on the gentiles; Let the rebellious not exalt themselves. Selah.

8 Bless our Elohim, you peoples! And sound His praise abroad,

9 Who keeps us in life, And does not allow our feet to be moved.

10 For You, O Elohim, have proved us; You have refined us as silver is refined.

11 You brought us into the net; You laid affliction on our loins.

12 You have let men ride at our head; We went through fire and through water; But You brought us out to plenty.

13 I enter Your house with burnt offerings; I complete my vows to You,

14 That which my lips have uttered And my mouth spoke in my distress.

15 Burnt offerings of fatlings I offer to You, With the incense of rams; I offer bulls with goats. Selah.

16 Come, hear, all you who fear Elohim, And I relate what He has done for my being.

17 I called to Him with my mouth, And praise was in my tongue.

18 If I have seen wickedness in my heart, יהוה would not hear.

19 Truly, Elohim has heard me; He has given heed to the voice of my prayer.

20 Blessed be Elohim, Who has not turned away my prayer, Nor His kindness from me!

67

1 Elohim does favour us and bless us, Cause His face to shine upon us. Selah.

2 For Your way to be known on earth, Your deliverance among all nations.

3 Let the peoples praise You, O Elohim, Let all the peoples praise You.

4 Let the nations be glad and sing for joy! For You judge the peoples uprightly, And lead the nations on earth. Selah.

5 Let the peoples praise You, O Elohim; Let all the peoples praise You.

6 The earth shall give her increase; Elohim, our own Elohim, blesses us!

7 Elohim blesses us! And all the ends of the earth fear Him!

68

1 Elohim arises, His enemies are scattered. And those who hate Him flee before Him!

2 As smoke is driven away, You drive *them* away; As wax melts before the fire, The wrong perish before Elohim.

3 But the righteous are glad, They exult before Elohim. And they rejoice with gladness.

4 Sing to Elohim, sing praises to His Name. Raise up a highway for Him Who rides through the deserts, By His Name Yah, And exult before Him.

5 Father of the fatherless, And Right-ruler of widows, Is Elohim in His set-apart dwelling.

6 Elohim makes a home for the lonely; He brings out into prosperity Those who are bound with chains; Only the rebellious shall dwell in a dry land.

7 O Elohim, when You went out before Your people, When You stepped through the wilderness, Selah.

8 The earth shook and the heavens dropped before Elohim, This Sinai, shook before Elohim, the Elohim of Yisra'ěl.

9 You, O Elohim, sent a shower of plenty, You confirmed Your inheritance, When it was weary.

10 Your flock dwelt in it; You provided from Your goodness for the poor, O Elohim.

11 יהוה gave the word; The women who proclaimed it was a great company:

12 "Sovereigns of armies flee in haste! And she who remains at home divides the spoil."

13 If you lie down among the sheepfolds, The wings of a dove are covered with silver, And her feathers with yellow gold.

14 When the Almighty scattered sovereigns in it, It did snow in Tsalmon.

15 A mountain of Elohim is the mountain of Bashan; A mountain of peaks is the mountain of Bashan.

16 O mountain of peaks, why do you gaze in envy At the mountain which Elohim desired to dwell in; יהוה even dwells *there* forever.

17 The chariots of Elohim are twenty thousand, Thousands of thousands; יהוה came from Sinai Into the Set-apart Place.

18 You have ascended on high, You have led captivity captive, You have received gifts among men, And even the rebellious, That Yah Elohim might dwell *there* .

19 Blessed be יהוה, Day by day He bears our burden, The Ěl of our deliverance! Selah.

20 Our Ěl is the Ěl of deliverance; And to יהוה, the Master, belong escapes from death.

21 Indeed, Elohim smites the head of His enemies, The hairy scalp of him who walks about in His guilt.

22 יהוה said, "I bring back from Bashan, I bring back from the depths of the sea,

23 "So that you plunge your foot in blood; That the tongues of your dogs Have their portion from the enemies."

24 They have seen Your goings, O Elohim, The goings of my Ěl, my Sovereign, Into the set-apart place.

25 The singers went in front, The players on instruments after them; Among them were the maidens playing tambourines.

26 Bless Elohim in the assemblies, יהוה, from the fountain of Yisra'ěl.

27 There is Binyamin, the smallest, their ruler, The leaders of Yehuḏah, their company, The leader of Zeḇulun, the leader of Naphtali.

28 Your Elohim has commanded your strength, be strong! O Elohim, this You have worked out for us!

29 Because of Your Hěḵal at Yerushalayim, Sovereigns bring presents to You.

30 Rebuke the wild beasts of the reeds, The herd of bulls, with the calves of the peoples, Each one humbling himself with pieces of silver. Scatter the peoples who delight in conflicts!

31 Ambassadors come out of Mitsrayim; Kush stretches out her hands to Elohim.

32 Sing to Elohim, you reigns of the earth, Praises to יהוה, Selah.

33 To Him who rides on the ancient highest heavens! See, He sends out His voice, a mighty voice.

34 Ascribe strength to Elohim; His excellence is over Yisra'ěl, And His strength is in the clouds.

35 O Elohim, awesome from Your set-apart places, The Ěl of Yisra'ěl is He Who gives strength and power to His people. Blessed be Elohim!

69

1 Save me, O Elohim! For waters have come up to my neck.

2 I have sunk in deep mud, And there is no place to stand; I have come into deep waters, And the floods overflow me.

3 I am worn out from my crying; My throat is dry; My eyes grow dim As I wait for my Elohim.

4 Those who hate me without a cause Are more than the hairs of my head; They are mighty who would destroy me, My lying enemies; What I did not steal, I restored.

5 O Elohim, You Yourself know my foolishness; And my guilt has not been hidden from You.

6 Let not those who wait for You, O Master יהוה of hosts, Be ashamed because of me; Let not those who seek You Be humbled because of me, O Elohim of Yisra'ěl.

7 Because I have borne reproach for Your sake; Shame has covered my face.

8 I have become a stranger to my brothers, And a foreigner to my mother's children;

9 Because ardour for Your house has eaten me up, And the reproaches of those who reproach You have fallen on me.

10 And I wept in my being with fasting, And it became my reproach.

11 And when I put on sackcloth, I became a proverb to them.

12 They who sit in the gate talk about me, And I am the song of the drunkards.

13 But as for me, my prayer is to You, O יהוה, At an acceptable time, O Elohim. In the greatness of Your kindness, Answer me in the truth of Your deliverance.

14 Rescue me out of the mire, And let me not sink. Let me be rescued from those who hate me, And out of the deep waters.

15 Let not a flood of waters overflow me, Nor let the deep swallow me up, Nor let the pit shut its mouth on me.

16 Answer me, O יהוה, for Your kindness is good. According to the greatness of Your compassion, turn to me.

17 And do not hide Your face from Your servant, For I am in distress; Answer me speedily.

18 Draw near to my being, redeem it; Ransom me because of my enemies.

19 You Yourself know my reproach, And my shame and my confusion; My adversaries are all before You.

20 Reproach has broken my heart and I am sick; I looked for sympathy, but there was none; And for comforters, but I found none.

21 And they gave me gall for my food, And for my thirst they gave me vinegar to drink.

22 Let their table before them become a snare, And a trap to those at ease.

23 Let their eyes be darkened, so as not to see; And make their loins shake continually.

24 Pour out Your wrath upon them, And let Your burning displeasure overtake them.

25 Let their encampments be deserted; Let no one dwell in their tents.

26 For they persecute him whom You have smitten, And talk about the pain of those You have wounded.

27 Add crookedness to their crookedness, And let them not enter into Your righteousness.

28 Let them be blotted out of the book of the living, And not be written with the righteous.

29 But I am poor and in pain; Let Your deliverance, O Elohim, set me up on high.

30 I praise the Name of Elohim with a song, And I make Him great with thanksgiving.

31 And this pleases יהוה more than an ox, A bull with horns *and* hooves.

32 The humble shall see, they rejoice, You who seek Elohim, and your hearts live.

33 For יהוה hears the poor, And He shall not despise His captives.

34 Let the heavens and earth praise Him, The seas and all that moves in them.

35 For Elohim shall save Tsiyon And build the cities of Yehuḏah. And they shall dwell there and possess it,

36 And the seed of His servants inherit it, And those who love His Name dwell in it a .

70

1 O Elohim, deliver me! Hasten to my help, O יהוה!

2 Let those who seek my life Be ashamed and abashed, Let those who are desiring my evil Be turned back and humiliated.

3 Let those who say, "Aha, aha!" Be turned back because of their shame.

4 Let all those who seek You Rejoice and be glad in You; And let those who love Your deliverance always say, "Let Elohim be made great!"

166

5 But I am poor and needy; Hasten to me, O Elohim! You are my help and my deliverer; O יהוה, do not delay.

75

1 We shall give thanks to You, O Elohim, we shall give thanks! And Your Name is near! Your wonders shall be declared!

2 "When I seize the appointed time, It is I who judge in uprightness.

3 "The earth and all its inhabitants are melted; It is I who set its columns firm. Selah.

4 "I said to the boasters, 'Do not boast,' And to the wrong, 'Do not lift up the horn.

5 "Do not lift up your horn on high (You speak with a stiff neck).' "

6 For exaltations are neither from the east, Nor from the west nor from the wilderness.

7 But Elohim is the Judge – He puts down one, And exalts another.

8 For a cup is in the hand of יהוה, And the wine shall foam; It is filled with a mixture, And He pours it out. All the wrong of the earth drink, Draining it to the dregs.

9 But I, I declare forever, I sing praises to the Elohim of Ya'aqoḇ.

10 "And all the horns of the wrong I cut off; The horns of the righteous are lifted up."

76

1 In Yehuḏah Elohim is known; His Name is great in Yisra'ĕl.

2 And His booth is in Shalĕm a , And His dwelling place in Tsiyon.

3 There He broke the arrows of the bow, The shield and the sword and the battle-axe. Selah.

4 You are resplendent, More excellent than mountains of prey.

5 The stout-hearted have been stripped; They slept their sleep; And none of the mighty men have found their hands.

6 At Your rebuke, O Elohim of Ya'aqoḇ, Both the rider and horse lay stunned.

7 You, You are to be feared; And who would stand in Your presence When You are displeased?

8 From heaven You shall cause judgment to be heard; The earth shall fear, and shall be still,

9 When Elohim arises to right-ruling, To save all the meek of the earth. Selah.

10 For the wrath of mankind praises You, With the remainder of wrath You gird Yourself!

11 Make vows to יהוה your Elohim, and pay them. Let all who are around Him bring presents To the One to be feared.

12 He cuts off the spirit of leaders, He is awesome to the sovereigns of the earth!

77

1 My voice is to Elohim, and I cry; My voice is to Elohim, and He listened to me.

2 In the day of my distress I sought יהוה; My hand was stretched out in the night And it did not cease, My being refused to be comforted.

3 I remembered Elohim, and groaned; I complained, and my spirit grew faint. Selah.

4 You ceased the watches of my eyes, I was too troubled to speak.

5 I have thought about the days of old, The years long past.

6 I remember my song in the night, I meditate within my heart, And my spirit searches diligently.

7 Would יהוה reject forever, And never again be pleased?

8 Has His kindness ceased forever, Has the promise failed for all generations?

9 Has Ěl forgotten to show favour? Has He shut up His compassions in displeasure? Selah.

10 And I said, "This is my grief: That the right hand of the Most High has changed."

11 I remember the deeds of Yah, For I remember Your wonders of old.

12 And I shall meditate on all Your work, And talk of Your deeds.

13 Your way, O Elohim, is in Set-apartness a ; Who is a great Ěl like Elohim?

14 You are the Ěl who does wonders; You have made known Your strength among the peoples.

15 By Your arm You have redeemed Your people, The sons of Ya'aqoḇ and Yosĕph. Selah.

16 The waters saw You, O Elohim; The waters saw You, they were afraid; The depths also trembled.

17 The clouds poured out water; The heavens rumbled; Also, Your arrows flashed back and forth.

18 The voice of Your thunder rolled along; Lightnings lit up the world; The earth trembled and shook.

19 Your way was in the sea, And Your path in the great waters, And Your footsteps were not known.

20 You did lead Your people like a flock By the hand of Mosheh and Aharon.

80

Give ear, O Shepherd of Yisra'ĕl, Who lead Yosĕph like a flock; Who dwell between the kerubim, shine forth!

2 Before Ephrayim, Binyamin, and Menashsheh, Stir up Your might, And come and save us!

3 Cause us to turn back, O Elohim, And cause Your face to shine, That we might be saved!

4 O יהוה Elohim of hosts, How long shall You be wroth Against the prayer of Your people?

5 You have caused them to eat the bread of tears, And have caused them to drink With tears, a third time.

6 You have made us a strife to our neighbours, And our enemies laugh among themselves.

7 Turn us back, O Elohim of hosts, And cause Your face to shine, That we might be saved!

8 You brought a vine out of Mitsrayim; You drove out the nations, and planted it.

9 You cleared a place for it, And caused it to take deep root, And it filled the land.

10 Hills were covered with its shadow, And the mighty cedars with its twigs.

11 She spread her branches to the Sea, And her shoots to the River.

12 Why have You broken down her hedges, So that every passer-by plucked her fruit?

13 The boar out of the forest ravages it, And the wild beast of the field devours it.

14 Return, we beg You, O Elohim of hosts; Look down from heaven, and see, And visit this vine,

15 And the stock which Your right hand has planted, And the Son whom You made strong for Yourself.

16 It is burned with fire, it is cut down; They perish at the rebuke of Your face.

17 Let Your hand be upon the One at Your right hand, Upon the Son of Aḏam whom You made strong for Yourself,

18 And we shall not backslide from You. Revive us, and let us call upon Your Name.

19 Turn us back, O יהוה Elohim of hosts, And cause Your face to shine, That we might be saved!

81

1 Shout for joy to Elohim our strength; Raise a shout to the Elohim of Ya'aqoḇ.

2 Lift up a song and beat the tambourine, The pleasant lyre and with the harp.

3 Blow the ram's horn at the time of the New Moon, At the full moon, on our festival day.

4 For this is a law for Yisra'ĕl, And a right-ruling of the Elohim of Ya'aqoḇ.

5 He appointed it in Yehosĕph for a witness, When He went throughout the land of Mitsrayim; I heard a language that I did not know.

6 *He says* , "I removed his shoulder from the burden; His hands were freed from the baskets.

7 "You called in distress, and I rescued you; I answered you in the covering of thunder; I proved you at the waters of Meriḇah. Selah.

8 "Hear, O My people, and let Me warn you, O Yisra'ĕl, if you would listen to Me!

9 "Let there be no strange mighty one among you, And do not bow down to a foreign mighty one.

10 "I am יהוה your Elohim, Who brought you out of the land of Mitsrayim; Open your mouth wide, and I fill it.

11 "But My people did not listen to My voice, And Yisra'ĕl would not submit to Me.

12 "So I gave them over to their own stubborn heart, To walk in their own counsels.

13 "O, if My people had listened to Me, Yisra'ĕl would walk in My ways,

14 "I would subdue their enemies at once, And turn My hand against their adversaries!

15 "Those who hate יהוה would cringe before Him; And their time *of punishment* be forever.

16 "He would feed them with the finest of wheat; And with honey from the rock I would satisfy you."

84

How lovely are Your dwelling places, O יהוה of hosts!

2 My being has longed, and even fainted, For the courts of יהוה; My heart and my flesh cry out for the living Ĕl.

3 Even the sparrow has found a home, And the swallow a nest for herself, Where she has put her young ones – Your altars, O יהוה of hosts, My Sovereign and my Elohim.

4 Blessed are those who dwell in Your house, They are ever praising You. Selah.

5 Blessed is the man whose strength is in You, *Your* Highways are in their heart.

6 Passing through the valley of weeping, They make it a fountain; The Teacher also covers it with blessings.

7 They go from strength to strength, Appearing before Elohim in Tsiyon.

8 O יהוה Elohim of hosts, hear my prayer; Give ear, O Elohim of Ya'aqoḇ! Selah.

9 O Elohim, see our shield, And look upon the face of Your anointed.

10 For a day in Your courts Is better than a thousand *days* . I have chosen rather to be a doorkeeper In the House of my Elohim, Than to dwell in the tents of the wrong.

11 For יהוה Elohim is a sun and a shield; יהוה gives favour and esteem; He withholds no good *matter* From those who walk blamelessly.

12 O יהוה of hosts, Blessed is the man who trusts in You!

85

1 יהוה, You shall take pleasure in Your land; You shall turn back the captivity of Ya'aqoḇ.

2 You shall take away the crookedness of Your people; You shall cover all their sin. Selah.

3 You shall withdraw all Your wrath; You shall turn from Your fierce displeasure.

4 Turn back to us, O Elohim of our deliverance, And cause Your vexation toward us to cease.

5 Would You be enraged with us forever? Would You draw out Your displeasure From generation to generation?

6 Would You not revive us again, For Your people to rejoice in You?

7 Show us Your kindness, O יהוה, And give us Your deliverance.

8 Let me hear what Ěl יהוה speaks, For He speaks peace to His people And to His kind ones; And let them not turn again to folly.

9 Truly, His deliverance is near to those who fear Him, For esteem to dwell in our land.

10 Kindness and truth shall meet, Righteousness and peace shall kiss.

11 Truth sprouts forth from the earth, And righteousness looks down from heaven,

12 Indeed, יהוה gives what is good, And our land yields its increase.

13 Righteousness goes before Him, And prepares a way for His footsteps.

139

O יהוה, You have searched me And know me.

2 You know my sitting down and my rising up; You understand my thought from afar.

3 You sift my path and my lying down, And know well all my ways.

4 For there is not a word on my tongue, But see, O יהוה, You know it all!

5 You have closed me in, behind and before, And laid Your hand upon me –

6 Knowledge too wondrous for me, It is high, I am unable to *reach* it.

7 Where would I go from Your Spirit? Or where would I flee from Your face?

8 If I go up into the heavens, You are there; If I make my bed in the grave, see, You are there.

9 I take the wings of the morning, I dwell in the uttermost parts of the sea,

10 There, too, Your hand would lead me, And Your right hand hold me.

11 If I say, "Darkness shall cover me," Then night would be light to me;

12 Even darkness is not dark for You, But night shines as the day – As is darkness, so is light.

13 For You, You possessed my kidneys, You have covered me in my mother's womb.

14 I give thanks to You, For I am awesomely and wondrously made! Wondrous are Your works, And my being knows it well.

15 My bones was not concealed from You, When I was shaped in a hidden place, Knit together in the depths of the earth.

16 Your eyes saw my unformed body. And in Your book all of them were written, The days they were formed, While none was among them.

17 And how precious are Your thoughts to me, O Ěl! How great has been the sum of them!

18 If I should count them, They would be more than the sand; When I wake up, I am still with You.

19 Oh, that You would slay the wrong, O Eloah! Depart from me, therefore, men of bloodshed!

20 They speak against You wickedly. Bring Your enemies to naught!

21 O יהוה, do I not hate them, who hate You? And do I not loathe those who rise up against You?

22 With a complete hatred I hate them; They have become my enemies.

23 Search me, O Ěl, and know my heart; Try me, and know my thoughts;

24 And see if an idolatrous way is in me, And lead me in the way everlasting.

140

1 Rescue me, O יהוה, from men of evil; Preserve me from men of violence,

2 Who have devised evils in their hearts; They stir up conflicts all day long.

3 They sharpen their tongues like a snake; The poison of cobras is under their lips. Selah.

4 Guard me, O יהוה, from the hands of the wrong; Guard me from a man of violence, Who have schemed to trip up my steps.

5 The proud have hidden a trap for me, and cords; They have spread a net by the wayside; They have set snares for me. Selah.

6 I said to יהוה, "You are my Ěl; Hear the voice of my prayers, O יהוה.

7 "O Master יהוה, my saving strength, You have screened my head in the day of battle.

8 "Do not grant the desires of the wrong, O יהוה; Do not promote his scheme. Selah.

9 "Those who surround me lift up their head; The trouble of their lips cover them;

10 "Let burning coals fall on them; Let them be made to fall into the fire, Into deep pits, let them not rise again.

11 "Let not a slanderer be established in the earth; Let evil hunt the man of violence speedily."

12 I have known that יהוה maintains The cause of the afflicted, The right-ruling of the poor.
13 Only, let the righteous give thanks to Your Name, Let the straight ones dwell in Your presence.

SEFER OF YESHAYAHU
SONGS & PSALMS STRATEGY OF WARSHIP FOR THE END DAYS

YESHAYAHU 12- SONG OF THANKSGIVING
And in that day you shall say, "I thank You יהוה, though You were enraged with me, Your displeasure has turned back, and You have comforted me.
"See, Ěl is my deliverance, I trust and am not afraid. For Yah, יהוה, is my strength and my song; and He has become my deliverance."
And you shall draw water with joy from the fountains of deliverance.
And in that day you shall say, "Praise יהוה, call upon His Name; make known His deeds among the peoples, make mention that His Name is exalted.
"Sing to יהוה, For He has done excellently; this is known in all the earth.
"Cry aloud and shout, O inhabitant of Tsiyon, for great is the Set-apart One of Yisra'ěl in your midst!"

YESHAYAHU 33- PSALM OF HOPE IN YAH
Woe to you ravager, while you have not been ravaged, and you treacherous, while they have not betrayed you! When you have ceased ravaging, you shall be ravaged. And when you stop betraying, they shall betray you.
O יהוה, show us favour, for we have waited for You. Be their arm every morning, our deliverance also in time of distress.
At the noise of the rumbling the people shall flee. When You lift Yourself up, the gentiles shall be scattered.
And Your plunder shall be gathered like the gathering of the caterpillar; as locusts rush about, they rush upon them.
יהו is exalted, for He dwells on high; He has filled Tsiyon with right-ruling and righteousness.
And He shall be the trustworthiness of your times, a wealth of deliverance, wisdom and knowledge. The fear of יהוה – that is His treasure.

YESHAYAHU 42- SONG OF THE SERVANT OF YAH PART 1
"See, My Servant whom I uphold, My Chosen One My being has delighted in! I have put My Spirit upon Him; He brings forth right-ruling to the nations.
"He does not cry out, nor lifts up *His voice* , nor causes His voice to be heard in the street.
"A crushed reed He does not break, and smoking flax He does not quench. He brings forth right-ruling in accordance with truth.
"He does not become weak or crushed, until He has established right-ruling in the earth. And the coastlands wait for His Torah."

SONG OF THE SERVANT PART 2

Thus said the Ěl, יהוה, who created the heavens and stretched them out, who spread forth the earth and that which comes from it, who gives breath to the people on it, and spirit to those who walk on it:

"I, יהוה, have called You in righteousness, and I take hold of Your hand and guard You, and give You for a covenant to a people, for a light to the gentiles,

to open blind eyes, to bring out prisoners from the prison, those who sit in darkness from the prison house.

"I am יהוה, that is My Name, and My esteem I do not give to another, nor My praise to idols.

"See, the former *predictions* have come, and new ones I am declaring; before they spring forth I let you hear them."

YESHAYAHU 42- HYMN OF TRIUMPH

Sing to יהוה a new song; His praise from the ends of the earth, you who go down to the sea, and all that is in it, you coastlands and you inhabitants of them!

Let the wilderness and its cities lift up their voice, the villages where Qěḏar dwells. Let the inhabitants of Sela sing, let them shout from the top of the mountains.

Let them give esteem to יהוה, and declare His praise in the coastlands.

יהוה goes forth like a mighty man. He stirs up ardour like a fighter. He cries out, yea, shout aloud. Over His enemies He shows Himself mighty.

"I have kept silent from of old, I have been still and held Myself back. Like a woman in labour I *now* cry out, I pant and gasp at once.

"I lay waste mountains and hills, and I dry up all their plants. And I shall make rivers become coastlands, and I dry up pools.

"And I shall lead the blind by a way they have not known – in paths they have not known I lead them. I make darkness light before them, and crooked places straight. These matters I shall do for them, and I shall not forsake them.

"Those who trust in idols, who say to the moulded images, 'You are our mighty ones,' shall be turned back, utterly ashamed.

YESHAYAHU 44- BLESSING FOR YISRA'EL

"But now hear, O Ya'aqoḇ My servant, and Yisra'ěl whom I have chosen.

Thus said יהוה who made you and formed you from the womb, who helps you, 'Do not fear, O Ya'aqoḇ My servant, and Yeshurun, whom I have chosen.

'For I pour water on the thirsty, and floods on the dry ground. I pour My Spirit on your seed, and My blessing on your offspring,

and they shall spring up among the grass like willows by streams of water.'

"One says, 'I belong to יהוה'; another calls himself by the name of Ya'aqoḇ; another writes with his hand, 'Unto יהוה,' and names himself by the name of Yisra'ěl.

YESHAYAHU 44- SONG OF JOY

Sing, O heavens, for יהוה shall do it! Shout, O depths of the earth! Break forth into singing, O mountains, forest, and every tree in it! For יהוה shall redeem Ya'aqoḇ, and make Himself clear in Yisra'ěl.

YESHAYAHU 48- SONG OF DEPARTURE FROM BABYLON

Come out of Baḇel! Flee from the Chaldeans! Declare this with a voice of singing, proclaim it, send it out to the end of the earth! Say, 'יהוה has redeemed His servant Ya'aqoḇ!' "

And they did not thirst when He led them through the deserts; He caused waters from a rock to flow for them; He split the rock, and waters gushed out.

"There is no peace for the wrong," said יהוה."

YESHAYAHU 49- SECOND SONG OF THE SERVANT OF YAH

Listen to Me, O coastlands, and hear, you peoples from afar! יהוה has called Me from the womb, from My mother's belly He has caused My Name to be remembered.

And He made My mouth like a sharp sword, in the shadow of His hand He hid Me, and made Me a polished shaft. In His quiver He hid Me."

And He said to Me, 'You are My servant, O Yisra'ěl, in whom I am adorned.'

And I said, 'I have laboured in vain, I have spent my strength for emptiness, and in vain. But my right-ruling is with יהוה, and my work with my Elohim.' "

And now said יהוה – who formed Me from the womb to be His Servant, to bring Ya'aqoḇ back to Him, though Yisra'ěl is not gathered to Him, yet I am esteemed in the eyes of יהוה, and My Elohim has been My strength –

and He says, "Shall it be a small *matter* for You to be My Servant to raise up the tribes of Ya'aqoḇ, and to bring back the preserved ones of Yisra'ěl? And I shall give You as a light to the gentiles, to be My deliverance to the ends of the earth!"

YESHAYAHU 50- THIRD SONG OF THE SERVANT OF YAH- A.THE SERVANT SPEAKS

The Master יהוה has given Me the tongue of taught ones, that I should know to help the weary with a word. He wakes Me morning by morning, he wakes My ear to hear as taught ones.

The Master יהוה has opened My ear, and I was not rebellious, nor did I turn away.

I gave My back to those who struck Me, and My cheeks to those who plucked out the beard, I did not hide My face from humiliation and spitting.

And the Master יהוה helps Me, therefore I shall not be humiliated. So I have set My face like a flint, and I know that I am not put to shame.

Near is He who declares Me right. Who would contend with Me? Let us stand together. Who is My adversary? Let him come near Me.

See, the Master יהוה helps Me. Who would declare Me wrong? See, all of them wear out like a garment, a moth eats them.

YESHAYAHU 50- EXHORTATION TO FOLLOW THE SERVANT

Who among you is fearing יהוה, obeying the voice of His Servant, that has walked in darkness and has no light? Let him trust in the Name of יהוה and lean upon his Elohim!

See, all you who light a fire, girding on burning arrows: walk in the light of your fire and in the burning arrows you have lit. From My hand you shall have this: you shall lie down in grief!

YESHAYAHU 52- FOURTH SONG OF THE SERVANT OF YAH

See, My Servant shall work wisely, He shall be exalted and lifted up and very high.

As many were astonished at You – so the disfigurement beyond any man's and His form beyond the sons of men –

He shall likewise startle many nations. Sovereigns shut their mouths at Him, for what had not been recounted to them they shall see, and what they had not heard they shall understand.

YESHAYAHU 59- A PSALM

Look, the hand of יהוה has not become too short to save, nor His ear too heavy to hear.

But your crookednesses have separated you from your Elohim. And your sins have hidden His face from you, from hearing.

For your hands have been defiled with blood, and your fingers with crookedness; your lips have spoken falsehood, your tongue mutters unrighteousness.

No one calls for righteousness, and no one pleads for truth. They trust in emptiness and speak worthlessness; they conceive trouble and bring forth wickedness.

They have hatched adders' eggs and they weave the spider's web. Whoever eats their eggs dies, and when one is broken an adder is hatched.

Their webs do not become garments, nor do they cover themselves with their works. Their works are works of wickedness, and a deed of violence is in their hands.

Their feet run to evil, and they hurry to shed innocent blood. Their thoughts are thoughts of wickedness, wasting and ruin are in their highways.

The way of peace they have not known, and there is no right-ruling in their ways. They have made crooked paths for themselves, whoever treads in them shall not know peace.

Therefore right-ruling has been far from us, and righteousness does not reach us. We look for light, but there is darkness; for brightness, but we walk in thick darkness!

We feel for the wall like the blind, and we feel as without eyes. At noon we stumble as at twilight, in deserted places, like the dead.

All of us growl like bears, and moan sadly like doves. We look for right-ruling, but there is none; for deliverance, but it is far from us.

For our transgressions have increased before You, and our sins witnessed against us. For our transgressions are with us, and as for our crookednesses, we know them:

transgressing, and being untrue to יהוה, and turning away from our Elohim, speaking oppression and apostasy, conceiving and pondering words of falsehood from the heart.

And right-ruling is driven back, and righteousness stands far off. For truth has fallen in the street, and right is unable to enter.

YESHAYAHU 63/64 - A PSALM

Let me recount the kindnesses of יהוה and the praises of יהוה, according to all that יהוה has done for us, and the great goodness toward the house of Yisra'ĕl, which He has done for them according to His compassion, and according to His many kindnesses.

And He said, "They are My people, children who do not act falsely." And He became their Saviour.

In all their distress He was distressed, and the Messenger of His Presence saved them. In His love and in His compassion He redeemed them, and He lifted them up and carried them all the days of old.

But they rebelled and grieved His Set-apart Spirit, so He turned against them as an enemy, and He fought against them.

Then He remembered the days of old, Mosheh, His people, "Where is He who brought them up out of the sea with the shepherd of His flock? Where is He who put His Set-apart Spirit within him,

who led them by the right hand of Mosheh, with His comely arm, dividing the water before them to make for Himself an everlasting Name,

who led them through the deep? Like a horse in the wilderness they did not stumble."

As a beast goes down into the valley, and the Spirit of יהוה causes him to rest, so You led Your people, to make Yourself a comely Name.

Look down from the heavens, and see from Your set-apart and comely dwelling. Where are Your ardour and Your might, the stirring of Your inward parts and Your compassion toward me? Are they withheld?

For You are our Father, though Aḇraham does not know us, and Yisra'ĕl does not recognise us. You, O יהוה, are our Father, our Redeemer – Your Name is from of old.

O יהוה, why do You make us stray from Your ways, and harden our heart from Your fear? Turn back, for the sake of Your servants, the tribes of Your inheritance.

For a little while Your set-apart people possessed it – our adversaries have trodden down Your set-apart place.

We have become like those over whom You never ruled – Your Name is not called on them!

Oh, that You would tear the heavens open, come down, that mountains shall shake before Your? –

as when fire burns twigs, as fire makes water boil – to make Your Name known to Your adversaries, so that nations tremble before You.

When You did awesome *matters* , which we did not expect, You came down, mountains did shake before You!

Since the beginning of the ages they have not heard nor perceived by the ear, nor has the eye seen any Elohim besides You, who acts for those who wait for Him.

You shall meet him who rejoices and does righteousness, who remembers You in Your ways. See, You were wroth when we sinned in them a long time. And should we be saved?

And all of us have become as one unclean, and all our righteousnesses are as soiled rags. And all of us fade like a leaf, and our crookednesses, like the wind, have taken us away.

And there is no one who calls on Your Name, who stirs himself up to take hold of You; for You have hidden Your face from us, and have consumed us because of our crookednesses.

And now, O יהוה, You are our Father. We are the clay, and You our potter. And we are all the work of Your hand.

Do not be wroth, O יהוה, nor remember crookedness forever. See, please look, all of us are Your people!

Your set-apart cities have become a wilderness, Tsiyon has become a wilderness, Yerushalayim a waste.

Our set-apart and comely House, where our fathers praised You, has been burned up with fire. And all that we treasured has become a ruin.

In view of all this, would You restrain Yourself, O יהוה? Would You keep silent and afflict us beyond measure?

YESHAYAHU 58:13-14 THE SABBATH

"If you do turn back your foot from the Sabbath, from doing your pleasure on My set-apart *day*, and shall call the Sabbath 'a delight,' the set-apart day of יהוה 'esteemed,' and shall esteem it, not doing your own ways, nor finding your own pleasure, nor speaking your own words, then you shall delight yourself in יהוה. And I shall cause you to ride on the heights of the earth, and feed you with the inheritance of Ya'aqoḇ your father. For the mouth of יהוה has spoken!"

YESHAYAHU 58- FAST APPROVED BY YAH

"Cry aloud, do not spare. Lift up your voice like a ram's horn. Declare to My people their transgression, and the house of Ya'aqoḇ their sins.

"Yet they seek Me day by day, and delight to know My ways, as a nation that did righteousness, and did not forsake the right-ruling of their Elohim. They ask of Me rulings of righteousness, they delight in drawing near to Elohim.

They say, 'Why have we fasted, and You have not seen? Why have we afflicted our beings, and You took no note?' "Look, in the day of your fasting you find pleasure, and drive on all your labourers.

"Look, you fast for strife and contention, and to strike with the fist of wrongness. You do not fast as you do this day, to make your voice heard on high.

"Is it a fast that I have chosen, a day for a man to afflict his being? Is it to bow down his head like a bulrush, and to spread out sackcloth and ashes? Do you call this a fast, and an acceptable day to יהוה?

"Is this not the fast that I have chosen: to loosen the tight cords of wrongness, to undo the bands of the yoke, to exempt the oppressed, and to break off every yoke?

"Is it not to share your bread with the hungry, and that you bring to your house the poor who are cast out; when you see the naked, and cover him, and not hide yourself from your own flesh?

"Then your light would break forth like the morning, your healing spring forth speedily. And your righteousness shall go before you, the esteem of יהוה would be your rear guard.

"Then, when you call, יהוה would answer; when you cry, He would say, 'Here I am.' "If you take away the yoke from your midst, the pointing of the finger, and the speaking of unrighteousness,

if you extend your being to the hungry and satisfy the afflicted being, then your light shall dawn in the darkness, and your darkness be as noon.

"Then יהוה would guide you continually, and satisfy your being in drought, and strengthen your bones. And you shall be like a watered garden, and like a spring of water, whose waters do not fail.

"And those from among you shall build the old waste places. You shall raise up the foundations of many generations. And you would be called the Repairer of the Breach, the Restorer of Streets to Dwell In.

Anointing Oil

Biblical use for consecration, prayer, healing & worship

by ABBA ANOINTING OIL(Reference Use)

TERMINOLOGY: To be "anointed" is, among other things, to be made sacred (consecrated); to be set apart and dedicated to serve God; to be endowed with enabling gifts and grace; to be divinely designated, inaugurated, or chosen for some purpose. We know this subject is important to God because the words *anoint* , *anointed* , and *anointing* appear in more than 150 Spirit-inspired Bible verses, including 22 New Testament Scriptures. Indeed, the English word *anoint* derives from the ancient Latin *inunctus* , meaning "smear with oil."

CONNECTION TO OIL: The *Bible Dictionary* mentions only two types of anointing: with oil or the Holy Ghost. In short, *anointing* and *oil* are much more integrally related than most people realize, which explains why Bible translators sometimes use *anoint* and *oil* interchangeably as synonymous verbs (*e.g.,* Isa. 21:5).

THE ANOINTED ONE: Both the ancient Hebrew form of *Messiah* and the ancient Greek form of *Christ* literally mean "anointed"; thus, "Jesus Christ" is more accurately rendered "Jesus the Anointed" (or as "Jesus, the Anointed One", or "Jesus, His Anointed"). This is one of the reasons our Savior first publicly announced Himself as the divine Messiah [Luke 4:18] by quoting Isaiah 61:1: "The Spirit of *Adonai ELOHIM* is upon me, because *ADONAI* has *anointed* me..." It's why Peter and John and the followers with them, inspired by the Holy Spirit, publicly refer to Jesus (*Yeshua*) as the "Anointed One" [Acts 4:26, NIV] and *NKJ, NIV,* and *NAS* Biblical versions translate: "Your holy Servant Jesus, whom you *anointed* ".

WHY FRAGRANT OIL: God is obviously a lover of sweet-smelling fragrances and perfumes since those words (or forms of them) appear 41 times and 35 times, respectively. Spices – in the context of anointing oils, perfume, food, and incense – are mentioned throughout the Bible: 16 verses containing *frankincense* , 17 with *myrrh* , five with *spikenard* , and many others featuring *cinnamon, cassia, calamus, camphor, stacte, aloes, onycha, cedar, honey, hyssop, henna, mandrakes, pomegranates, lilies, roses,* and *saffron* . Our faith is deepened and we are enriched and brought closer to God as we begin to study and understand the spiritual meaning of these exotic biblical fragrances.

FIRST SCRIPTURAL REFERENCE: The great Hebrew patriarch Jacob (divinely renamed "Israel") makes a sacred vow to God after *anointing a stone pillar by pouring oil on top of it* [Gen. 28:16-22; 31:13; 35:14]. Jacob names the pillar's locale "Bethel" (or *Beit-El* , meaning "House of God.) The editors of the *Ryrie Study Bible* comment that by pouring this anointing oil, Jacob "consecrated" the pillar, thereby rendering it an altar holy unto God.

THE HOLY ANOINTING OIL: In Exodus chapter 30:30-34, the LORD tells Moses to make a very special and "holy anointing oil" of "the finest of spices", including "flowing (liquid) myrrh", "sweet-smelling cinnamon", "fragrant cane", "cassia", and "olive oil". This highly perfumed oil was used to consecrate (set apart) the articles used in Temple worship, including the ark of the testimony, the holy tabernacle, and all its furnishings, which made them "Holy" (Kadosh in Hebrew) unto the Lord. However, Yahweh gives an admonition NOT to reproduce the exact formula or use it on ordinary humans—an admonition that ABBA takes seriously. (We do not attempt in any way to reproduce this formula).

THE LAMPSTAND: In Biblical times light was usually provided by oil lamps (or *menorahs* , a Hebrew word translated "lampstands", "lamps", or, less accurately, "candlesticks"). Often made of clay, brass, silver, or gold, these simple "lamps" slowly burned oil – typically olive oil. This explains verses such as Exodus 27:20 ("...order the people of Israel to bring you pure oil of pounded olives for the light, to keep a lamp burning continually"); Exodus 35:14 ("...the *menorah* for the light, ... and the oil for the light, spices for the anointing oil and for the fragrant incense..."); and Exodus 35:28 ("...oil for the light, and for the anointing oil..."). It also deepens our understanding of the parable of the wise and foolish virgins [Mat. 25:1-12].

PRIESTS: In *Exodus* , the LORD identifies anointing oil as an acceptable *offering* unto Him [Ex. 25:6]. Furthermore, He directs that Aaron and his sons be anointed, consecrated, and sanctified as holy priests to minister unto Him [Ex. 28:41 and that Aaron be anointed as Israel's High Priest through the pouring of anointing oil on his head and garments [Ex. 29:7,21,29]. (Psalm 133:1-2: compare harmonious brotherhood to "fragrant oil on the head that runs down over the beard of Aaron...").

KINGS: In Scripture's first *kingly* anointing, the prophet Samuel pours oil on the head of King Saul [1Sa. 10:1].

DAVID'S ANOINTING: David, the "man after God's own heart," is officially anointed with oil (by others) not once but *three* times [1Sa. 16:12-13; 2Sa. 2:4; 2Sa. 5:3]. In Psalm 23:5, he says to God, " *You* anoint my head with oil." This is confirmed by Psalm 89:20-21, wherein God declares, " *I* have found David my servant and anointed him with My holy oil. My hand will always be with him." In addition, David *anoints himself* while trying to shake off grief over the death of his child and just before entering the Temple to worship God [2Sa. 12:20].

QUEEN ESTHER & OIL OF MYRRH: In Esther's era any Queen-to-be had to undergo a year of preparations prior to coronation [Est. 2:3, 6-13]. Esther underwent "a six-month treatment with *oil of myrrh* and six months with perfumes and other aloes". One translation states it as "… *with olive oil and myrrh…*" In ancient times, the average woman's perfume *was* her anointing oil.

MARY OF BETHANY & SPIKENARD OIL: One of Scripture's most poignant, bittersweet scenes [Mat. 26:6-13; Mark 14:3-9; John 12:3-5] memorializes Mary of Bethany: A woman with an alabaster jar filled with very expensive perfume (pure spikenard oil worth an average laborer's annual wage) approaches *Yeshua* , breaks the jar, and begins pouring the precious oil over His head and feet. As the house fills with the oil's pungent fragrance, the Lord says to those nearby: "She has done a beautiful thing for me…She poured this perfume on me to prepare my body for burial…I tell you that throughout the whole world…what she has done will be told in her memory." Obviously, our Lord was deeply touched by Mary's unselfish, thoughtful, heartfelt, sacrificial expression of devotion and profound love. Some Bible commentators deem Mary's faithful act as the utmost example of what God desires in believers.

FRANKINCENSE & MYRRH: The "Magi from the east" honored the child Messiah with gifts of gold, frankincense, and myrrh [Mat. 2:11]. The gospels recount that before His death, Yeshua (Jesus) was offered myrrh mixed with wine, which He refused, and that after His death His body was treated with "a mixture of myrrh and aloes." Frankincense has come to be associated with Messiah's role as our intercessor (the bowl of incense in Rev 5:8 is frankincense, representing the prayers of the saints), myrrh with His suffering and death. In Song of Songs the writer refers to the bridegroom (Yeshua) as "who is He coming in a pillar of smoke smelling of myrrh & frankincense?" Many have suggested that the gold, frankincense, and myrrh represent the three roles of Yeshua respectively: King, Priest and Prophet.

FRAGRANCE OF MESSIAH: The apostle Paul writes: "…thanks be to God, who in the Messiah constantly leads us in a triumphal procession and through us spreads everywhere the *fragrance* of what it means to know Him! For to God we are the aroma of the Messiah, both among those being saved and among those being lost; to the latter, we are the smell of death leading only to more death; but to the former, we are the sweet smell of life leading to more life." [2Co. 2:14-16]

YAHUSHA'S COMMAND: According to Revelation 3:18 (NAS), *Yeshua* Himself says to the believing community in Laodicea: "I advise you to buy from Me gold…white garments…and *eye salve to anoint your eyes* , that you may see." Speaking of "white garments", consider the advice of King Solomon: "Always be clothed in white, and always *anoint your head with oil* ." [Ecc. 9:8, NIV]

BELIEVERS ARE ANOINTED: Believers are "in *Yeshua* "(Jesus) and He is "in us"; thus we, too, have been and are divinely anointed, as affirmed by both 2 Corinthians 1:21-22 ("…it is God who sets…us…in firm union with the Messiah; He has anointed us, put His seal on us, and given us His Spirit") and 1 John 2:20, 27 ("…you have received the Messiah's anointing…the Messianic anointing you received from the Father remains in you…His Messianic anointing continues to teach you about all things…so remain united with Him.") So, whether or not you use anointing oil, you're already one of God's anointed!

OTHERS CAN & SHOULD BE ANOINTED : Some believe oil should be used to anoint *only* kings and priests; according to Scripture, however, believers in *Yeshua* as the divine Son of God and as their Savior and Lord *are* "priests" [1Pe. 2:5,9]; they *are* kings (by virtue of having the *King* of Kings " *in* them" [Gal. 2:20]); and they may justifiably view their being anointed with oil as a *physical manifestation* of their being filled continuously with the Holy Spirit [1Jn. 2:20; 2Co. 1:21-22]. Indeed, according to most Bible scholars, in God's Word anointing oil typically symbolizes the Holy Spirit. Furthermore, "ordinary" ancient Israelites anointed themselves and each other with oil [Ruth 3:3; 2Ch. 28:15; Dan. 10:3; Amos 6:6], and the *B'rit Hadashah* (Hebrew for *New Covenant)* actually *directs* "ordinary believers" to do this [Mat. 6:17; James 5:14].

WHY & WHEN TO USE BIBLICAL FRAGRANT OIL TODAY:

· As an act of consecration and dedication, a setting apart for a special purpose in God's kingdom. Houses, structures, articles of worship, clothing and people can be anointed as a sign of consecration to God. Consider anointing yourself every morning, praying Scriptures over your mind, heart, ears, eyes, hands and feet. It WILL change your day!!

· As the Priests of the home, husbands are encouraged to anoint their wives and children for consecration, protection, peace, pronouncing a blessing upon them as did the Fathers of Old!!

· As a preparation to bible study, devotional time, fasting, and praise and worship

· In times of sickness, fear, anxiety, oppression of the enemy, end of mourning, ALSO in foot-washing ceremonies

· As bath oil—the olive oil is great for your skin and the fragrance is divine!

ALL OF ABBA'S ANOINTING OILS ARE MADE FROM EXTRA-VIRGIN, KOSHER OLIVE OIL FROM ISRAEL, BLENDED WITH PURE ESSENTIAL OILS AND SPICES, USING SOME OF THE SAME APOTHECARY METHODS AS IN BIBLICAL DAYS.

SCRIPTURAL FRAGRANCES AND THEIR SPIRITUAL SIGNIFICANCE

Frankincense : used on the Altar of Incense in temple times, one of the 3 gifts brought to Messiah (intercession) Song of Songs 3:6, Isaiah 53:5, Hebrews 3:24

Myrrh : Queen Esther bathed in oil of myrrh for six months before her presentation to the King (purification, dying to self, and preparation for the KING) Esther 2:12, Song of Songs 1:13

Hyssop : exotic Biblical plant used in cleansing rituals and in certain sacrifices of the Hebrews (cleansing, purification) Psalm 51:7

Cedars of Lebanon : fragrant wood used to build Temple and also to anoint a restored leper's house (strength, permanence, wholeness, restoration) Psalm 92:12

Pomegranate: highly prized fruit from ancient times, its motif was used to decorate the temple and was embroidered on high priest's garment (fruitfulness, abundance, blessings, favor of God) Numbers 13:23

Spikenard : fragrant oil used by Mary to anoint head & feet of Jesus (intimacy, extravagant worship) John 12:2-3

Rose of Sharon : flower depicting the beloved (beauty of the bride) Song of Songs 2:1

Cassia : one principal spice of the Holy Anointing Oil used to anoint priests, kings and their garments. The coming King Messiah's robes will smell of cassia (humility, being stripped of pride, set apart or holy with a servant's heart) Psalm 45:8

Covenant: a special blending of the fragrances of the Bridegroom (Frankincense & Myrrh), the Bride (Spikenard) and the Spirit of G-d (Hyssop/Holy Fire) *(marriage covenant in Hebrew)* Ex 24:1-8

How Sound Relates To Healing and Deliverance

The sound released by prayer, praise, and worship affect things in the spiritual and the physical realm. Sounds are vibrations that travel through the gaseous matter (air). Sound can also travel through solid matter. Sound affects things. The Scriptures record that Yahuah actually inhabits the sounds of praise. Think about that from a physical standpoint.

Verbal praise to Yahuah – the sound of humans praising Elohim– affects matter in such a way that YAH is said to inhabit it.

With the creative force of the Ruach HaQodosh that inhabits the sound of prayer to YAH or praise and worship to YAH, matter and the spiritual are impacted.

The impact is so significant that if humans did not praise Yahuah, the "rocks would cry out" in praise. I suppose that means the vibrations recorded in the crystal structure of rock would continue vibrating and fill the vacuum of praise.

Biblically, this is demonstrated multiple times, but the creation account recorded in Bereshiyth/Genesis is a good example. The sound of the voice of YAH released Yahuah's will and changed matter. It brought order to the chaos. Prayers do the same thing today (on a microscale, of course).

Actually, the vibrations caused by sound can be recorded in matter, and they can affect the air around it in certain conditions. Have you ever listened to a recording of a congregation singing praise and worship to Yahuah... *and the atmosphere around you changed?* Yahuah inhabits praise... even recorded praise.

How sound interacts with different kinds of matter may explain the healing power that was stored in the clothes referenced in the verses above, and it may account for why historically salt and oil that have been prayed over have been successfully used in healing and deliverance.

(NOT) Quantum Vibrations-

RULE OF THE VICTOR
STATEMENT OF RULE OF THE VICTOR:

WE exercise *"Rule of the Victor"* over all the demonic regions that have set their will against <u>MY FAMILY, MINISTRY, MARRIAGE, HOME, LAND, & ASSIGNMENTS FOR YAH__</u> ,

WE exercise "Rule of the Victor" against all those demonic regions that have permitted spirits ***in or through*** their territory.

WE command that they be **CUT OFF** from *ever* receiving power from darkness again.

WE require the immediate disbursement of all their funds from the kingdom of darkness into the Kingdom of Light (spoils of war),

WE require the immediate destruction of all their books and artifacts of sorcery, and

WE require the immediate reversal of all their schemes.

Penalties applied. INTO the pit! *In YAHUSHA HAMASCIACH'S NAME!*

The ancient walled city of the Scriptures had the most in common with the modern city. It was most often a center of apostasy, a base for imperialism, a treasure trove for plundering tyrants, a monument to human pride, vainglory and rebellion against Yahuah... The city provides no ideal for culture since it is opposed to biblical culture. Like Babel, the prototype, it has been erected in defiance of Yahuah's design for a decentralized agrarian civilization." Howard King- "A Christian-Agrarian Critique of Technological Society"

Food for Thought

Time, Place, Proximity, Mutual Concerns, and Mutual Kindness

By time, I mean years. The more the better. Generations are best.

By place, I mean a home where a family lives, on a section of land that the family has, over time (maybe even generations) cared for and grown to love. Proximity is the state or quality of being near. A new kind of community has emerged in recent years with the advent of the internet. Such a community can be good. But it can never be a best form of community because there is little proximity. Virtual proximity just isn't the same as physical proximity and never will be. Mutual concerns arise out of a mutual worldview. Worldview boils down to fundamental ideas about what is right and wrong, good and bad. Worldview is at the root of religious belief. Generally speaking, rural folks share similar belief systems. They may not all agree on religious doctrines but they think alike on many core issues. One example of this becomes clear during a national election when the rural areas of the nation typically vote the same (i.e., the "red states"). Mutual kindness is when people in the community interact by speaking, visiting, working, caring, sharing, and giving to each other in some way, to some degree, preferably on a daily basis. This kind of best community was once the norm in most rural areas of America. It was also found in small rural towns and villages. But as agrarian culture has given way to modern, industrialized culture, the social fabric of rural communities has become more and more threadbare.

Atmosphere has fervently shifted---the fragrance of freedom has evaporated and the stench of lawlessness fumes.

It is the beginning of the eternal collapse of this universe. Starting today, every action step will be down. Get ready. We all have been warned, the beginning of the end began in February 2020. Soon every Believer and Follower of Messiah Yahusha will be considered a domestic terrorist. We are now enemies of the state. We are the most hated and pursued sect of people as the WORD says.

Advance the Kingdom of YAH through revelation. Revelation is YAHUAH revealing HIMSELF to us.

My life must reflect that of a life not of this world. Key is living in this realm but not be of this realm. Every action I take must be that of a reaction living from the Kingdom of YaH. Dress like I am not of this world. Talk in a manner unworthy of this world having Kingdom perspective. Think of Enoch, Abraham, Moseh, YAHUSHA.

Deuteronomy 13 test for the Natsarim

Translated into YAH's LOVE! Become YAHUSHA's LOVE

BLESSING: *May YAHUAH ELOHIM give you eyes to see and ears to hear so that you can make it all the way to the Great Wedding Feast of the Lamb and be a blessing to others as you travel there in obedience! May the God of Abraham, Isaac and Jacob bless you with health and prosperity as His will desires.*

TEN WORDS- THE LAW OF THE MOST HIGH YAHUAH
SHEMOTH 20

And Elohim spoke all these Words, saying,

"I am יהוה your Elohim, who brought you out of the land of Mitsrayim, out of the house of slavery.

"You have no other mighty ones against My face.

"You do not make for yourself a carved image, or any likeness of that which is in the heavens above, or which is in the earth beneath, or which is in the waters under the earth, you do not bow down to them nor serve them. For I, יהוה your Elohim am a jealous Ěl, visiting the crookedness of the fathers on the children to the **third** and **fourth** generations of those who hate Me, but showing kindness to thousands, to those who love Me and guard My commands.

"You do not bring the Name of יהוה your Elohim to naught, for יהוה does not leave the one unpunished who brings His Name to naught.

"Remember the Sabbath day, to set it apart. "Six days you labour, and shall do all your work, but the seventh day is a Sabbath of יהוה your Elohim. You do not do any work – you, nor your son, nor your daughter, nor your male servant, nor your female servant, nor your cattle, nor your stranger who is within your gates. "For in six days יהוה made the heavens and the earth, the sea, and all that is in them, and rested the seventh day. Therefore יהוה blessed the Sabbath day and set it apart.

"Respect your father and your mother, so that your days are prolonged upon the soil which יהוה your Elohim is giving you.

"You do not murder.

"You do not commit adultery.

"You do not steal.

"You do not bear false witness against your neighbour.

"You do not covet your neighbour's house, you do not covet your neighbour's wife, nor his male servant, nor his female servant, nor his ox, nor his donkey, or whatever belongs to your neighbour."

And all the people saw the thunder, the lightning flashes, the sound of the ram's horn, and the mountain smoking. And the people saw it, and they trembled and stood at a distance, and said to Mosheh, "You speak with us and we hear, but let not Elohim speak with us, lest we die."

And Mosheh said to the people,

"Do not fear, for Elohim has come to prove you, and in order that His fear be before you, so that you do not sin."

So the people stood at a distance, but Mosheh drew near the thick darkness where Elohim was.

And יהוה said to Mosheh , "Say this to the children of Yisra'ĕl: 'You yourselves have seen that I have spoken to you from the heavens. ' You do not make besides Me mighty ones of silver, and you do not make mighty ones of gold for yourselves. 'Make an altar of earth for Me, and you shall slaughter on it your burnt offerings and your peace offerings, your sheep and your cattle. In every place where I cause My Name to be remembered I shall come to you and bless you. 'And if you make Me an altar of stone, do not build it of cut stone, for if you use your chisel on it, you have profaned it. 'Nor do you go up by steps to My altar, lest your nakedness be exposed on it.'

ORACLE- YESHAYAHU 42

Thus said the Ĕl, יהוה, who created the heavens and stretched them out, who spread forth the earth and that which comes from it, who gives breath to the people on it, and spirit to those who walk on it:

"I, יהוה, have called You in righteousness, and I take hold of Your hand and guard You, and give You for a covenant to a people, for a light to the gentiles, to open blind eyes, to bring out prisoners from the prison, those who sit in darkness from the prison house.

"I am יהוה, that is My Name, and My esteem I do not give to another, nor My praise to idols.

"See, the former *predictions* have come, and new ones I am declaring; before they spring forth I let you hear them."

Sing to יהוה a new song; His praise from the ends of the earth, you who go down to the sea, and all that is in it, you coastlands and you inhabitants of them!

Let the wilderness and its cities lift up their voice, the villages where Qĕḏar dwells. Let the inhabitants of Sela sing, let them shout from the top of the mountains.

Let them give esteem to יהוה, and declare His praise in the coastlands.

יהוה goes forth like a mighty man. He stirs up ardour like a fighter. He cries out, yea, shout aloud. Over His enemies He shows Himself mighty.

"I have kept silent from old, I have been still and held Myself back. Like a woman in labour I *now* cry out, I pant and gasp at once.

187

"I lay waste mountains and hills, and I dry up all their plants. And I shall make rivers become coastlands, and I dry up pools.

"And I shall lead the blind by a way they have not known – in paths they have not known I lead them. I make darkness light before them, and crooked places straight. These matters I shall do for them, and I shall not forsake them.

"Those who trust in idols, who say to the moulded images, 'You are our mighty ones,' shall be turned back, utterly ashamed.

"Hear, you deaf! And look, you blind, and see.

"Who is blind but My servant, or deaf as My messenger whom I send? Who is blind as he who is at peace, and blind as servant of יהוה?

"You see much, but do not observe; ears are open, but do not hear."

It has delighted יהוה, for the sake of His righteousness, to make the Torah great and esteemed.

But this is a people robbed and plundered, all of them are snared in holes, and they are hidden in prison houses. They have become a prey, with no one to deliver – for plunder, and no one to say, "Restore!"

Who among you gives ear to this, pays attention and hears for the time to come?

Who gave Yaʿaqoḇ for plunder, and Yisra'ĕl to the robbers? Was it not יהוה, He against whom we sinned? For they would not walk in His ways, and they did not obey His Torah!

So He has poured on him His burning displeasure and the strength of battle, and it set him on fire all around, yet he did not understand. And it burned against him, yet he did not take it to heart!

Brother's and Sisters; if you have been woken in the past four to six years to return to Torah, to observe the Sabbath and keep YaH's Appointed Feast Days and other Biblical truths that have been hidden for so long, then I truly believe that you and I are the Natsarim and some of us are even Sons and Daughters of Zadok. We have each been given unique and authentic gifts for specific assignments in these end days. We will all be brought together as one body with many moving parts moving in unison!! We have moved out of the Age of Grace into the time of Judgement ; many things are happening right now before us all at one time, we must be Watchmen and Watchmaiden's. By that desire we have been set apart through the offering of the body of יהושע Messiah once for all. And indeed every priest stands day by day doing service, and repeatedly offering the same slaughter offerings which are never able to take away sins. But He, having offered one slaughter offering for sins for all time, sat down at the right hand of Elohim, waiting from that time onward until His enemies are made a footstool for His feet. For by one offering He has perfected for all time those who are being set apart. And the Set-apart Spirit also witnesses to us, for after having said before. Much of this book is for reference purposes. Simple reminders in the Scriptures to use as a tool of our warfare. Truly, we have entered into a time of WAR. I pray that you will hold tightly to your Scriptures/Bible to the very end. The times we face are such as never been before and never will be again. We must survey our heart daily and pray for YAH to create a clean heart in us so we truly become the pure & spotless Bride that Messiah Yahusha is coming for!

"This is the covenant that I shall make with them after those days, says יהוה, giving My laws into their hearts, and in their minds I shall write them," Hebrews 10: 10-16

Salt & Lyte Gypsy Ministry

LEAVING BABYLON A NATSARIM'S TOOLKIT FOR TRIBULATION

Printed in Great Britain
by Amazon